Further praise for *Queering Psyc*

"The discipline of psychotherapy is unavoidably implicated in the structure of the society in which it operates. The only way to ensure it doesn't replicate embedded social inequities and harms is for it regularly subject itself to intense critical examination from a wide diversity of perspectives. *Queering Psychotherapy* is a shining example of this kind of inquiry and should be a compulsory read for anyone in the field, however they choose to identify." – **Dr. Aaron Balick, psychotherapist and author**

"The space of therapy can feel claustrophobic. If you're queer or trans and working with a heteronormative therapist, the room itself can feel airless especially when you are trying to establish a workable relationship and understanding about your identity. An airless room fraught with misunderstandings. This book is a reservoir of information, knowledge and professional understandings which seek to widen out that space into a comfortable queer landscape. Invaluable." – **Juno Roche, author of *Trans Power and Queer Sex***

"*Queering Psychotherapy* is a dynamic collection featuring important, intersectional perspectives. It tackles big topics, such as trans desire, lesbian erasure and navigating shame, with nuance and care. Brimming with powerful insights, this book is a vital resource for professionals and fascinating reading material for us all." – **Roxy Bourdillon, Editor-in-chief of *DIVA* magazine**

"A stirring and necessary contribution to the field! In this liminal time, when a new generation of clients and students are calling psychotherapists and training institutions to accountability, *Queering Psychotherapy* can offer a compelling compass for reorienting and reimagining our field. The collaborative format of the book embodies the message vividly, by calling us all in, to critically and heartfully join the creative project of querying and queering the underpinning of our theories and practices." – **Shoshi Asheri, psychotherapist, educator and creative collaborator at Aashna UK**

"This excellent book takes an intersectional approach in the understanding of psychotherapy through a queer lens and is essential reading, therefore for those who are from the LGBTQ+ community or are working within said communities such as myself. That this book has been brave enough to include such a wide range of voices and perspectives, angles, cultures, and races is a testament to just how psychotherapy can come together when it steps outside of the heteronormative, able-bodied, white, middle class constraints within which it has been entangled almost since its inception. This book is essential reading and needs to be studied on courses around the country." – **Dr Dwight Turner, psychotherapist, Supervisor and Workshop Facilitator**

"Passionate, thoughtful and opens a much-needed discussion with the mainstream therapeutic community who often do not understand the needs and lives of LGBTQI+ clients." – **Matthew Todd, author of *Straight Jacket***

For my parents

QUEERING PSYCHOTHERAPY

Edited by Jane Chance Czyzselska

KARNAC

KARNAC

First published in 2022 by Karnac Books, an imprint of Confer Ltd.

www.confer.uk.com

Registered office:
Brody House, Strype Street, London E1 7LQ

1 3 5 7 9 10 8 6 4 2

This is a work of nonfiction. Any similarity between the characters and situations within its
pages, and places, persons, or animals living or dead, is unintentional
and co-incidental. Some names and identifying details may have been changed or
omitted to protect the privacy of individuals.
Every effort has been made to trace the copyright holders and obtain permission to reproduce
this material. If you have any queries or any information relating to text,
images or rights holders, please contact the publisher.

British Library Cataloguing in Publication Data
A catalogue record for this book is available from the British Library.

ISBN: 978-1-913494-73-5 (paperback)
ISBN: 978-1-913494-74-2 (ebook)

Typeset in Berling by Bespoke Publishing Ltd
Printed in the UK

Contents

About the authors

Meg-John Barker (they/them) is a writer and writing mentor who trains therapists and others in gender, sexual and relationship diversity (GSRD) and other skills. They identify as queer, trans, plural, relationship anarchist and kinky. Key intersections are white British, mixed class background, dis/abilities around hearing, post-traumatic stress, survivor and English speaker. They worked as a psychotherapist from 2006 to 2019 following training in existential psychotherapy. They are also strongly influenced by Buddhist, systemic and somatic approaches. An academic psychologist since 1995 teaching and researching primarily GSRD and mental health-related topics, they have also written many books including *Rewriting the Rules, Life Isn't Binary* and graphic guides and self-help books on gender and sexuality, as well as zines and other resources. They also wrote the BACP resource on GSRD.

Anthea Benjamin (she/her) is a black, cisgender, heterosexual, working-class female who practises as an integrative arts psychotherapist, group analyst, supervisor, trainer and organizational consultant for culture change in institutions. Anthea is interested in intersectionality, anti-oppressive practices and racial trauma in racialized/othered bodies.

Kris Black IAP, UKCP, MBACP, ISN, LLB (hons) (they/them) is an integrative clinical supervisor, trainer, integrative arts psychotherapist and child and adolescent counsellor in private practice. They are an Advanced Accredited Gender, Sex and Relationship Diversities Therapist and they live and work within the QTIBPOC communities in London. Kris has worked extensively within the education and LGBTQIA+ charity sectors with young people. Kris is a committee member of the Coalition Against Conversion Therapy. Kris is a working class, BPOC, Queer, Non Binary Trans, Disabled Elder who has survived institutional and interpersonal violence.

Sabah Choudrey (they/them/theirs) is a psychotherapist in training, trans youth worker, public speaker and writer. At time of writing, they are between the second and third year of their Masters in person-centred psychotherapy. Sabah co-founded Trans Pride Brighton in 2013 and made The Rainbow List in 2015, celebrating 101 of the most influential LGBT people in Britain. Sabah has built a presence across UK and Europe, speaking at TEDx Brixton 2015, ILGA Europe 2016, IDAHOT Brussels 2017 and Malmö Pride 2017/18/20 about intersectionality, identity and inclusion. Sabah has been a proud trans youth worker since 2014 and Joint Head of Youth Service at Gendered Intelligence since 2020, trustee for Inclusive Mosque Initiative, co-founder of Colours Youth Network supporting LGBT+ BPOC young people in the UK. They are the author of *Supporting Trans People of Colour: How to Make Your Practice Inclusive* (2022). They have also conducted therapeutic work in the community, facilitating groups for trans people or trans people of colour, holding therapeutic spaces with queer trans people of colour with the QTIPOC collective Misery in 2020. Sabah is the winner of the Gay Times Future Fighter Honour 2021.

Jane Chance Czyzselska (they/she) prefers to be called Chance and is a white queer non-binary trans relational integrative psychotherapist and counsellor in private practice. They are also a writer. Their therapeutic thinking and being is influenced by feminist, queer, trans and decolonising ideas and practices. They are an editorial advisor for *Therapy Today* as well as being on the organizing committee of The Relational School. They have volunteered at London's Step Forward charity and at the LGBTIQ+ charity London Friend. From 2004 to 2017, they edited *DIVA*, the magazine for LGBTIQ women and non-binary people, and they write for a range of national and international mainstream and psychotherapy publications.

Dominic Davies (he/him) has worked as a counsellor, psychotherapist and sex therapist for over 40 years, setting up, in 2000, the UK's largest dedicated independent therapy service for queer clients, Pink Therapy, after successfully completing the co-editing of the final two volumes of the Pink Therapy trilogy with Charles Neal. Dominic works integratively and specializes in working with gender, sexuality and relationship diverse clients. He and his team of queer tutors also run internationally renowned post-graduate training for therapists working with GSRD clients. He is an older, disabled, white, cis, gay male who has always been involved in consensual non-monogamy (CNM) relationships and for the last 15 years has been out as kinky. As well as offering therapy to queer clients, he also ran a supervision group for kink-identified therapists. He co-authored a chapter on dual relationships with former BACP chair Lynne Gabriel in *Issues in Therapy with Lesbian, Gay, Bisexual and Transgender Clients* (2000).

Bay De Veen (she/her) is a therapeutic practitioner and supervisor working mainly online. She is an older, white, European, asexual, anarchist lesbian who is genderqueer. Influences include philosophy, science and nature, narrative and story, migrations, poetry, writing and creative approaches to holistic healing that include conversations with the body, the care of self and others, as well as an appreciation for and special interest in the situational and contextual intersections of living a complex life in a wonderful, crazy world.

Robert Downes (he/him) practises as a psychotherapist, supervisor, teacher and student drawing from a range of traditions: queer theory, Black feminisms, critical theory, relational psychoanalysis, philosophy, music and literature, alongside the spiritual teachings and practices of the Diamond Approach.

Paul Harris (he/they) is a white, Welsh, cisgender, working-class, gay male working as an integrative child psychotherapist and consultant supervisor. His specialism in working with complex development trauma is underpinned by over 20 years of work within the field of somatic psychotherapy and the healing arts generally, with both children and families across a wide range of public and private services.

Ellis J. Johnson (he/him) is a psychodynamic psychotherapeutic counsellor who works mainly alongside trans/non-binary, queer and questioning people in private practice. He offers training to fellow therapists in working affirmatively with gender diversity, and has previously worked as a mental health advocate and provided counselling in higher education and NHS Wellbeing services. He now works as a supervisor for QTIPOC and trans/non-binary people across the third sector and also delivers training in anti-racism and trans inclusion to organisations across the UK and internationally. His work draws on anti-racist and decolonial approaches to gender, sexuality, spirituality and the human experience. He describes himself as a Brown, mixed, working-class trans man with roots stretching from Yorkshire to Jamaica to South Asia.

Dr Gail Lewis (she/her) is Reader Emerita in the Department of Psychosocial Studies at Birkbeck College, Senior Visiting Research Fellow at the Department of Gender Studies, LSE and Visiting Professor at Yale University in the academic year 2021–22. She trained, first, as a psychodynamic psychotherapist and then as a psychoanalytic psychotherapist at the Tavistock Clinic. Her political subjectivity was formed in the intensities of Black feminist and anti-racist struggles and through a socialist, anti-imperialist lens. She was a member of the Brixton Black Women's Group and one of the founder members of the Organisation of Women of African and Asian Descent, Britain's first national organization for Black and other women of colour. She is currently writing a book on Black feminism in Britain and has written on feminism, intersectionality, the welfare state and racialized-gendered experience. Her publications include *Race, Gender and Social Welfare: Encounters in a Postcolonial Society* (2000), Polity Press; *Citizenship: Personal Lives and Social Policy* (2004), ed. Polity Press; 'Birthing racial difference: conversations with my mother and others' (2009), *Studies in the Maternal*; 'Unsafe travel: experiencing intersectionality and feminist displacements' (2013), *Signs: Journal of Women in Culture and Society*; 'Where might I find you: popular music and the internal space of the father' (2012), *Psychoanalysis, Culture and Society*; 'Questions of presence' (2017), *Feminist Review, 117*; 'Black feminism and the challenge of object use' (2020), *Feminist Review 126 (1)*. She works alongside artists and other creative practitioners to explore, disrupt and offer alternatives to the violent and violating representations of Black and queer lives. She and Foluke Taylor were in conversation, discussing 'Black feminisms in the consulting room', as part of Confer's module *Women on the Couch* (2020). She, along with Barby Asante, Foluke Taylor and others, did a recorded reading of M. NourbeSe Philip's essay *Caribana: African Roots and Continuities* for the podcast *Dipsaus*, first available to coincide with the online version of London's annual Notting Hill Carnival in 2020. She also participated in NourbeSe Philip's *Zong! Global 2020*. She believes that intergenerational conversations, as part of the process of ancestral connection and guidance, are among the most urgent in these times. She is an Arsenal fan.

Amanda Middleton (she/her) is a white, queer, femme antipodean who thinks a lot about gender. For the last 20 years, she has fought passionately to put queer lives at the centre of knowledge making. Obsessively immersing herself in queer theory as a survival skill, she wonders how we, as queer people, can reshape our relationship to power and resist oppressive forces to take up more space. Initially, she qualified as a psychologist in Australia, and then as a family and systemic psychotherapist in the UK. A UKCP registered psychotherapist in independent practice, Amanda works primarily with relationships, gender, sex and sexuality, specializing within the LGBTIQ communities. She has extensive experience in the NHS and social care and has previously worked as a specialist in the areas of sex and sexuality, dual diagnosis, HIV and sexual health, drug and alcohol use and domestic violence. Her practice home is The Pink Practice, and she is also an associate lecturer at the Tavistock and Portman Trust, and supervisor at Gendered Intelligence.

Igi Moon (they/them) is a chartered psychologist and Fellow of the British Psychological Society (BPS). Igi's work focuses on psychotherapy, gender, sexuality and emotion. It is an interesting combination! They have published two edited books, *Counselling Ideologies: Queer Challenges to Heteronormativity* (Routledge, 2010) and *Feeling Queer or Queer Feelings: Radical Approaches to Counselling Sex, Sexualities and Gender* (Routledge, 2007). They are presently working on developing a Trans-therapeutic approach to working with trans and non-binary people and establishing a therapy clinic at Roehampton University. Igi represents the BPS on a number of committees, and they are presently involved with extending the Memorandum of Understanding against Conversion Therapies to protect trans and non-binary people. They are also an Associate Fellow at Warwick University in the Department of Sociology. Most of all they like playing with ideas. And the cat!

Charles Neal (he/him) has been connected with psychotherapy for 50 years. A breakdown aged six led to twelve years of formal psychoanalysis, with a series of further breakdowns and hospitalization in adolescence in a therapeutic community. He specialized in developmental psychology when training to teach. After a few years' break from therapy, he saw humanistic therapists for over 35 years as a client and trainee, mainly at Spectrum Therapy in London. Since 1990, he has worked as an independent therapist, consultant and group facilitator in public and private sectors. His therapy practice has focused on sexualities, creativity and existential issues. Co-founder of the European Association for Lesbian, Gay & Bisexual Psychologies in the early 1990s, Charles founded and chaired its British wing. With Dominic Davies, he edited the Pink Therapy trilogy of practice handbooks (McGraw Hill, 1996, 2000) and later became Honorary Clinical Associate of the Pink Therapy organization, which arose from that. He held their Certificate of Advanced Gender and Sexual Diversities Therapy and, for 20 years, offered workshops on their training programmes. He was an editorial advisor for *We Are Family* queer families magazine and led the world's longest-running gay and bi men's therapy group, Coming Home, for 25 years. In 2014, he published *The Marrying Kind? Lives of Gay and Bi Men Who Married Women* (CreateSpace) and is now in semi-retirement. Although he now identifies as a gay man, 'maleness' has been a difficult identity since childhood. He lived a bisexual life for the first part of his volitional sexual and relational history. He is a survivor of sexual abuse, alcoholic parenting, violence and bullying as well as of very many accidents and illnesses. He deeply enjoyed being married to a woman for 12 years and feels massively grateful in having two, now adult, incredibly kind, talented, loving sons. For the past 40 years, he has lived in a gay partnership. His partner has a teenage son, and they now also enjoy grand-parenting two very special Kiwi girls together.

Karen Pollock (they/them) is a therapist offering online counselling, training and supervision. They have specialist training and experience of working with gender, sexuality and relationship diverse communities and have a Post Graduate Diploma in Gender, Sexuality and Relationship Diverse Therapy awarded by Pink Therapy. After studying philosophy at the LSE, Karen worked in southeast Asia for a number of years as a teacher and trainer before returning to the UK. Karen is especially proud of being an Academic Archers Research Fellow and their queering of the fictional character Shula from the British BBC Radio 4 soap opera The Archers. They recently contributed to the book *Non-Binary Lives, An Anthology of Intersecting Identities* and lead training across the UK and online for counsellors and others to improve access and inclusion for all.

Beck Thom (they/she) is a white, queer, non-binary human from the middle of the UK, who happens to have certified in sexological bodywork. Beck has said for a long time 'everything I touch turns to queer' and that describes the evolution of their work. Beck has a background in LGBT youth work and therapeutic social work, specializing in children with sexual behaviour problems, and they have somehow combined their endless fascination with human sexuality and sex education with a queer community close to their heart. Quintimacy (Queer Intimacy) is their offering of one-to-one work and online and in-person workshops aimed exclusively at queer and trans people. They also promote queer and trans orientated somatic sexuality work, offering mentoring and training to other practitioners. Beck is ethically non-monogamous, kinky and neurodiverse, and believes that everyone, not only LGBTIQ people, benefits from queer sexology.

Valentino Vecchietti (she/they) is an award-winning writer, artist and equality campaigner. In 2019, she founded Intersex Equality Rights UK, an intersex-led organization which campaigns for equity and supports organizations to ethically include people with intersex variations. In May 2021, Valentino redesigned the Progress Pride flag to include the intersex community, creating the Intersex-Inclusive Pride flag.

Jake Yearsley (he/him) is a white, heteroflexible trans man living in the South West, UK. Working as an integrative counsellor and psychosexual therapist, he specializes in GSRD therapy, with a commitment to continually evolve and learn from the developing models of GSRD, in particular trans theory. Trans theory emphasizes the lived experience of a trans person as what matters most when working with this client group. Jake has worked therapeutically within trans communities for over ten years. This has included FTM London support group, the Metro in London, LGBT Switchboard, All Sorts project and the Clare Project, Brighton. Jake works in private practice and teaches GSRD therapy at the Minster centre, London. Jake says, 'Acknowledging my trans identity and history is important for me and the work I do. This honours who I am and the trans clients that I see. Not being open about who I am perpetuates the shame of being trans.'

Neil Young (he/they) is a white, English, working-class, queer man working with young people and adults in private practice as an integrative arts psychotherapist. Neil has 25 years' experience as an organizational consultant, facilitator, researcher and youth work manager specializing in the lived reality of diverse gender and sexual identities. Neil founded Mosaic LGBT Young Person's Trust [https://www.mosaictrust.org.uk], advised the first two Mayors of London on LGBT+ issues and wrote 'Young people: not straight, not narrow' (BACP University and College Counselling, 2017) [https://www.bacp.co.uk/bacp-journals/university-and-college-counselling/september-2017/young-people-not-straight-not-narrow/].

Acknowledgements

This book is an infusion from the last few decades of life learnings, philosophies, mistakes, insights and wisdoms absorbed and digested from others – inside and outside of the therapy world – about the lived experiences of queer and trans people, underpinned by queer, intersectional feminist and decolonial thinking. There are many people who have helped me in my learning and whose ideas have contributed to the collective consciousness-raising, from my ancestors – especially Paul, who was denied life because of his variation in sex characteristics, and my queer grandmother, Marianne – to people that walk the earth today. The names that come to mind here are the closest to home and there are many people beyond this list who have taught and lifted me, including my family. We continue to learn, making missteps and more skilful steps along the way, so that we may also leave something for those who come after us. I'm grateful to those who came before me and who are also alongside me. Bay, our journey and growth together has changed my life. Juno, thank you for your luminous brilliance. Thank you to the friends, colleagues and others who have taught and continue to teach me so much: Aashna's Pretish Raja-Helm, Shammi Kohli and Jamie Crabb, Anando Emryss, Anita Gaspar, Bird La Bird, Campbell X, Diane Torr, Michele Aaron, Michelle Butler, Fox Fisher, Harriet Mossop and Stillpoint Spaces' Other Women reading group, reading group, Jacky Fleming, Janice Acquah, Jennifer Fear, Judy Yellin, Kayza Rose, Kristiene Clarke, Vajralila (Lea), Leticia Valles, Louise Hide, Mary-Jayne Rust, Paris Lees, Dr Phyll Opoku-Gyimah, Shoshi Asheri, Toni Hogg, The Anti-Discrimination Focus' Mamood Ahmad and Sam Jamal, and everyone at London Friend. Thanks also to those from whom I have learned through their writings and practice in and out of the therapy room: Adrienne Rich, Angela Davis, Jane Elliot, Janina Fisher, Jessica Benjamin, Joan Nestle, John Bowlby, Karen Maroda, Kate Bornstein, Maggie Nelson, Patrick Califia, Peggy Mackintosh, Peggy Page, Pat Ogden and Ruella Frank. Thanks to my writing mentor, MJ Barker, without whom this book probably wouldn't exist. Christina Wipf Perry and Liz Wilson at Confer and Karnac, thank you for believing in me and this book and for answering my endless questions. To my clients with whom it is a privilege to work and learn. And to my brilliant, generous co-contributors, it has been a humbling joy to learn from your insights, knowledges and wisdoms. I am grateful for the work you all do in our communities. The world is better for your being in it.

COVER ILLUSTRATION NOTE TO THE READER

The first rainbow flag was designed by gay rights activist Gilbert Baker in 1976. Each colour represented an aspect of the LGBT movement. In the decades since, the flag has evolved into the Intersex-Inclusive Pride Flag that adorns the cover of this book. A rough timeline of the flag's evolution includes American trans woman Monica Helms' transgender flag, created in 1999 and proudly carried on Pride marches all over America and worldwide in the twenty-plus years since. In 2013 Morgan Carpenter of Intersex Human Rights Australia designed the intersex flag featuring a purple circle, which symbolizes "wholeness and completeness," on a yellow background. In 2017, under the leadership of American civil rights activist Amber Hikes, Philadelphia's Office of LGBT Affairs developed the rainbow flag, incorporating black and brown stripes in reference to queer black, brown and people of colour. In 2018. Daniel Quasar redesigned the flag incorporating Helms' design, to include trans people, creating what is now known as the Progress Pride flag. In May 2021 Valentino Vecchietti of Intersex Equality Rights UK developed the Progress Pride flag further still, to create the Intersex-Inclusive Pride flag. By June 2021 it had gone viral on the internet and was internationally welcomed as the new Pride flag, reflecting the ongoing expansion of queer family.

Introduction

by Jane Chance Czyzselska

In spring 2020, the Covid-19 pandemic and national lockdown started to change lives as we had lived them. Workplaces and meeting spaces emptied like caves. Days and weeks slowed down. Roads cleared of traffic birthed quiet and birdsong. Space opened up for a collaborative psychotherapeutic cross-fertilization. Following a conversation with Dr Gail Lewis (Chapter 1) in which she notes some of the ways that Black lesbian poet and author Audre Lorde's ideas seem to echo the work of white heterosexual male psychoanalyst Wilfred Bion, I re-read Lorde's essay 'Poetry is not a luxury' and was struck by the therapeutic message in her description of poetry. Reflecting on the form as a revelatory 'distillation of experience' that makes it possible to 'give name to the nameless so it can be thought' (2017, p. 8), Lorde's words sound not dissimilar to what white psychoanalyst Christopher Bollas conceived with his 'unthought known' or the exploration of what we unconsciously learn of the object world as infants and how we can harness it in the service of our psyches.

It wasn't the first time I had felt that Lorde's words convey something vitally important about how we can examine and regulate our emotions. So, it's not only poetry that is a vital place for self-reflection and understanding, as I believe therapy can also be, but also decolonial, Black lesbian feminist, queer and trans perspectives that can bring richness to our profession, a richness that often goes unacknowledged or is even rejected as 'too political', as if the therapy encounter is a politics-free space.

It is because of the politics inherent in our lives, the inequalities that are endemic to it, that therapy, however, *can* often be a luxury and also a privilege, especially for those in the LGBTIQA+ and QTIPOC communities. Therapeutic outcomes for these client groups also vary, perhaps sometimes because of this unwillingness to accept that all of our identities are politicized under white cis hetero-patriarchy.

Indeed, Crawford *et al.* (2018) found that people from sexual and ethnic minorities were more likely to report experiencing lasting bad effects from therapy. Rimes *et al.* (2019, p. 577) also found that 'compared to heterosexual women, lesbian and bisexual women had higher final-session severity for depression, anxiety, and functional impairment and increased risk of not attaining reliable recovery in depression/anxiety or functioning'. Similar results were found among bisexual men. In research by Stonewall (Bachman & Gooch, 2018) one in twenty LGBT people and one in five trans people reported they had been pressured to access services to change or suppress their sexual orientation and/or gender identity. Therapists already have an ethical obligation not to practice so-called "conversion therapy" but these harmful practices do take place. Further, as this book goes to press, many therapists are expressing their opposition to the government decision to exclude trans people from the ban on so-called "conversion therapy" practices despite the fact that more recent statistics indicate that trans people are twice as likely as cisgender LGB people to be offered or subjected to conversion practices (BCTC, 2022).

Anecdotally, I have heard from QTIPOC individuals in therapy that it can be as much of a lottery to find therapists who are able to work with embodied racialized trauma given its neglect in training institutions alongside the lack of rigorous work around whiteness. The same can be said for finding therapists who have been well prepared for working with gender and sexuality diversity. And as Amanda Middleton (Chapter 7) notes, there are no guarantees about cultural competency regarding these intersectional markers. Both Sabah Choudrey (Chapter 14) and Robert Downes (Chapter 3) observe that there simply isn't enough thought given to marginalized identities in most therapy trainings. The research on therapy outcomes made me think again about the relative paucity of therapeutic literature available to those who work with clients from LGBTIQA+ communities and about who creates this literature and how knowledge is generated. This book aims to contribute something towards filling the gap of knowledge that exists in text form and we could do with several more volumes still. Sabah Choudrey launched their book *Supporting Trans Clients of Colour: How to Make Your Practice Inclusive* (2022) earlier this year, and Dominic Davies (Chapter 15) with Silva Neves are currently updating the ground-breaking Pink Therapy volumes first published in 2000.

One of the queering practices of this book is that, as editor, I have worked collaboratively, asking participants to reflect on non-normative thinking and practice in a variety of therapeutic situations. A journalist before I became a therapist, I started by speaking with each contributor, not setting the agenda other than to ask them to decide on three or four key considerations to share with fellow colleagues about their work and experiences as therapists and therapists in training. Many of the books we read as trainees and beyond elevate the medical model approach with its diagnostic categories which, although undeniably useful, can also lack the nuance of the actual people we are and of those who come to our therapy rooms. So, with some contributors, topics known to be of interest to them were suggested, while others brought their own preferred talking points. In some chapters, I was present as an enquiring other mind and in others I was mostly absent. When Bay De Veen suggested writing an imagined conversation with a supervisor, I was reminded of the Black feminist practice of fabulation and Saidiya Hartman's *Wayward Lives, Beautiful Experiments* (2019) and of Jose Esteban Munoz's *Cruising Utopia* (2009) and the importance of creating stories about the future that act as a kind of springboard to the worlds we dream of living in. So, this book is a collection of conversations, some real and some imagined. I have found them all to be thought-provoking, healing and challenging and, although I have spent almost all my working and personal life in queer community, the ideas contained in these chapters show me there is always so much more to learn.

The normative conventions of discourse that exist in the multiplicity of cultures we navigate infuse many of our profession's theories and belief systems and they also frame and reproduce the inequalities that impact not only LGBTIQA+ therapists' lives but also those of our clients. Which is to say that those who hold positions of power, either in social status, in publishing, in institutions or in communities, including in the fields of psychotherapy and psychoanalysis, have until recently preferred so-called 'experts' to write and share knowledge in a format that aligns with academic structures and strictures. This form of knowledge creation and dissemination can often use language that is inaccessible and, although there are some ways in which technical jargon can help us to understand the detail of clients' experiences, these are not necessarily what we would share with clients, even if they too happen to be therapists. Indeed our field's rarefied language is one of the many ways in which the asymmetry of power in the therapeutic relationship can be evidenced, but there are others, especially so if the therapist is operating from within a framework that doesn't consider how the positionality of the person in front of them might impact them, and this is where the conversations and essays in this book come into their own. What could happen between therapists or clients if they were to speak together and not be bound by the conventions of normative therapeutic culture? Does not the therapeutic space hold a kind of magic that is born from implicit and explicit conversations between therapist and client?

When I was studying to be a counsellor and then psychotherapist, I would have loved to have been accompanied by a book which offered a sense of eavesdropping on the most fascinating queer clinicians, and which reflected the dynamic nature of the therapeutic relationship. How might a collection of conversations in book form mirror and support some of the kinds of conversations or reflections we have both with clients and between peers and supervisors? Such conversations we know can be life-shaping and world-changing, as well as modelling of the queer and decolonizing philosophies that underpin this book which reject the notion of the therapeutic 'expert', drawn as it is from what Robert Downes calls 'Empire Mind'. So, the conversing subjects of this book have a range of professional, lived and reflective experiences to offer and share and their insights refashion the limitations of the way we are taught about each other, as well as those who are othered. There can be a tendency, even in therapeutic books, to remain in an intellectual register, even when covering deeply emotive subjects. This can be a particular risk when dealing with themes of gender and sexuality, given the ways in which marginalised groups have often been pathologized and dismissed by associating us with feelings and bodies rather than rationality and minds. In this book contributors were invited to express themselves as fully as possible, and to include the deep range of feelings that circulate around the issues and experiences being discussed. An intersectional vein runs through this book because, despite living in a society that does its best to subsume the complex subjectivities of race, class, ability, gender, cis or transness, sexuality and faith, we know that these markers of difference impact significantly on how each of us moves through the world. The chapters are ordered in such a way as to make it possible to dip in and out as time and interest permits. If you are unfamiliar with this territory, hopefully the first two chapters introduce some of the ideas that many other chapters are building on.

Lorde wrote prodigiously about the importance of recognizing how our differences must be acknowledged and leveraged as a source of strength and pointed to the limitations of living in 'the European mode' which posits that life is 'a problem to be solved' (2017, p. 8) and ideas – rather than the body – are the route to freedom. I understand the space of this book, which moves around queer and queered bodies, as my relationship to my own body and ergo identity has shifted during its creation. Alongside my first conversations in 2020, I also started to explore the shape and contours of my body through conversations with my therapist and the significant others in my life. These conversations moved me from considering myself as a cis queer woman considering a breast reduction to a gender non-conforming person electing to have chest surgery and whose identity is not – perhaps was never – in alignment with the gender assigned to me at birth based on my biology. So, in some conversations, keen-eyed readers will notice that I refer to myself, and am related to, as cis and, in Chapter 5, written closer to the publishing deadline, I have shifted to a trans position, moving from Jane to Chance. I understand transness to be, in the Rocheian sense, 'a new space. Uncontrolled and uncontrollable' by Euro-centric white patriarchy, and 'a destination' (2019, p. 255). Trans as in a way of being that is 'beautifully cut adrift from the endless layers of performativity that have weighed me down my whole life', (2019, p. 11). May we and our clients also find such lightness in our ways of being.

Queering the Black feminist psychoanalytic

Gail Lewis PhD

We are embedded in and socialized by colonial history and culture, and much of mainstream therapy is based on Euro-centric theories that replicate this same colonial history. This mindset is not inclusive of other cultures or ethnicities. On the rare occasions that other cultures are acknowledged in the literature or elsewhere in our field, they are often based on the racist stereotypes that have existed since the early days of our profession at the turn of the twentieth century. As sensitive clinicians, we need to interrogate and investigate how these ideas show up in therapeutic practice. There are, however, notable exceptions, says Dr Gail Lewis, who offers new ways to think about what colonial era psychoanalyst Wilfred Bion can offer to queer white and QTIPOC clients.

Wilfred Bion and Audre Lorde: queer bedfellows

JANE CHANCE CZYZSELSKA: I'm really interested in what you find valuable in Bion's work. I'm curious about how you queer or decolonize his thinking. I want to know about a queer Black feminist analytic.

GAIL LEWIS: I'm a Kleinian. I was trained at the Tavistock. I align to it, it makes sense to me in its own terms, but it makes sense to me in the way that any learning that I've done through institutions and the fields of theory and practice they teach, you know, pedagogical practice, makes sense to me, in that they *all*, all of them, come from a framework of modernity, and modernity produced the hierarchies of value of personhoods and instituted all the normative subject positions that we could occupy.

Theory and practice come from a framework which produced hierarchies of value of personhoods

JC: Yes, true.

GL: Including obviously the racialized one that I think is quite primary, I think that gender comes out of that because I think it's also central to racial capitalism. So just as we can really be critical of any mode of psychanalytic, psychotherapeutic learning, all the schools we went to – even now, though there are attempts now to make changes – they are not really fundamentally trying to change, I don't think. I mean, some people in them are making inroads but is that really radically different from anthropology, from sociology, philosophy, history or literature studies? I mean, I don't know whether anything is innocent or more innocent in one disciplinary area than others. We can do our own hierarchies of value and say, 'Oh well, the psychoanalytic orthodoxies are more toxic, more about instilling the normative than the stuff we get in the university, or in the school that's guarded by police', and you know all of that, so I'm aligned in that way, in that I've learned from all of them and I'm suspicious of all of them.

JC: Right, OK. So, under racial capitalism, the economic set-up is structured to privilege white people and that makes race a primary subject position which creates further hierarchies – is that what you're saying?

GL: It is the economic set-up as *part* of the whole social set-up – a 'social' set-up that includes the psychic, cultural, epistemological 'set-ups'. And within that are the 'ontological' set-ups – the range of subjectivities and senses of self that are possible. Racial capital is a structure/manifestation of the organization of the world through the prisms and knowledge frame and hierarchies of value of human and non-human life. Within that there are categories of gender but increasingly – in the wake of Atlantic enslavement, I think – gender is finally understood as a category of whiteness and thus as a structure of power and normativity. So, it's in that sense.

JC: Yeah, OK.

GL: So that then requires of us, I think, a kind of insistence on trying to do two things: the first thing is to know what it is we are being taught. So, for me, it's 'what is it that Klein and the Kleinians are saying?' Let me take it at face value and learn it, pay due respect, and learn from it, with it, through it.

JC: Yeah, yeah.

Respect the theory and put it in critical but creative dialogue with other thinking

GL: So pay due respect and then when I feel I've learned it – and I in no way, Jane, think I'm an expert on any of that, on any particular body of theory really – so I get what I can from it, take it seriously and then having taken it seriously, put it into real critical but creative dialogue with these other ways of thinking; bodies of theory that also deliver something and steal something.

JC: Yeah.

GL: But, of course, the other thing is to put that under the scrutiny of the lens of lived experience and activist claims, actually not just claims but activist modes of saying, 'We can be different, something different can happen so different personhoods can emerge.' So, when you try and scramble all that and you're in your consulting room, and in walks someone who says, 'X or I found you through Y, they said you might be good' and you know immediately you hear that that they are really putting you under scrutiny to test whether they can reach you and you can reach them.

JC: Mm, yes.

GL: Then they come in and they say, 'Well, I came here because something's not right. I'm not feeling OK, I'm under pressure, or I'm at the point of collapse,' or whatever they present with, but they come because something is not quite working for them in their lives, and we know immediately if we have a queer person before us or someone who doesn't even necessarily know that, but you feel a bit of a vibe ...

JC: Right, right.

Part of the trouble is we're just being minoritized

GL: Or someone who has been racialized as minority and maybe has a racialized identity, but you also get a vibe just being 'minor' isn't OK. Part of the trouble is we're just being minoritized: as queer, as Black, as trans*, as feminine – in whatever body – that somehow that's not OK, or a particular kind of masculine as well. All the ways in which the normative structures of power are impacting on this person's life, and they come in and say, 'And I am hoping you can walk with me and get me somewhere different.' And you think, 'This is really a big task.' So, for me what's really important then and this is why – thinking about that bringing-together – why I feel Bion, a very strange, interesting man from what I gather, gives us the first tool that we need, I think, and it's built on Klein and that's to stay open to curiosity, to be open but without having a desire for a particular outcome.

JC: Oh, yes.

Lorde and Bion both seem to be saying that we need to be open enough to ourselves

GL: Who do we have before us? In a real way, not in a kind of 'let me pathologize', but really who do we have before us? What is it that they are asking me to walk with them about, and can I think, Bion says, again building out of Klein and post-Kleinian thinking around counter-transference, can I stay open enough to know what I can and can't offer? My capacities and my limitations? I think of that and

Bion and that's like his container/contained idea, his idea of maternal reverie, all of that. The capacity to really stay with someone in their pain, hold it, receive it from them, process it and give it back in a way that feels more bearable for them; that's what they mean by that container/contained and maternal reverie. And then immediately I think of Audre Lorde and *Uses of the Erotic* (1984) because she – it seems to me – is saying exactly the same thing. We need to be able to be open enough to ourselves and the ways in which feeling – the capacity to acknowledge and use feeling for understanding, a capacity that we've been cut off from – those feelings help us to know something that structures of power don't want us to know.

JC: Yes!

GL: That the normativities through which you're supposed to be a proper, adapted person, like of 'respectability' and 'self-possession' – talk about a discourse of property! – and rationality, etc., etc., all the things through which all of us are judged and we judge ourselves, as 'proper', 'adjusted', 'deserving'. Of course, through a Black queer feminist lens, these normativities are named 'whiteness', with the accordant economies of gender, and once we see that, then it's clear that the powers that be – including the epistemological powers within theoretical positions – don't want us to know our queer selves and the creative potential of that. They don't want us to know so curiosity is cut off. Lorde says we need to touch our feelings to get back in touch with that, but so does Bion (not perhaps in explicit terms about queer subjectivities but in terms of what he calls O, that cannot be represented but is 'the truth' of us. See *Attention and Interpretation* [Bion, 1970], especially Chapter 11). So, Bion's theory of thinking is all about how thinking comes from, is a product of, a capacity to stay with the feelings that feel unbearable, and Lorde is saying the same thing and it's like 'what the fuck?!' How come these two, seemingly, radically different people, with radically different experiences, come to such similar positions?!

Through a Black queer feminist lens, normativities are named 'whiteness'

JC: Yeah. I wonder if she read Bion or if she came to a similar way of thinking through her lived experiences?

GL: Yeah, that question is really begged, isn't it? I guess this is just an example of how we and all things are connected, and there are certain metaphysics that 'know' the world and the space/place of the human in it, in ways that are radically different to the normative frames of modernity we were talking about a minute ago. African and/or Indigenous metaphysics. And that's one of the paradoxes for me of psychoanalysis: that it is so much a discourse of modernity, yet its radical outside (well, inside – the theory of the unconscious!) declares its link to more ancient understandings – as Audre would name them – or what Bion would call O, as I said. But to get back to the point! When I started my training, I knew Lorde first and then I go into my classes, and I get this thing called a 'theory of thinking' (1962) or 'attacks on linking' (1959) from Bion and I'm thinking, 'God, this sounds really like Audre. How can that be?' Because he is, I assume, upper class English, an Indian colonial aristocrat. And then I learn, ah, but he had his first eight years with his Ayah.

JC: Yes, the Indian woman his parents paid to mother him!

GL: So this is another source of knowing I expect through her practices of care that help him to tap into what Audre would call the spiritual-stroke-psychic-stroke-emotional that for her is the erotic – that's what the erotic is for her.

JC: Mm yes, a more expansive idea of the erotic than the popular usage, that's only connected to the sexual?

GL: Yes, for sure. In fact, if you read the essay 'Uses of the erotic: The Erotic as power' (1984), you'll see that she explicitly says that this is far wider than the sexual, though it incorporates this as an aspect. But it is, in perhaps more psychoanalytic terms, a deeply libidinal impulse that reaches out from within and is 'ancient'. And so now I'm thinking, 'Oh, lesson learned here, Gail.' Sometimes, to our surprise if we're open enough, if we can hold that stance of curiosity, those who are positioned as our antithesis – who we are other to – can really reach us and teach us. I now think that is a 'truth' despite the concrete social realities of normative power and its multiple regimes of epistemological and ontological violence, but because as persons those social realities are never totalizing, we always exceed them, that's why we exist, otherwise we couldn't exist. Black life as – I don't just mean as anti-racist life – but Black life as living for itself, under the radar, you know, outside the stereotypes of us, Black life couldn't exist if all this was totalizing as it were. So, the lesson is, can I learn something then from this figure who is apparently the opposite to me? Older – of course, I'm already old – dead, white, male, aristocratic part of the imperial, at least his family and whatever he did, and he was in the army. And here's this man who's speaking to me with a different terminology but a similar language to Audre Lorde.

JC: Yeah!

GL: Wow!

JC: I know, I know and I'm just thinking back to Audre Lorde and bell hooks, both of whom talk about emotionality and how white people project their own inability to be emotionally expressive onto Black people.

GL: Yeah, yeah.

JC: And Black life being the site of so-called 'unruly' emotionality; that's being shut down as well.

GL: Exactly! So for both of them, Bion and Lorde – obviously it's my interpretation, who knows? – both of them are saying, if we are going to allow ourselves to find and hold on to, in a way that doesn't feel like it fragments us, what we might for want of a better word call an authentic self – slightly bringing in Winnicott (1982, 1990) – in a sense, that kind of feels like who I am; this kind of feels like I'm not having to split myself up to be this here and that there, to be secret about aspects of me, you know, to be the compliant Black girl, you know, because of the stereotype of the angry Black woman?

JC: Yeah, yeah.

GL: … to hide my queerness, whoever I'm lovers with, because it is under very real attack but somehow I need to be able to hold these together, and being able to do that requires being able to touch deep into the forms of knowing that come from our emotionality, our capacity to feel and not just have sensation. Our capacity to feel, know and seek connection.

JC: Yeah, so what you're saying is there is some kind of expansive potential, as Bion says, and both in his ideas and in Lorde's there's something of the spiritual, and entering that realm?

GL: Totally, totally.

JC: And openness?

GL: Totally. As long as we don't think of the spiritual as about some kind of thing called God, that isn't about life, isn't about the totality of connectedness, because what the logics of racial capitalism, the frameworks of modernity require is that we mustn't have interdependency, we must have the capacity to dominate and have others know their place, and to command, and everything; whereas when you get into the realm of the spiritual where it is about the interconnections, that is frightening because they make us vulnerable. I mean, we know in the room sometimes the moment when you've got someone – well, it doesn't even have to be someone, it can be me in my distress, when I was in my first analysis. Let's turn it the other way round. In my absolute distress, in a way not even knowing what it was at some level, not able to articulate it, or having an intellectualized sense but not a *felt* sense of just what was my deep pain and trouble; and trying to be able to be with a white woman therapist and I'm finding myself talking about right up-close everyday racism inside the family. And I am literally collapsed in a heap on the floor, cowering in the corner of the room next to a blanket box, sobbing because suddenly something's happened, that the knot of feeling and pain and agony and fragmentation really has been pierced a little bit. Of course, what do I do after I get up off the floor and go out and come back for my next session? I completely attack: 'Don't you ever fucking come near my family again in your talk. You fuck off!'

JC: Yeah, yeah, yeah!

Containing clients and offering back what they can bear

GL: Because actually she'd gotten up close and she'd hinted that we could stay with it. And in that moment – and there were several moments like that over the years – in the early years, it was unbearable and eventually it could become bearable, and we could stay with it. And when I'd say, 'You're just not getting this,' she could admit it and say, 'No, I'm not getting it. I can't know what you're talking about in terms of micro-aggressions of racism, the pain you felt and feel about that in your family.' Because people can get the big sociological patterns of racism – let's hope therapists can anyway – but the micro-aggressions, I don't know whether they can because they are right in the room. But because she could say, 'You're right, I can't be there or know it, but you have the feeling and let's work with that,' we could stay with it and gradually put me together a bit. I have to say my presentation was much more around the terrible effects of racism on me than homophobia, anti-queerness in a way, but in reassembling me and detoxifying the racism, even the less acute internalized homophobia could get nullified because I was able to say, 'But this is me, not all of me – yes, all of this stuff has produced me but I'm more than it and therefore I can be more authentically me. More of a sense of an alignment.'

JC: So there was something about your analyst's – to use Bion's understanding – containing capacity?

GL: Yeah, absolutely, and to sort of show me and use with me what I came to understand as my projections and projective identifications, and she could use her counter-transference. I was trying to communicate something about the unspeakability, almost the unthinkability, of some of the micro-aggressions around racism, so I could communicate that and she could kind of receive it and hold it and stay with it until she and I, we together, could think it through more and begin to articulate it but also to know when I was doing a whole set of projections or projective identifications that were much more evacuative, chucking into her. 'Don't fucking come near my family,' I said because I was thinking, 'How can I go near them? How can I dare to reveal and speak that this was also an aspect of our domestic life? Not just the loving bits or the socialist bits.' And in my training, I came to know this through a kind of Kleinian approach – an approach that insists on the need to hold both 'love' and 'hate' as a prerequisite or process really toward and in the 'Depressive Position' and what Bion thought of in terms of K and -K (where K stands for 'knowledge' and the desire and capacity to seek knowledge from experience; and -K is the opposite, the destruction of that capacity and desire for an ongoing process of transforming experience into knowledge) – a reaching toward the unknown and a capacity to see and hold 'links' and to find a place of quietude inside, kind of thing. She could contain and I could increasingly hold together the 'love' and 'hate': mine as well as that of beloved family members – not that of those family members who were not beloved. But what was vital for me, you know, in both my being on the couch and then in the clinical seminar, supervision and psychoanalytic theory room, was that I had Black feminist thinking like that of Audre to build this new learning upon, learning as a patient in analysis and as a trainee.

JC: I love how you describe your process. Can you say more about the origins of projection?

GL: So the tiny infant in the paranoid schizoid position from birth to three or four months is constantly projecting, has to split and project in order to survive because it is such a tiny helpless dependent infant human. Then Bion picks it up and says we have to take this really seriously and use these projective identifications in our technique because if we close ourselves to them, we won't be able to take the communications that are coming from the patient or client and that are trying to tell us something. Just as the infant projects into the maternal figure, whoever that is – the maternal object – the unbearable feelings, the fear of death, and that maternal figure needs to be able to receive this and not give it back straight away, not just say, 'Oh, there, there, baby, here you are; feed you.' But just as in the feeding or change, you attend to the physical needs of the baby, in the psychological aspect of that process, you hold on to what's being projected into them – let's use that pronoun – and try to make sense of it enough to understand what the infant is feeling, just as you do when you say, 'Oh, why are they crying? What is it?' And then you think, 'Oh, maybe it's this?'

JC: Yeah, yeah.

GL: I mean, I've only done it as an auntie, not as a birth mother, but it seems to work, you've found something. So Bion says just as that happens with the infant and there's a maternal reverie where the maternal object can act as a container of what's being projected out, process it and give it back in a digestible form. So, he is saying we need to be able to do the same in the room with the people we are sitting with and trying to walk with – listen to them, watch them, take all the modes of communication that they are giving to us and say, 'I can receive it. I can hold it and it can help both me and you process it, and then we can work further with it.' And Bion says that sometimes, even when we receive it, we might work so fast and give it back that for the patient it feels like we have not stayed with it at all. We have again broken down the link between container and contained, analyst and patient, because we have not been able to hold onto what they have brought to us, to try to help us feel as well as think about.

JC: Right. So, basically you haven't metabolized what the client has projected into you or the field sufficiently in you.

GL: Yes, exactly, and then the feeling of it is unbearable and that might be a repetition, so you walk into the room, and someone says, 'You know what? I'm gay, I'm lesbian, I'm bi, I'm trans, I'm non-binary and I'm trying to tell my parents or whoever and they just went crazy and chucked me out or went cold and said, "Do you want chicken with your potatoes?" Cut it off.' And then if in the room, we do the same, in some form or another, either turn away or say, 'Well, I can give you this food but I can't give you the food that says let's talk about this, let's think this through, that's OK, that's OK for us to think about and then what we think about might be all sorts.' It's not about thinking to change them; it's saying, 'What has it meant to you to bring that to us today? What's the pathway we need to walk to feel and think this thing through further, to hold this container/contained relationship in a way that helps you to integrate, embrace, redefine whatever it is that happened? But yes, it's OK for you to be right here and we'll stay looking at it on the table.'

JC: Yeah, yeah, beautiful.

When the activist bodymind speaks to/with the analyst bodymind

GL: And for me, you see, what's extraordinary is that capacity, despite some of my teachers saying things like, 'Oh, X doesn't know whether they're Arthur or Martha' – that awful phrase – to show me in a room when they were talking about a clinical process note, an actual clinical sample of how to stay open with curiosity to that same person that in the theory lecture they'd said Arthur and Martha about – an extraordinary disjunction.

JC: Wow! It's interesting to hear that sometimes a therapist's lack of awareness or their political insensitivity won't necessarily negatively impact on the client or the work.

GL: I think the training that I got – even with aspects of my teachers who thought questions of racism were wider cultural/culture and not of any relevance to their unconscious effects, as though there was a difference – showed that kind of disjunction between their ideological/theoretical position and their position actually in the room. It's weird and maybe I am being too generous, yet that is what I think. But I think, too, that what I had as a resource was that I heard people like Audre Lorde (1984) and Hortense Spillers (2003). I had my activist history which was like, 'You know what? You taught me something but you ain't getting this and we're going to have to do this work, do this theoretical development and practice, we'll use what's good from you and we'll not take everything. We'll alloy it with other stuff, and we'll develop it ourselves.' But just as I've not thrown all my sociology away, or all my Marxism or other things away, I don't throw the Kleinian theory away that I was trained through.

JC: I can relate to what you are saying because I was an active Marxist when I was at uni in my twenties and for a few years after that. I got involved in campaigning against Section 28 and the anti-abortion Alton Bill.

GL: Yeah, yeah.

JC: So I have been aware of how lives are politicized by those who aren't like us for a long time – those who are not queer and female and, in your case, those who are not Black – so then as editor of *DIVA* magazine I developed a greater awareness of lesbian, bi, queer, trans, intersex, QTIPOC lived experiences and then gradually also becoming more aware about whiteness and trying to address that. So that was what was going on in and around me when I was doing my training. My life has been a political training of sorts. So, I'm interested in this thing about politics because for me, as a girl, a lesbian, there were times when I felt as if my voice didn't matter as much as boys' or men's. So, meeting a communist and Marxist ideology shortly after I had come out, almost being given the words to say by comrades, words that were powerful and 'won' arguments, I finally felt my own insides. I had structure internally: my voice *did* matter, and I could be listened to and have impact, effect change.

GL: Yeah, yeah.

JC: It was like scaffolding for my personhood. In recent years, I've noticed that when I have challenging conversations with cis-het people about transness and some white folk about whiteness I often move away from my emotional into my political discourse. In those moments, it can sometimes feel difficult to talk about the emotional aspects. Have you had something similar? Is it to do with becoming politicized as a young person when you feel your voice isn't heard in your family? I became a journalist to have a voice and then as an editor commissioned others to give them a voice. I suppose you could say therapy is about creating a space for clients' inner voices and being heard. Our lives are politicized whether we want that or not, but how do we bring it into the room? It's about bringing it in with care, isn't it? I know I sometimes do it in a clumsy way: I might say, 'Is there something about race going on here?' with some clients of colour or 'Is there something about gender or something transphobic going on here?' to create space for that to be talked about.

GL: Yeah.

JC: Does that speak to you?

GL: Yes, it does, it really does, and I suppose a bit like you I was an active activist. It was manic actually. It was absolutely needed, just as now, you know, we need to be pressing, pressing, pressing, even though we need to rethink a lot. I don't think we know how the political reformation and structure of ideas would be exactly, or what shape our demands would take, how we could articulate across all those demands because things are so changed, it seems to me.

JC: Mm.

GL: The old off-the-shelf things just don't have resonance but that is not the same thing as saying you can't learn from them. I was really active in anti-racism, all London anti-fascism within feminism and Black feminism and the lesbian Left back in the late 1970s, early 1980s, all that kind of stuff, all the time. And I think it was because that was needed in the world out there but, in my internal world, I needed to avoid the very thing that I collapsed on my analyst's floor of, by the blanket box in the corner weeping, weeping, saying, 'This is all that stuff out there but fuck, it's been inside me and it's just messed me up. There's a bit of me' – and that was the mania – that was the thing I was defending against. So, within Black feminism now, absolutely put at the forefront by the younger generation with thinkers/activists, has been the need to not only practise care but to understand that self and collective care is a powerful politics. It absolutely is in Marxist terms. We could think about that practice of self-care as a rejection or refusal of the very alienation that comes from racial capitalism – which is to say 'capitalism' because it *is* racial capitalism.

JC: Yeah, yeah.

GL: Trade union struggles to shorten the working day is about shifting the balance of power but care, that's what the women do. Now the younger Black feminists have put that on the agenda and they link it to a much more environmentalist consciousness about the destruction of the world, so there has been a real shift and what that helps me to do is think 'OK' – this is to think not necessarily to succeed in the consulting room. 'Then what does it mean to really slow down? Because obviously the work is there – because from a Black feminist field of practice and a therapeutic practice we try to go slow.' If someone wants to move too fast, we might say, 'You've moved rather fast, we might think about it.' You know? We do that so we slow down but to slow down in a way that enables connections between inside and outside, the so-called 'outside' that in some therapeutic or analytic minds feels as though it is a completely separate world. Not in our minds precisely because of what we are trying to struggle with: the toxicities of normativities of all kinds. And we are not trying to fix the people we work with in a way that makes them more so-called normal, whether that is white normal, hetero normal, gender normal, ability normal. We are trying to say, 'This is a reality. The world out there with its toxicities and how it can get inside us. And what we're trying to do here is make it that you can feel legitimate and relatively whole. Authentic. Stitched-enough-together to feel you can manage your life and you come to try to manage something that feels unmanageable. We are trying to help you manage that. Not to make you "normal".'

JC: Yes, and not to fit you into the small shape that is created for you.

GL: Yes, exactly, that's what I mean exactly. To hold onto your own capacities, your own 'good enough' self, while, just like Black feminism theorizes and shows, if we can be constantly open to the learning that comes from understanding that normativities are toxic because they construct and materialize hierarchies of human value; while *also* knowing that those outside the normative live anyway, live otherwise, then transformation and change can follow, and therefore expansion and growth. It's kind of like a model of what we might achieve in the room (with 'clients', 'patients', 'analysands' or whatever terminology we use), what we might help produce in the room between us. And by extension we get it too, they give us that, but it can be really hard. I think I find my manic political voice starts to get going almost like it's the slogans on the march rather than, 'Am I really thinking about why that slogan has come up now in my mind in the light of what you said? Can it help me to think about what it is you're telling me?' I don't always make that move successfully at all!

JC: No, I don't think I do either!

GL: But I know it has to be done and one can try and retrieve it and that's OK because otherwise we are trying to model ourselves in the image of whiteness, which is to be perfect.

JC: Well, yes, that's it. That's why I love what Bion says about not knowing. It is something that Robert Downes often says: 'What if it's OK to not know? Let's try and hang out with that feeling and where you're at right now' (Downes, personal communication).

GL: Yeah, and usually something will come then.

JC: Yeah, but I also notice what he refers to as 'Empire Mind', which is often present in me when I'm with a client who doesn't know and who really wants to. Those moments seem to demand of me that I need to know, I need to get it right.

GL: Exactly, exactly.

How can we think together about a queer Black feminist analytic futurity?

JC: What do we do with the 'Empire Mind' when it comes? If you think about Munoz and queer futurity (Munoz, 2009) and also Afro-Futurism, the idea of a future that we fantasize about because the present isn't ours, is not made for us: it's made for white straight, cis – it's made for white people more than people of colour (POC) but not so much if you are queer female or gender non-conforming – how can we touch into this future? Is that what Audre Lorde means when she talks about the possibility of what could be? She describes the kind of world she wants to live in and co-create in the present.

GL: Yes, and within a Black feminist logic, theory, practice, the idea of futurity is about what we want that isn't now. OK, but it's understood as what has to happen now to make *then* possible?

JC: Yeah.

GL: And what has to happen now to make *then* possible is things like you getting together this book as a resource. It is things like people going on the streets and saying not anti-racism but Black Lives Matter. That is such a profoundly different kind of slogan.

JC: Yeah, yeah.

GL: The ways in which trans* is both a declaration of people saying that binary is fluid and also unintelligible if you're non-binary – it makes no sense – but that both holds open the possibility of a different kind of future. So, there are all sorts of ways that there is a future in the making by the stuff that's going on now that gestures towards – not with guarantees – something being different, while claiming that the status quo is not liveable, it is not liveable. You know?

JC: Yeah, that's really powerful. The present structures make lives not liveable.

GL: Anti Blackness and its consequences is not liveable. Gender tyranny is not liveable and the way that segues into queer suggests something in the making. It is outside the bounds of intelligibility. It can't be fixed and yet there are traces. There is a wonderful article by a Black anthropologist called Vanessa Agard-Jones called 'What the sands remember' (2012). It is all about the ways in which she does some ethnographic work in Martinique as a queer of colour anthropologist scholar and starts noticing queer bodies around her. Then somebody says, 'Oh no, you have to go to …' and then she goes to this beach and on this beach, which is just the sand and the trees, is a cruising ground but it's more than a cruising ground. It's not just about moments of sex but it's moments of coming together.

JC: Right.

GL: And it's all in the sands and it's got a long, long queer history. So, it's those sorts of traces that we are trying to lay down.

JC: I would love to read that.

GL: It's a really nice piece. And then there's Tina Campt's talk on futurity and fugitivity (Campt, 2014, 2017). Do you know her work?

JC: No.

GL: She talks about futurity as being what has to happen now for *then* to happen, to be a bit simplistic about it. She has done a couple of books, but one is called *Listening to Images* and she looks at photos and listens to them. That is the kind of thing when we are in our therapy room – someone comes in, in whatever distress, upset that they need to think through, work through, and sometimes what you get before is really a stereotype – a kind of performance of a stereotype, that's what I mean by that. Obviously because they think they have to be in front of you, but they also give you a sense of who they think they have to be in front of several people. And if you think about that thing – about listening to images, as Tina Campt does – she sees mugshots or reads passport photos and she listens to the frequency of the images that suggest, 'You think I'm here to get my passport photo done, but I'm just going to show you a little of who I am,' and that's the kind of listening that we do in the room, no? We listen not only to words but to all the other ways in which we are being communicated to.

JC: Yeah, and I like the sound of her work – no pun intended!

GL: And that again is all from Black feminism and a Black feminist approach to the world that says we can be brave enough to sit with what you know and what you don't know. Be curious about it and listen for it, as it links – to go back to Bion – with this person in the room with you today and tomorrow and next week. And in that linking, can you bear the linking to happen? Not just can *they* bear it, but can *you* bear the linking to happen, so that something creative can emerge from it? And that's what he has done with the Kleinian idea of the epistemophillic instinct.

JC: Woah! What's that?

GL: Klein talked about a kind of instinct of enquiry and curiosity and wanting to get into the mother's body's contents and all of that and that's what generates our thirst for knowledge, but can it be borne because it can be too frightening and hence Bion's theory of K and minus K.

JC: Right, OK. Yeah. I'm curious about the impact of only having heterosexuality mirrored to queer kids by their primary caregivers. Obviously, there are queer people today who have been brought up by lesbian, gay or bi and/or queer parents, but I wonder what kind of a lack might be experienced by queer children brought up by hetero parents who – even if they are openly affectionate – don't experience a mirroring of their queer desire? Being queer is still shamed in our culture, after all. I'm thinking of Halberstam's *Queer Art of Failure* (2011), as in we have failed at being heterosexual.

GL: Yeah.

Working with our ancestors

JC: But also what freedom and joy that can be created if we can somehow challenge that experience. For instance, me learning a few years ago of a queer ancestor who was lovers with Freud's lesbian patient.

GL: Oh wow! Really? That's amazing!

JC: I know! Completely amazing. It was my grandmother. She invited Freud's lesbian patient to stay with her a few times and they had an affair.

GL: And where was this?

JC: In Vienna and Prague.

GL: Oh right, wow.

JC: It blew my mind! Discovering that changed something in me in that moment forever. She existed. I never met her: she died before I was born, but there is something about a repair of the lack or absence of mirroring within a culture that doesn't celebrate non-normative love and desire.

GL: Yeah.

JC: You know? And my Black queer friends talk about how Black queer love is celebrated even less.

GL: Yes, totally.

JC: And most of the relationship stories you get – often made by white people, that is – they don't work, or it is difficult. It is so rare to see Black gay or lesbian love stories represented in film or TV about queer Black love.

GL: Yeah, yeah. It's interesting. It is part of why Michaela Coel's *I May Destroy You* (BBC One, 2020) was important: it was showing the quandaries of what's abusive and what's not.

JC: Yeah, yeah.

GL: Different people negotiating sexual lives, and that was the queer guy as well, and so I thought that was important. I don't know. What's running through my mind is two tracks of a response. One is to not know the possibility, or to not see echoed in the world out there the possibility, of one you can feel; it is totally distressing, erasing, negating, all of that, and casts one adrift until you start finding – as you did, say – or being able to see the signs of you in family histories, in community life, in the ways in which X is spoken about, you begin to hear. But that absence can be part of what brings people into the room, and one hears of so many stories, a bit like yours, of finding someone back in the family tree and thinking, 'Oh, I see.'

JC: Yeah.

GL: Or it reminds me of the first time I went to Jamaica as an adult in the village really and realizing that everyone was clocking me. I went with the woman who was my partner at the time, and it was her village. I wasn't saying anything, everyone was clocking us.

JC: Yeah.

GL: We weren't out. And so you start realizing as they are clocking us, they are clocking another two women who are living in the village, not visiting from London. So that there's a way in which queer life is there but disavowed. So there are those things: yes, it can be really hard and you have to develop a lens and discover things, but the other response in me is to say that even when there is a severance and the painful costly severance of a kind of legacy of our existence, even when that happens, and in some senses there is no greater collective manifestation of that than the Black diaspora in Europe and the Americas where we don't know where we came from. Enslavement was a legitimate severing of that. We don't know.

JC: Yeah, yeah.

GL: And we can go in search of it and start to clock it. So, what I'm saying is there is a whole collective experience of not having a mirroring or a history and even within that a capacity to build life, not life without loss – it's not life absent of the experience of profound loss and severance, but to build life in a way that taps into forms of knowledge that we forgot we knew. Which goes back to Audre Lorde and Jacqui Alexander (Alexander, 2005), for example. In which we tap into a source of knowing that is deeply rooted in our capacity for feeling and tapping into the ancestral that helps us to not know for certain, but to know through feelings of a presence that is perhaps ghostly, a presence of ancestors. Ancestral spirit. Where this stuff about 'these two genders only' and 'have to be lived in that particular way in the image of whiteness', is meaningless.

JC: Right.

GL: And could we bear to travel between that as a framework of understanding our present here and now, which is very much in terms of everyday Black life – under-the-radar Black life, Black life not lived through the stereotypes, of knife-crime and baby-mother, baby-father and all this stuff, but another kind of Black life?

JC: Yeah.

GL: Could we travel into queer community, into gay and lesbian experience that says we can know our presence even if we haven't had it mirrored to us in the immediate family context?

JC: Yeah.

GL: So, it is two responses: yes, it's deeply painful but then there's something else as well about surviving. I hate the word surviving really but living through and with absence and finding ways to touch into a knowing presence in us.

JC: I generally only hear Black therapists talk about the ancestors. I guess some therapists talk about intergenerational trauma, and that, I think, comes from post-Second World War Jewish psychoanalysts. But it feels like it's rarer to hear about the strength we might glean from our ancestors. I would like to be able to talk about my ancestry which is part-Jewish and part not-Jewish.

GL: But that's part of the Black life lived otherwise. Saidiya Hartman (2021) talked about that, under the radar of the status quo that would say you are not legitimate life at all, hardly life at all. And that sense of ancestral connection or touching the ancestors' spirit – they are all part of everyday terminologies that speak to what Lorde would say, 'tapping into that source of generativity that we've been so severed from', that that white hetero-patriarchy wants to sever us from. That.

JC: It is interesting but there are two kinds of not knowing: there is the way we have been forced to not know, particularly if you're a straight white male, our feelings, and ancestors whatever and then there's us talking about the value of inhabiting a not-knowing approach; it's a different kind of not knowing.

GL: Yes, it is a different kind of not knowing. The second version is an ability to stay with not knowing and not turn away from it and in the consulting room – thinking with Bion – we need to notice when there is a turning away from not knowing and, even more than that, an attack on the potential of knowing.

CHAPTER 2

On working with trans and gender-expansive clients

Ellis J. Johnson

In therapy trainings and culture, cisgender identities and roles are centred, leaving trans and gender-expansive clients at risk of being othered, misunderstood and pathologized. Psychodynamic psychotherapeutic counsellor Ellis J. Johnson suggests alternative ways of working with, thinking about and supporting trans and gender-expansive clients.

Be wary of the idea of the authentic self with trans people

ELLIS J. JOHNSON: Authenticity, or expressing the authentic or true self, is assumed to be both an aim of transition and a goal of therapy. However, I think it takes on a very different valence when we think about trans lives and identities. I think the ideal of reaching 'the authentic self' is damaging to the trans community and as therapists we need to interrogate that notion when we are supporting trans people.

JANE CHANCE CZYZSELSKA: Interesting, say more!

EJ: There is an expectation that trans people are always trying to get to a core version of who they are, and when they get to live it out, they live happily ever after. This is a huge amount of pressure; who truly can say what their authentic self is? And if you can, how can you prove it to people who are demanding proof? I believe there is expression that feels better, easier, more peaceful and more aligned with other parts of the self, expression that is constantly constructed, not something pure and final. For that reason, we can instead think about authentic selves, authentic expressions, instead of an aim of finding and living an authentic self.

Trans questioning people in therapy can hold a huge amount of distress around the question of who they 'truly' are, and I can often visibly see the tension drain from their faces when we begin to expand our curiosity away from the binary of 'are you or aren't you trans?' The idea of the authentic self also gives very little space to fluidity and our constantly changing versions of ourselves. The goal of reaching a 'true self' can be a painful expectation for gender-fluid people, for example, because it can be more difficult for other people to accept that fluidity if we are stuck focusing on a singular, ultimate destination. So, when I approach my trans clients, I'm not thinking, 'What is your true self?' I'm thinking about them exploring incrementally about what feels easier or better, more peaceful, more joyful, more aligned or less painful in this moment, at this time, as opposed to asking, 'What is the core truth?'

Gender consistency is a cis myth

JC: Absolutely. Some trans people might try different names out with friends or partners or even their therapists, to see how it feels to have other people use it and for them to use it themselves. There is this demand within white cis hetero-patriarchy for consistency, particularly regarding identity, even though we all change through a lifetime, so I think it can be harmful to expect consistency, particularly with trans and non-binary people and others who are gender-expansive.

EJ: Yes, and the idea of consistency being a cis myth makes me think about the importance of categorization for white supremacy; that we have to be able to categorize people especially when thinking about race, sexuality and gender, interestingly enough all things to do with the body, in order to create hierarchy, which can then justify dominance. Consistency is necessary for categorization, and categorization is necessary both for white cis hetero-patriarchy and for the survival of the 'psy-complex', meaning the ways in which psychology has tried to categorize the human condition; the Diagnostic and Statistical Manual of Mental Disorders (DSM) being a perfect example. Mary Watkins and Helene Shulman write about this in *Toward Psychologies of Liberation* (2008).

JC: Yes, true.

EJ: Unless as a therapist you can answer for yourself what makes you authentically 'you', and unless you have the luxury of being that one hundred per cent of the time, then you shouldn't expect trans people to be able to demonstrate, explain, prove and live within their version of that one hundred per cent of the time either. We don't owe anyone consistency. Unfortunately, we are in a moment where trans people are often expected to demonstrate consistency in order to get access to medical care, so this is truly a flaw in the medical model, and I think we need to challenge that in therapeutic spaces.

JC: Mm, yes.

EJ: Most of my work has been with trans clients over the last seven years and the majority of people I speak to don't come to therapy to question or figure out their identity. Maybe there's a belief amongst cis therapists that people will come through the door and want you to help them decide 'if they're a man or a woman', but in my experience, most of the distress I see with my clients is around them trying to figure out how to explore/express their gender without being disowned, attacked or expelled to the margins of society; it is preparation for hard conversations, and exploring very legitimate fears around losing relationships, employment, medical care and, more broadly, safety. These are the things that seem to take up much more space and can often obscure the bigger questions about what the client actually wants for themselves.

Perhaps I just happen to see people who already have a strong, clear sense of their gender, but for those clients who are deeply questioning themselves, the sessions often turn, almost immediately, towards their fears about other people's reactions and whether transition is 'worth it' as opposed to whether it holds some meaning for them personally. So, we then get to a place where we are talking about giving or gaining permission, from the self or from others, not just authenticity. Lots of trans people are constantly navigating a trade-off between being themselves and being safe; focusing on authenticity negates the very real intersections of oppression that they must survive under.

This is also very relevant when we think about people who detransition, as research shows that some people revert to living as the gender they were assigned, not because they were mistaken, but because it was impossible to live as the gender they felt they were for reasons such as social or familial rejection, isolation, lack of support, difficulties finding employment, etc. – see Torrey Peters' *Detransition, Baby* (2021) as an example of this. These are people who may have experienced a great deal of pain at probably the sharpest end of gender trauma.

JC: Yes.

EJ: Gender may be personal, but it is largely played out socially, meaning that we need others to reflect it back to us in order to feel that we have a place in the world. That to me is the trauma, not the trans identity.

JC: And are you talking about work with adult clients?

EJ: Yes, I work with over-16s.

JC: Also the authenticity issue is a transphobic narrative, isn't it? It is the question that asks, 'What's a real woman, what's a real man?' That question comes from the outside, not the inside. Of course, the two things aren't separate, so there is perhaps an internalization of the external cis questioning of transness that happens and that creates a lot of self-doubt among trans clients.

Transphobia is internalized cis normativity

EJ: Yes, absolutely, and that self-doubt can be absolutely debilitating. Sometimes it is very difficult for trans clients to navigate around the toxic narrative that their feelings around gender are 'perverted' or that their 'condition' is actually a sexual fetish; those narratives affect how trans people feel about and attempt to understand themselves as well as how others see them; we might even say that some have internalized cis normativity, or cis-ness, as a 'good object'. I think what many people talk about as being internalized transphobia is actually internalized cis normativity. Transphobia is cis normativity in action.

JC: I hadn't thought about that before but yes, of course it is.

EJ: Yes, I believe the term internalized transphobia is just a fear of not living up to the gendered norms that traumatize everybody – both cis and trans people. It is the grappling with something that everybody grapples with: that pain of having to fit into very narrow expectations. So, if a trans client says, 'I don't look like a woman' what she is really saying is, 'I don't look like what we're told a woman should look like.' But she is a woman, so of course she looks like a woman; she is what a woman looks like. I think that framing it in this way de-centres transness as the issue and re-centres cis normativity as the problem. Externalizing that narrative can be very powerful. Authenticity, or individualism, assumes that people have agency and assumes that they can choose who they are, and that it is a real possibility to move around in the world on their own terms. This really is the way (some) white cis people are allowed to exist, but people of colour, and of course trans people, are not allowed this same agency because they live under the lenses – and structural realities? – of white supremacy and white cis hetero-patriarchy. This also applies to the working classes, disabled people, immigrants and refugees – what freedom and choice do they have, and just how complicated is it to pursue their own freedom? Oppression – and capitalism – doesn't afford us the luxury of choosing authenticity over safety in many cases, especially when we are preoccupied with surviving, and it limits our choices. It's also interesting that society simultaneously glorifies 'being yourself, being unique' while making it almost impossible, and dangerous, to do so.

JC: Yes, that's really true. If only it was that easy.

EJ: So the idea of authenticity is really a myth, in my opinion, and should not be an expectation on trans people when we live under white cis hetero-patriarchy. Looking forwards, maybe what we mean by authenticity is thinking or being in the world in a decolonized way. Maybe we can replace the pressure to find our authenticity – which is a goal that the trans population is particularly burdened with, in my opinion – with the goal of decolonizing our minds, our bodies, our gender, our sexuality and our spirituality, and unburdening ourselves from oppression.

We can't think about gender without thinking about race

EJ: So let's talk about the link between our understandings of gender and race. We can trace the beginnings of our current understandings of race back to the mid to late seventeenth century in the Caribbean with laws such as the Barbados Slave Code of 1661. The modern, western categorizations of race began to be encoded in law around the mid to late seventeenth century, when it became necessary to differentiate between the rights of enslaved Africans, Indigenous populations and white European indentured servants in the Americas and in the Caribbean. This was followed by the development of the field of what we would now call scientific racism, with Carolus Linnaeus' 1758 edition of *Systema Naturae* classifying and ranking four different 'varieties' of human beings. A whole discipline was developed with the aim of separating out humans by race and creating a hierarchy, where white Europeans were seen as the most civilized, intelligent and rational of the 'races' (or 'species') and, almost universally, Black Africans were placed at the bottom.

One thing which perturbed white Europeans seems to have been the ways in which different cultures around the world expressed gender in a multitude of ways; white Europeans took this to be evidence of how they were savage, animalistic, uncouth. In order to maintain the illusion of superiority, diverse sexual and relationship practices, such as non-monogamy, were denigrated and continue to be, to this day. In their wonderful book *Gender Trauma* (2020), Alex Iantaffi talks about how the settler colonial project wiped out indigenous, expansive expressions of gender and forcibly replaced them with white European versions, which enforced the gender binary. We can say the same about expansive sexualities, and about

Indigenous religious practices and spirituality. So scientific racism and the gender binary are linked together. Maria Lugones writes about this in *The Coloniality of Gender* (2016). That project is ongoing, and it is ongoing in the therapeutic traditions, which hold core assumptions about the parameters of human behaviour, what is 'normal' and what needs to be 'fixed'.

JC: Speaking of scientific racism, around the same time, European white sexologists like Kraft-Ebbing (1886) wrote 'the higher the development of the race, the stronger the contrasts between man and woman'. In other words, the white gender binary denotes a more superior culture than Black and Brown cultures and societies and that was in relation to biological and non-biological gender markers. This belief was very much in play in the creation of medical protocols for people born with variations in sex characteristics too. The racialization of gender is everywhere!

EJ: Yeah, it's really fascinating, and it shows how important it is to know your history, know where these categorizations and assumptions have come from.

JC: Yes, Amanda Middleton (Chapter 7) also says 'know your history' in relation to how our profession has pathologized LGBTIQ+ patients and clients over the decades and centuries.

EJ: Absolutely.

Gender variance is a human norm

EJ: Gender – and sex – variance is a human norm. The white, cis experience is not the most accurate or only way to understand human sexuality or gender. Those very narrow expectations really do cause harm in the therapeutic space, and in general.

JC: Yes, and Myra Hird (2003) describes how Fairbairn, who worked with an intersex patient in the 1930s, focused the analysis on establishing the patient's 'true sex' despite her wanting to explore her gender identity. And according to Hird, he seemed to be assuming that the patient must be a woman because she was attracted to men. The question is why?

EJ: I think that's a great example of the fallacy of the psy-complex, a very basic flaw in its understandings of human sexualities, sex and gender, built on miscalculated categories, built on colonial brutality. Why can't we embrace experiences outside of these binaries when variance is a human norm? The variations in sex characteristics embodied by intersex individuals prove that the body naturally transcends those binaries in different ways; sex is bimodal, not binary.

JC: Oh yes, of course. That makes sense.

EJ: Those who don't fit the categories easily are projected upon and othered. In his book *Intersections of Privilege and Otherness* (2021), Dwight Turner explains how whole groups will project and split off unwanted aspects of their group identity onto the collective other, resulting in oppression of that which gets driven into the shadow. Trans people, in their transgression of white cis hetero-patriarchy, are or represent those parts that are driven into the shadow. For example, I think that cis men who direct such brutal anger towards trans women are expelling the hatred, disgust or fear of their own femininity; the femininity they are not allowed to express or love for themselves. Perhaps gender-critical women find something particularly galling about what trans women mean for their own relationship with their gender, too. Trans people are gender trauma writ large for the cis population, and many of them cannot face it when they see the fallacy of the gender binary in front of them.

JC: It is so important that therapists are taught about othering. I think othering is present when doctors and surgeons enact and enforce surgeries on infants born with genital variations that can't be categorized as male or female, too. That may also be something to do with the surgeons who feel they must control and categorize these 'wayward' bodies. I also think there's maybe something unmetabolized and unprocessed about their own bodies and gender that they then project onto the othered intersex infant bodies, and the result can be multiple surgeries through infancy that are incredibly invasive and often very damaging to those bodies.

Interrogating gender trauma and the violence of the gender binary

EJ: Exactly, and I am really pleased there's a growing movement of intersex activists saying, 'We want control over our bodies, we don't want unnecessary surgeries.' I try to shine a spotlight on the experience of intersex people when I can because while the intersex experience is not the same as the trans experience, I think some intersex people experience the gender binary literally being written onto their bodies with a scalpel, especially as, from what I understand, some surgeries are performed solely with the goal of ensuring that intersex children will be able to engage in heterosexual, penetrative sex when they are older. I understand that sometimes surgery is necessary for functional or medical reasons, but sometimes it isn't. Heterosexism and cissexism intersect here, I think.

There's an outdated trope that trans people were 'born in the wrong body' and that we always wish we were cisgender, but I don't experience that as the whole truth, and I don't believe it should be presumed to be a goal for trans people to live as close to a 'cisgender experience' as possible. I believe that we can think of cis as a stand-in for other words, such as acceptance or love or ease; maybe what we'd like, or perhaps what I'd like, is safety. Perhaps we should see cis-ness as a metaphor for safety when really what I want to say is, 'Can't we be loved and be safe exactly the way we are?'

I don't necessarily subscribe to the idea that trans people are 'born in the wrong body'. A body is just a body. It is the meaning we ascribe to that body, what it is expected to do and perform that is the problem. Having said this, for some clients, that feeling might be exactly correct, but we need to move away from this as an expectation and as the only 'true' experience of being trans.

JC: You're blowing my mind with this. What I'm really loving is that I'm looking at gender through your trans lens and I do try and do that myself but I'm cis. Well, I'm gender non-conforming but I'm cis, I guess. I have a lot of de-programming to do but I relish looking at the world through a trans lens and destabilizing and de-centring cis-ness. Thankfully, it is beginning to happen.

EJ: There is so much to be gained for cis people in interrogating gender trauma and the violence of the gender binary.

JC: Absolutely, as queer culture has been liberating for heterosexuals, so transness is liberating for cis people. You might be coming to this but I'm curious to find out more about the trans and gender-expansive clients who ask how to deal with coming out and the fear of rejection.

EJ: Great question, and there are a few things to consider. In my experience, clients who are just coming out might be scared that as soon as they tell one person, they will have to tell everyone and that maybe things will snowball out of their control. I have found it useful to explore how clients can keep their boundaries and manage those conversations in ways that feel safe – for example, being clear about what they want to happen next or what they want from the person they're telling, being clear about how much they're prepared to talk about or that they don't have all the answers yet but they are sharing as much as they feel comfortable with at that time.

With trans lives being so much in the public eye, unfortunately the first hurdle is often having to undo a lot of misconceptions about what being trans means before anyone can begin to actually hear what they are saying about their own experience; the vitriolic dialogue around trans issues in this country makes it so much harder to begin on neutral ground. It is important to acknowledge that and remind trans clients that they do not owe it to anyone to be experts in gender theory! They don't even have to be experts in their own experience or have all the answers, but they do need to decide what they want from coming out, on their own terms, instead of feeling pressured to do so.

I think preparing for all sorts of responses is wise and spending time exploring what they imagine it could be like if rejection does happen, which it very well may do, and spend time with that fear until it no longer feels as threatening. What might the consequences be and how have they survived past experiences of rejection? Can we acknowledge that it probably won't be a one-time conversation, so let's take the pressure off getting it right the first time; giving themselves permission to not have all the answers.

And lastly, making space for practical considerations of safety – for example, is there someone safe they can go to if things don't go well? Find an ally if you can. Contingency planning can help clients to feel more prepared and in control.

There have been trans and gender-diverse people for millennia

EJ: I'm thinking of how difficult it can be for trans people to connect to ancestral wisdom. There is always this idea that trans people are 'the first' to do anything. You know, the first trans man to have a baby, or the first trans couple to get married – there's a powerful narrative that we're very new and a fad, and it's meant to position us as a threat, I think.

And this is why I think so much about history. There have been trans and gender-diverse people for millennia. We're nothing new, and to say, 'I'm part of a lineage of people who span back to the dawn of time, I'm not here by myself; there are people who lived outside of the gender binary who have survived and thrived before me' is so important. I think about being an ancestor and that there will be trans people after me; what stories can I leave behind for them to show them that they are not new either?

There is something really important about elders in the community who might seem to be missing from community spaces. They may be poor, disabled, isolated. Hearing and seeing our community's stories such as in The Museum of Transology is vital.

JC: The exhibit that was in Brighton Museum in 2020? Is it still there?

EJ: Yes, it moves around the country and is now available online, I think. It helps to normalize, and in a way also defetishize, the trans experience. We have existed for a long time and will continue to do so. We can communicate our understanding of that to our clients in lots of subtle but powerful ways.

JC: By defetishize, you mean it's not a fad or a trend as some transphobes say?

Consider what you don't know about trans lives

EJ: Yes, I mean moving away from treating trans clients as a novelty or treating the topic as something salacious and risqué. There can be a little bit of 'cis-saviourism' too, where cis therapists feel sorry for trans clients and want to become experts in order to 'save' trans people, instead of working in allyship with the trans community or other trans therapists.

Often trans clients tell me they have seen cis therapists who may be well-meaning but can only see them or relate to them through a cis lens. In fact, I have seen lots of clients who have had great relationships with past therapists but have ultimately been let down by how they have responded to the client beginning to explore gender, which has led to endings in what have otherwise been great experiences. So, we are not just talking about 'bad therapists' here, but competent people who are under-prepared to work outside of their own experience.

JC: For those who don't understand the term cis lens, how would you explain that?

EJ: OK, so a word that comes to me is a comparison; a subconscious belief in cis experiences as the 'natural human norm', and anything else as an anomaly or a deviation from the norm. Expecting that everyone will be cisgender unless they say otherwise, which is cis normativity; not being able to de-centre your own experience or reflect on your own positionality – that is, where you are placed within structures of oppression, and not having any self-awareness of how this might be affecting how you view your clients, or how they view you.

At its sharper end, a cis lens will result in the implicit – or explicit – belief that deviation from the cis norm should be understood as pathological, which can also contribute to that feeling of 'novelty' around the trans experience. You might be expecting clients to explain themselves to you in a cis-normative way, using language which suits your view of the world and that you will understand – perhaps they don't yet have adequate language to explain what they are trying to explain, and perhaps sometimes it just feels like talking another language.

Cis normativity, to me, is a baseline flaw which obscures the complexity, wonder and brilliance of the human experience. There is work that you can do to undo that – you can expose yourself to more trans stories and histories for a start and start to truly accept that there are so many more layers to gender than you might yet understand. This includes considering your own gender! You can start with *How to Understand Your Gender* by MJ Barker and Alex Iantaffi (2017). It takes acknowledging and moving past our defences and humbling ourselves to be in a position of not knowing and not being expert, which I think is notoriously difficult for many therapists!

JC: Sure. Sometimes I might say, 'Let's look at this through a trans lens, rather than through a cis lens,' but as a cis person suggesting a non-binary or trans person does this, it can feel a bit awkward. It's similar when I talk about racism with clients of colour from my white perspective. Do you know what I mean?

EJ: Yes, and I think it's that white guilt or that cis guilt to know the right thing to say all the time and be the expert when it comes to this stuff. The rest of the time we allow ourselves to be curious and not-knowing but when it comes to things that are complicated like racism and transphobia, we put a lot of pressure on ourselves to know the answers. And that does a disservice to everybody in the room. There is so much emotion and guilt and shame around these topics that it can make it quite fraught in the space.

JC: That guilt and shame can lead some therapists to think it's best to treat everyone the same?

EJ: Yes, I come across this often. The question we must then ask is, the same as what? Or the same as who? Where is your starting point? I meet lots of therapists who feel they don't need to learn about what we might call 'otherness'. I hear lots of people say, 'I treat everyone the same so I don't need to learn about every different type of client that I might see,' perhaps because they are encouraged to think that their own position of counsellor/therapist is neutral. Often, this is white cis therapists who, implicitly, think of themselves as 'just normal' – that is, not trans, not gay, not of colour. We are encouraged to think of the power dynamic in the room in terms of client/therapist, and sometimes – binary – gender comes into it; for example, how might it impact the relationship? But we can certainly do better than that. It's part of interrogating cis-ness and whiteness, I suppose; those with privilege never need to be aware of difference or their identity because they are in the middle, the centre, of society. They assume this makes them normal and therefore neutral. It is actually an arrogance and a disservice to all clients.

We all benefit from learning about de-centring cis-ness.

JC: For me, looking at the world through a trans or an intersex lens and learning through listening to and speaking with friends as well as reading has been liberating. I benefit from learning about de-centring cis-ness because it's a liberation.

EJ: I couldn't agree more.

JC: One question I have is when our own gender stories are similar to those of certain clients. How might our shared narratives and relationships to our own bodies and gendered identities impede work with our clients?

EJ: I mean, we do need to be aware of overidentifying with clients in general; however, this is the same for cis therapists who work with cis clients too, or any therapists who have something in common with their clients, which I would say is not uncommon.

For me, while there is certainly a shared language with my trans clients and we are operating in the same 'gender-plentiful universe', all their experiences are so diverse! So, while we have something in common to a degree, overidentifying isn't really an issue. I wonder if it's a question of being mindful about our own need for connection or seeing ourselves or our experiences reflected back in our clients, and more practically, checking out our understandings/assumptions with clients in a more active way.

I can also imagine there could be some tenderness around

comparing our own experiences of transition with our clients' – perhaps some difficult feelings around shame or loss could be triggered – but I think that kind of empathy can be extremely powerful for the relationship. Ultimately, and as always, it's important to make good use of supervision in these cases.

JC: One other question I have is why, when we're learning about attachment theory and developmental trauma, don't we reflect on the trauma of white cis normativity? Maybe you've already answered that in a way that white supremacy tries its best to hide all that?

EJ: Well, I think that we do, but we don't call it cis normativity, we call it 'gender', as if it is an absolute, an unmoving thing. We consider gender variance but only insofar as it relates to cis-ness and its deviance from it, so our starting point is really quite poor. I think in many ways we do reflect on gender trauma in psychotherapy, but we haven't yet reached a point where we have dislodged white cis hetero-patriarchy as the standard or the starting point, and sadly this means that unless we do more learning and un-learning, there is a whole universe of human experience that we can't even comprehend is existing and thriving all around us. There is a real lack of imagination in cis-consciousness. More broadly, I think white supremacy violently seeks to protect itself at all times, and the profession stands on the shoulders of lots of very white, privileged people, largely cis men. So, of course we don't consider white cis normativity. Why would we, when whiteness/cis-ness always seeks to protect itself as a good object, violently and consistently?

JC: I suppose to think about it means you have to unpick so many presumptions and the structure of how you understand the world. Perhaps it's too overwhelming or disruptive – as you've mentioned – for some?

EJ: Yeah, disruptive is the word, profoundly disruptive. Perhaps also because psychology as a discipline is often concerned with the empirical, the rational, the scientific, and what we are talking about is difficult to categorize. I believe this again is the result of white supremacy, needing to categorize and predict and find certainties and to establish the parameters of 'normal', and in fact a lot of what we are talking about here is about expansive expressions of gender, sexuality and relationships. We are also talking about spirituality and ancestry.

JC: And an adherence to the white Euro-centric medical model as well.

Don't focus only on despair with trans clients, focus on trans joy equally

EJ: Yes, which is a model which has always pathologized diversity. Cis, straight identities have not been included in the DSM or ICD (International Classification of Diseases). It might sound shocking to some, but some trans clients may not be traumatized by their gender at all and may not find it necessary or helpful to focus on it as a site of trauma. Of course, distress is posited as a prerequisite for a diagnosis of 'gender dysphoria', which is a necessary label if you want to gain access to medical interventions, but in reality, distress and dysphoria should not be seen as an inherent part of being trans; lots of trans people do not experience profound distress and dysphoria. In other words, being completely and painfully miserable is not an inherent part of being trans, although I once heard someone describe dysphoria as 'heartbreak' and I think that can be a really profound feeling for some.

Gender can be fun! It can be neutral, boring, painful, but also freeing, exciting, dangerous. I often speak to clients about allowing themselves to not be sure and to be curious and playful around their gender and their expression. Don't forget to explore it as a celebration with your clients – when I came out, only one person said congratulations, and I will never forget that they did.

More broadly, I think that gently revisiting positive/joyful childhood experiences of gender exploration can be very meaningful. There was a reason that we began moving towards a different sense of gender than that which was expected; this means there had to have been something positive in there, or if not positives, then at least something – or some things – more comfortable or meaningful, or less painful. Something that 'disrupted' the expectations others held for us. It can be easier to feel compassion for a child/child self where we can connect to the innocence of gender – we have been taught that it's only deviant, adult, sexual, but many parts of it aren't.

There is so much to celebrate about being trans and about gender euphoria – the antonym to dysphoria – in which people feel elation in being seen, seeing themselves or expressing themselves in a way which aligns with their felt sense of self. It is important to spend time exploring how to find those feelings, and how to follow them. Sometimes I will say, 'How can we follow the good feeling?' and that might be changing some small thing, like cutting your hair a little bit shorter, and seeing how that feels, then trying out a different style or fit of jeans, and seeing how that feels, then trying a different piece of jewellery. I think gender can be experienced as incremental joys, instead of always pushing for the 'big wins'.

Understanding terminology makes a huge difference to trans and gender-expansive clients

EJ: On a very basic level, understanding terminology makes a huge difference to trans and gender-expansive clients. It can feel daunting to engage with the language since nobody wants to get it wrong and 'offend' – or hurt, I think is a better word – their clients; ironically, it's often the therapists that want to get it perfectly right every time that can feel debilitated by not knowing the exact right words to use, which helps nobody in the end. It's always right to ask, 'What does that word mean to you?' since words mean different things to different people, especially when we are talking about something as subjective as gender. However, having a command of some of the basics will really help you ease into, and normalize, that discussion, which can be a very powerful experience for a client who otherwise might live with feeling othered and 'abnormal' the rest of the time. It also avoids the dispiriting experience of being the therapist's 'teacher', which is extremely common and profoundly disappointing and damaging to the relationship and essentially, I think, it's unethical. On a basic level, using correct pronouns is a vital starting point in avoiding harm; a study for the Trevor Project in 2020 found that trans and non-binary youth who had their pronouns respected attempted suicide at half the rate of those who did not.

JC: It's important to interrogate the way we use language. It's so second-nature and it forms our way of thinking and constructing the world. It creates or recreates the world that comes from the dominant and othering ways of thinking and talking.

EJ: Absolutely.

JC: Therapy culture is white, cis, middle-class and heterosexual, so even if we don't belong to all or any of those categories, we can reinforce that normativity, not think about language use, etc. We are bound to get terms wrong as language is always evolving, even among people from within the same 'group', so we need to keep listening and learning.

EJ: Yes, I think as therapists you inevitably represent systems – cis hetero-patriarchy *and* therapy – that are extremely likely to have caused pain and trauma in the past to trans communities. Unless you have an understanding of and are working consciously to unravel white supremacy and cissexism, you are almost certainly recreating it in the room; we must see race and gender as a 'known unknown'. In the same way that we must be actively anti-racist instead of passively being non-racist, we must also be active in our dismantling of cis normativity because these two intersections go hand in hand. Only by accepting this as a starting point can we begin moving towards the creation of a society (including a therapeutic society) which embraces gender diversity, and by extension, human diversity as a whole. It's liberation not only for trans people, but for everyone.

CHAPTER 3

Queer shame: notes on becoming an all-embracing mind

Robert Downes

Shame stories frequently show up in the lives of LGBTIQA+ clients. Reflecting on how we accompany queer shame, both within and beyond the therapy room, psychotherapist Robert Downes offers some notes.

Shaming is one of the deepest tools of imperialist white supremacist, capitalist patriarchy

JANE CHANCE CZYZSELSKA: I was thinking about how to start this conversation with you. Should I ask you for your definition of shame or how it manifests both within us and between us and our clients in the room? What are your theories about it? Where would you like to start?

ROBERT DOWNES: Yes, a good place to start, definitions. I collect them, or more accurately, I collect definitions, descriptions, theory and narratives relating to shame from a variety of sources across disciplines and practices. I have found this gathering to be essential to my own personal exploration and reckoning with shame which shapes my practice as therapist and educator. When I refer to queer, I am referring to LGBTIQ+ and in doing so I envision all of our embodiments and manifestations while recognizing that I cannot account for us all completely; the answers to your questions will offer a sketch from this particular subject.

So much is shamed about so many queer bodies that to be radically inclusive requires extensive interdisciplinary study and embodied practice to build up a capacity to be with the shame-inducing legacies that our various embodiments carry in the face of multiple oppressions. For some of us, there are mortifying humiliations to contend with: I recall the collective shaming rituals that I encountered in the so-called playground at school and what it took to revisit those moments that were also years.

Michael Eigen's simple but potent definition of shame as an 'ever self-persecuting I' is a useful starting point. We can then get curious about the origins of this persecuting one that takes up residency within our psyche soma. In all my studies and explorations, belonging is seen as a fundamental driving force behind shame, our need for relationship and the excruciation when connection is lost in feeling cast out.

I draw from a lot of early developmental theory alongside relational psychoanalytic thought and teachings on narcissism. Patricia De Young's (2015) work on chronic shame has been fundamental, alongside Michael Eigen's (2015) words on shame. Frantz Fanon (2008), James Baldwin (1990) and, more recently, Tarana Burke (Me Too) and Brene Brown's collaboration, *You Are Your Best Thing: Vulnerability, Shame Resilience, and the Black Experience* (2021), have all contributed to an ever-expanding intersectional lens through which I view shame as located in the social world in need of a social analytic.

In the 1990s, I was reading Gershen Kaufman and Lev Raphael address shame in relation to lesbians and gay men in their book *Coming Out of Shame* (1996). They write about how internalized shame has to be returned to its interpersonal origins, the realm of intersubjectivity. This is extended by returning it to its systemic origins that bell hooks refers to when she says: 'Shaming is one of the deepest tools of imperialist, white supremacist, capitalist patriarchy because shame produces trauma and trauma often produces paralysis' (hooks and Harris-Perry, 2013).

When I teach about shame, I start with bell hooks to see what this perspective on shame evokes. I start there because I think shame gets too readily located in the maternal parental environment and a white heteronormative, able-bodied, parental environment at that, so that needs disrupting from the get-go.

The problem of locating shame primarily in the mother–baby dyad

RD: Locating shame primarily in the mother–baby dyad I take to be problematically reductive, leaving mothers navigating a lot of shame about their parenting rather than locating the issue within a system that is actually hostile to parenting and children, into a system that primarily seeks bodies that will shop and work while creating hierarchies of value and visibility, marking out some embodiments as ideals and others as more disposable than others. Thus, I think it is essential to consider shame via a range of critical lenses.

⟋ For all queer embodiments, this is a significant notion to return shame to the systems, to relieve ourselves and our clients of the tendency to blame ourselves for the harm that got into our queer selves. We came here really just wanting to be ourselves and we arrive to pre-existing trouble that inevitably gets in. My working definitions and descriptions of shame need to be rooted in this perspective because we internalize systemically created harmful narratives. We can sadly make them our own while they are born of dominant discourses. Thankfully, for many of us, something about our nature contends with these arrangements that are innocently downloaded while we resist and insist otherwise.

To respond to your question about how shame manifests in us and between us in the therapeutic dyad, I will say this for now. One of the challenges of working with shame is the shaming agents that operate in our psyches about the shame we experience. Part of the work is coming to terms with the multiplicity of our own minds and how agents of hate and shame are internalized and will be triggered and enacted in the therapeutic matrix. So far in my experience they don't go, I just become more able to respond creatively to their presence, including in my practice. I often think of the work of living with shame as an ongoing process of befriending ourselves and the array of voices and characters that reside in the realm of our psyche soma, including a befriending attitude towards the sometimes vicious occupants. So, shame work for all queer embodiments requires a comprehension of how heteronormative, white, racialized, gender-binaried patriarchal culture conflictually resides in our psyches, how we might reckon with that as an ongoing practice in life and within therapeutic practice – and humour is essential.

JC: Yeah, I agree. In his book *To Be a Gay Man*, Will Young (2020) talks about the bigger picture too. He talks about his school experiences in the 1990s and things were not great even then for gay kids. So, he locates shame in the culture, in schooling and his gay shame which he felt came in to being because of all the characteristics that are associated with being gay in a white cis heteronormative patriarchal world that says that men should be and behave in a 'manly' way and being gay wasn't/isn't considered manly, for example. So, I'm wondering, when we therapists are in the room with that gay shame, queer shame, how do you suggest we approach it?

RD: Yes, how do we welcome shame when it is born of an unwelcome which has us trying to hide to protect ourselves while we are also wanting to come to life?

I suggest we get ready for its inevitability, that we energetically expect and welcome it because it will come and needs to come so that we can have some freedom and ease. It certainly helps to have done our own work around shame and, in my experience, I recognize it as an ongoing theoretical and experiential study and practice. I meet shame in myself most days, as well as in the consulting room with clients, fellow students, supervisees. At the same time, we need to extend our knowledge of shame beyond our own personal experience and examine shame through the lenses of racism, anti-Blackness, misogyny, trans-antagonisms, body problematics, narcissism, white supremacy, disability, gender binaries, class, colonial legacies and what Lynne Layton calls neoliberal subjectivities (Layton and Leavy-Sperounis, 2020).

Stepping into the matrix of shame

RD: We need to be able to step into the matrix of shame when it manifests because it is always there in the background until something is disrupted in the contact that makes it more figural. The magic happens when we are open to it and the reality that, within each therapeutic relationship, we might co-create a crucible for working with shame. It helps to name shame directly and to share stories about particular aspects of shame so that we can feel and think about it together. I directly invite shame out of the closet that we usually attempt to keep it in. For some queer clients, I have offered readings that speak to something of their experience of shame so that it becomes something we can mutually explore with more symmetry.

So, in time I invite myself and my clients to breathe into shame, to embrace it with the breath, to make room for the painful stories and realities that usually unfold from shame. We don't think too well in the immediacy of shame, so we need punctuation with the breath, by inviting time and making space so that we can return to thinking and relating from within the shame. That takes practice because of our habitual relationship to shame; we need to allow not knowing so that what has been contained within shame can reveal itself so that more of our spirit can live within our embodiments.

How we approach shame needs some thought but not too much hesitancy; we need to model the embodiments that were missing for us as part of our raising. We need to be and become bodies upon which shamed self-states can land and be received, bodies that can tolerate and enjoy the embodied erotics and plurality of gender that need an alternate meeting ground to the one most of us were formed within. The more we have explored these realities in ourselves, the more of a receptive meeting ground we become. To receive and accompany another's shame is a privileged alchemical practice.

JC: Yes, and then I suppose some people can feel shame about shame; shame that they have the shame.

RD: Yes, shaming of the shame, like a double up. I recall it was such a relief when I was able to feel into this and understand what it was. Before that, there were movements to hide or get away from this doubling up of shame because shame can be experienced as scorn from within and without. It is often accompanied by such a sense of deficiency, an absence of agency and belonging. We tend to feel so young and defenceless that we take the lack to be a personal deficiency. This often-sudden loss of some sense of capacity is what can make us feel doubly shamed. In these moments, personally and in my work with people in these states, I invite a breath to feel into and make space for the deficient states, the one that attacks and the one who is being attacked, to get really intimate with this matrix that Donald Kalsched (2013) calls the self-care system.

Once I had the formulation made available to me, it meant I could be more open about this shame matrix and more able to inquire into it. Once clients have an understanding of shame, the more able they are to go towards it to retrieve what it holds as we unravel from shame woven out of our personal history as well as multiple forms of oppression.

The antidote to shame is giving yourself to yourself as you are

JC: Yeah, I remember in your shame training you talked about the antidote to shame as being able to give yourself to yourself as you are.

RD: Yes, that is the powerful bit, as you are. A living embodied radical acceptance that for me has taken time and a lot of gathering to be able to formulate experiences of shame into narratives, to get to a place where I can be with those moments of fragmentation and meet them creatively. I recall in my training that I tried to hide shame; no one had offered a teaching and invitation to be with shame in as explicit a manner that I and many others needed. To give yourself to yourself as you are requires practice – on trainings and sometimes with clients, I make the invitation and repeat it: 'If you give yourself to yourself as you are in this moment, what do you find?' Repeating the question invites a deepening into the unknown as well as creating a self and other intimacy that can enable some relaxation of the self-care system.

We long for intimacy with ourselves and others, yet our compulsions to belong often override meeting these self-states that haven't had a reception. This orientation towards an intimacy with ourselves moment-to-moment develops through practice because to give ourselves to ourselves as we are also includes recognizing when we don't want to, when we can't, when we are in hate with ourselves. This needs to get spoken too, in my experience.

Shame has us leave ourselves frequently and as a wider culture there isn't a critical mass of skilfulness when it comes to being with and tending to a fragmented shamed psyche soma. When we feel undone, fragmented, broken, most of us don't usually report on the reality of that directly; we often meddle with these states. It is only by allowing such states and building the capacities to be with these states that something else gets to happen. This has to become an everyday practice for many of us.

We might not want or be able to speak of how we really are from within shame, where we imagine and take ourselves to be unlovable, broken, not at our best in the company of the unlovable, often hateful states that ultimately need a witness. Shame would have us hide those things for fear of further shame, loss of connection and belonging. If we stick with shame and its revelations, we might be able to allow ourselves to be as we find ourselves, wreckage and all. I recall the relief of finally being able to speak from shamed states unfiltered. I am mindful of the shame playlist, and the track *So Broken* by Björk where she sings directly of feeling broken, and H.E.R.'s relief in singing the words, 'I'm not OK.'

JC: Yes, and I remember you saying that tending to shame was a portal back to our vulnerability and sensitivity, that shame is a colonizer and that it needs to be in the company of someone, or bodies that can receive it. That really resonated with me because it can create the space and welcoming environment that you are talking about.

RD: Yes, the colonizer – sometimes colonizers – there can be multiple occupants in this psychic residency. I sometimes lighten the situation by suggesting to clients that the psyche is multiple and that we are recognizing and learning to live with and respond to sometimes very difficult psychic flatmates.

Becoming more of the 'all-embracing mind that sees me'

RD: There is a line from a Rilke poem that I use for myself and the shame workshops: 'How I yearn to belong to something, to be contained in an all-embracing mind that sees me' (2005). In time, I realized that I was becoming more of the all-embracing mind that sees me as my studies and explorations deepened. The work began to settle a lot of the seeking from the other to see me, to receive me – for what was really in need of being embraced and seen was the queer kid who went unseen, the queer kid who felt so hated, the queer kid who simply wanted to express love and desire as well as be desired, free of all the repressive inner technology that acts as both protector and persecutor within the self-care system that turns aggression against ourselves as a crude protector. This is why I speak of the portal back to our vulnerability and sensitivity; as we gather compassion and understanding for what we have survived and lived through, our implicit lovability often returns to our own awareness more fully, more fleshly. I make words up.

JC: Ha, yes. I get it though. You talked about how shame can be preverbal, and I was wondering about how that might happen.

RD: Colwyn Trevarthen's work points to this (Trevarthen and Aitken, 2001). In his videos of parent–child interactions, we can see and think about early intersubjectivity and the infant's sensitivity to contact and responses to contact that aren't quite right for the infant. His work really points to attunement and calibrating contact where shame can be observed in the infant, a movement away from the adult and what occurs to re-establish contact. His work is useful in that it assists us in becoming able to carefully notice such subtleties in our work with adults. What I am interested in in relation to his work is how the infant needs to be with a parental body that can hold and receive shame, read it, absorb and be with whatever state the infant is in. When the parental field begins to pick up something in the infant that is a little queer, non-normative, then that can be experienced as an unwelcome to that particular soul. I think some of us pick up rejection of our particular embodiments very early on, before we even get to words.

I recall a scene that remains with me from my early training. My gestalt teacher was doing some work with me in the group that was shame related. At some point, she came to sit near me and offered me the tip of her finger, to me this looked like a lot to offer. I felt her measured presence. I moved slowly and met her fingertip with my fingertip and that moment was one of the many moments that began to undo something of the conviction of being a hated subject which lies at the heart of shame.

JC: Yeah.

RD: That's quite a lovely thing.

JC: It's beautiful.

RD: And we need that kind of measured contact to come back into the world, to find our way back, a much more subtle form of coming out. When we re-discover and reclaim these implicit movements experientially, the impulse to police the need to be seen and for contact relaxes and shame no longer needs to function in getting us to pull away from the other, from need and ultimately from our desire for relatedness and intimacy. That's one way I have come to understand it anyway.

JC: Yeah, and going back to the macro: 'being needy' has got a bad rap. It's not a good look for people, especially those socialized as male. There's shame about need. So, over a lifetime if the shamed parts of us are not addressed, we really suffer. I'm also thinking about the different layers of shame: the preverbal shame that gets stoked by racialized or gendered shame, or shame about sexual orientation and trans shame.

Most embodiments get shamed in some way

RD: Yeah. And this is where the bell hooks quote is useful again: most embodiments get shamed in some way. Very particular embodiments are celebrated, offered as the standard and idealized. The rest of us navigate the diminishment as well as offer the critique and disruption to the normative hegemonies.

JC: Yeah, and I'm thinking about intersex infants who are operated on because their genitals don't conform to what's expected of 'male' or 'female' biologies in a binary sex and gender framework, and how that body shame starts so early on.

RD: And what that sparks in me is that shame is related to belonging and our need to belong. I can see that people who decided that they needed to operate on intersex bodies are trying to make some kind of belonging in the gendered body binary, rather than imagining and making a world and culture that has room for accepting all the ways we manifest beyond the binaries.

JC: That some surgeons can justify surgery on infants' genitals for essentially cosmetic reasons is a delusion and it's torture, according to Mendez (2013), that is based on the white patriarchal medical model, which insists that bodies are gendered in a binary way despite the physical, biological evidence.

RD: Yes, that has been the practice for many institutions, to uphold a normative gender and body binary. I think we are in a moment where the critique and unravelling of gender is opening up while also being vehemently defended against. We are in transition and trouble.

JC: And what you are saying here is that shame in our cultures is a given, so why do we not tend to learn much about it in our initial trainings? Is it because there isn't much theory written about it?

We are fixated on diversity rather than decoloniality within the institutions

RD: There is more than enough material about shame from a variety of perspectives and experiences for us to draw from. White, heteronormative patriarchy is so embedded and reinforcing of itself that some work has to take place to centre the other and the theories and practices of the other. This happens when training institutions focus on delivery and not on doing the deep study and practice to really reckon with the trauma of the systems we live in that should then inform the trainings we do. We are predominantly fixated on diversity rather than decoloniality within the institutions. Both deep study and re-organizing the relations of power is yet to take place in the field, so thankfully there are those who practise otherwise. I am appreciative of the analytics that get practised and taught beyond the dominant training institutions. Resmaa Menakem, Prentice Hemphill, Dr Jennifer Mullan, Adrienne Maree Brown, Meg-John Barker and Ellis J. Johnson are some of the people who have been contributing to theory and practice that brings together social justice and therapeutic thought and practice.

The Black gaze as a site of critique and resistance, as bell hooks points out in 'Eating the other' (1992), has not been internalized by the bodies that 'govern' the field of therapy, let alone the ways we teach and what we teach. What is reproduced maintains antagonisms to Black and queer embodiments. We have collectively created a lot of theory that lives and remains marginalized because the analytics about maintaining power and status are not reckoned with institutionally. Some are wise not to wait and carry on.

I think a queer and anti-racist approach to therapeutic study and practice is a lot more interdisciplinary, extending the curriculum to be much more inclusive of voices and approaches beyond what we are usually offered. I wrote a chapter with my friend and colleague Foluke Taylor (2020) that is a story of two students describing a therapeutic training re-imagined, infused with critical thinking and practice. I think institutions are not necessarily doing the re-imagining. I also think that to really address trauma through an intersectional lens, curricula and practice is a stretch for institutions that are not humble enough to reconsider their work.

To work with shame is to reveal to ourselves in the company of another the wretchedness inside

RD: To really work with the shame means we get to reveal to ourselves in the company of another/others the wretchedness inside, the devastation, the unmet need, the desire, the shapes we take in the face of hatreds, the destructive aspects of ourselves that we often struggle to contain that we turn against ourselves. Maybe our relationship to shame has something to do with how limited our trainings are in working with shame. Maybe it's something to do with money. I don't know whether it's because it takes us to the heart of the devastation or whether it is assumed that it will take place in the privacy of the dyadic therapeutic relationship.

It really is a practice of developing an inner receptivity to shame, to be able to read the story it tells us as we feel into it, to have enough mental space to think alongside it and that for most of us is a developmental process, one that comes with extensive practice. Hence, I offer some clients practices and readings to deepen their understanding of shame so that they can then develop their embodied practices to contain shame and then make use of it within themselves and interpersonally. Where we are left is that many of us are not as resourced to work with the complexity of shame that we encounter, particularly with an intersectional lens. I also see that shifts are taking place beyond the institutions.

JC: How did shame get developed for you, if that's not too personal a question?

RD: Shame didn't get very developed, worked through for me in one-to-one therapy and I found aspects of my training reinforced the existing shame I was troubled with. Hence, I took to studying it because it was an almost daily companion that would keep me awake at night.

I think my self-care system in relation to shame was so formidable it made it hard to really make use of therapy and the therapeutic relationship, to operate as a student in class, to be in my skin and transparent about what felt so shamed in me. Sexuality, being raised in a family with an alcoholic father, with an Irish ancestry, with parents who were ashamed of their class status at times meant for multiple registers of shame. The extensive shame studies that I undertook personally and in dialogue with a few friends and colleagues meant many nights exploring and inquiring into shame. I also joined a school, the Diamond Approach, where shame and the super ego were explored deeply alongside extensive explorations into the shapes we take in relation to wounds of value that we call narcissism. Being offered teachings really supported the development of the capacity to be curious in the face of shame as opposed to avoidant. Deeper work into spiritual perspectives on shame and narcissism really helped transform my relationship to shame. And it continues.

As I explored shame in the here and now, with teachings that aided that practice, the more intimate I became with shame and the more access I had to that which lay behind or wrapped up in it. When you did the shame training where I invited people to share something that had felt shamed about them, the collective sharing really changes the field, evoking spirit and the presence of love. That's what makes shame work worth it.

JC: Yes, I loved your shame workshop. I would love to do more. It's interesting because – to go back to Will Young – he said talking about gay shame in a group was one of the most healing things because it was no longer hidden. Perhaps more powerfully than in a therapy room with an individual therapist. In your shame training, it felt incredibly powerful to share – not more or less powerful than in a therapy session – but it was meaningful to give voice to hidden shame and to not know how it would land with others. Taking a risk with others rather than just one person, and hearing others doing the same, the multiplicity of shame. Sharing shame stories and feelings took it to a different level.

Sharing shame stories helps undo the shamed and the aloneness

RD: Yes. I think sharing shame stories in a group does a lot of undoing of the shamed and the aloneness; it re-establishes connection and undoes isolation. It brings joy often; most of the shame events ended with the presence of joy.

I will say two more things about this. When I came out, I came out and then there is this assumption of pride, and what I found was missing was the journey from shame to pride. The space for recovery where the internalized shame and hate could be metabolized. That's what was missing for me personally and what is missing more generally given the attacks on youth work with queer young people. Thankfully, there are resources online in social media that meet some of this need.

JC: Yeah, that resonates with me in terms of working with gay, queer and trans shame and the deprivation we experience when we aren't welcomed by others or the culture. The deprivation of an experience of community, of any kind of culture, for those queer people who haven't yet found community. Maybe they go to clubs but hide their gayness in some parts of their lives, so life feels as if something is missing, without culture, support and the community healing that we need.

RD: Having a group environment is powerful because shame is about belonging: being in the group or out of the group and shameful disclosures as a kind of practice with others who have had similar shamings becomes a practice of reconnecting, because most of us experience our oppressions as very internal kind of toxins and it's only when we hear other people's personal revelations that re-connection and unravelling from self-blame narratives can begin to occur.

JC: Yeah.

RD: This is why, I guess, I became a gay youth worker in my twenties because I was already in therapy then and I was introduced to that therapeutically minded space for recovery and revelation. So, we would sit and have a circle and people would share and we would have themes to reflect on and much of it was pointedly healing work, sharing shames and sore spots, which was relationship and community-making for that particular group. Self-care systems got shared and identified in the presence of understanding and love. So, we offered the other kind of space compared to the bars and the clubs that was very powerful work.

The hope was that the opposite of shame is pride but maybe love is the opposite of shame

JC: Yeah, I can imagine. And I'm thinking about this quick leap from shame to pride. It's interesting that in the LGBTIQ+ community globally that's been the direction or the aspiration: to move away from the shame towards pride rather than tending to the shame. And maybe the hope has been that the opposite of shame is pride but maybe love is the opposite of shame?

RD: Yes, nice. Love, openness, transparency, uniqueness and the capacity to be ourselves as we are, rather than trying to shape ourselves in relation to the ideas and images that the internalized colonizers keep in mind for us. The move into pride can be an inflation in place of a growing up and what needed to happen for many of us, for me, was a growing up, because there hadn't been the formative experiences of normalizing and celebrating desire with men. I came out to something that I was not emotionally or psychologically equipped for, neither were many of the young people I was working with. We used to do a lot of mopping up with the young men who would go out and get into situations they weren't ready for. Some weren't able to stay close to themselves to see what was right for them. Shame work brings you back into a sensitive caring relationship with yourself. A lot of what looks like freedom to some was not freedom; it was trouble. Because the shame work hadn't recalibrated them into a caring relationship with themselves, if that makes sense?

JC: Yeah, I'm thinking about my first experiences of London Pride and a Stop Section 28 event in Manchester. I had never seen so many lesbians or gay men in one place. So, from going from complete deprivation of lesbians to seeing thousands of them was the most incredible, empowering, tearful experience. Section 28 wasn't a Pride event, so there was anger there but the Pride event also had tens of thousands of lesbians and gay, bi, trans and intersex people who were there – it moved me. I still cry at my local Pride event. It touches me that there are straight local people, business owners, old people waving with love and in support from their balconies. Reflecting on those parts of me that have felt so unloved and how much they are received at Pride contrasts with the daily queer unlove. So, Pride can be a beautiful thing.

RD: And when it hits you like that, years later, as it still hits me, at a queer gathering like that, it's a kind of marker of the deprivation of what was and the power of a little bit of love and coming together. The love that was missing, the reception and the recognition that was missing, it's almost like my body can forget it, then I get a big reminder when we come together – some of the time. I also don't want to idealize this coming together because we still encounter problematics around race, gender and disability within what some call the LGBTIQ+ community. I have trouble with calling it a community when there are splits and conflicts that are quite harmful that continue to take place. So, there is both grief and relief in these gatherings.

JC: Yes, a relief and a grief. Going back to what you said about moving too fast from shame to pride, I'm thinking of chemsex and self-care and the hurt that can be inflicted on the self in pursuit of a particular kind of belonging and that can become a kind of self-harm.

Addictions are attempts to know freedom but that freedom can be costly

RD: Yeah, there are lots of different thoughts to be had around chemsex. It's not an area of expertise for me but in terms of thinking about it in relation to shame: unravelling from shame is a long game. It really is a difficult, painful thing, and not everyone knows about therapy and other practices that might unravel them from shame to some sense of freedom beyond the internalized embodied, structural kind of hatred. I can see chemsex as an attempt at and practice of freedom from a harmful, shaming, normative culture. I can see how drugs, drink or chemsex are attempts to know a freedom but, as you pointed to, sometimes in that freedom what gets thrown under the bus is care, of self and other, so that freedom can be costly to some degree because it's not very conscious.

JC: Yes, it's still so much in the culture that to be gay – or to be anything other than white male, cis and straight – will come with shame.

RD: I guess we need a lot of practice to become ordinary and we need to hear ordinary dialogue between queer folk, between straight and queer people along the gender continuum centring Black, Brown, people of colour voices and attempting to have dialogue that addresses trans lives without the violence that is so frequent a presence these days. I don't know that there is enough actual dialogue beyond the reactivity we witness so much on social media. We need learning environments, spaces for practice where we can stumble and find our way to learning to live and love with one another.

I'm 56 and the topography of the LGBTIQ+ landscape has changed significantly in my lifetime that I am catching up and being made anew through exchanges that I am having now as I listen to and study with the multiple voices that insist speech otherwise. To really practise care in amongst a topography of queer manifestations requires a lot more thought, study and care. It requires space where we can download that thought and practice and when I say practice, I mean the practice of regarding one another, really listening to one another in an age of individualistic attachment to opinions, being right and defending lies about what it is to be human. Despite my own predilections to being right and certain, my practice is to orient to the possibility of being undone and remade in all kinds of interactions within and beyond the consulting room, to recognize when I am fixed and to loosen that up and be willing to be loosened up while bearing that which might feel shameful at the same time.

JC: I feel my own tension and shame about not knowing enough slipping away as I listen to you. It's healing. Thank you. When you speak of individualistic attachment to opinions, being right and defending lies about what it is to be human, I think about the white cis-gay Tories [politically right-wing] I've met!

RD: Yes, a significant number of white gay men make use of the privileges afforded some versions of masculinity and whiteness. They think of themselves as being closer to the idea of straight white male embodiments; there's a bit more of a willingness to participate in the system that harms you less than others and to throw those not so near to it under the bus. I remember when I met my first Tory gays, I was stunned that they could exist! In my teens, I was a little naïve when coming out. I assumed other gay men would have an intersectional perspective, would already be aligned with feminist and anti-racist discourse and stuff but that isn't to be assumed. I feel ashamed of these little white gay boy racist fascists who have such big social media profiles and propagate lies and lack any kind of critical thinking. What happened to them? So, I see how, for some, shame compels a refusal of interdependency, of care, of linking. They choose their comforts and privileges and align themselves often with bigots in the hope of some sense of belonging and assimilation, I guess.

JC: Yeah, that's a whole other way of dealing with shame. Going back to what you said about how we are born into a culture that traumatizes and shames us: it's as if the dominant class knows that traumatizing people is a way to control; as bell hooks said, shame is something that is built into the way that society operates. The domineering, angry boss, or partner. The institutionalized and systemic hostile arrangements. How do we transform it beyond the therapy room?

How do we transform shame beyond the therapy room?

RD: That is a big question. I don't have an answer; that answer has to be made and lived collectively, as stressed by many of the Black feminists who inform my thinking. Waking up practices, movements, resistance and action are required. We are living in a moment where there is so much to draw from about how we might live otherwise, yet the monster of capital and its adherents is formidable in its attempt to destroy and quash critique and transformation. The right is so well mobilized to attack Black lives and anti-racism, trans rights, queer lives, womxn's lives and bodies and to justify the object use of all bodies in the service of capital and empire. It is quite disturbing to consider that many governments and corporations see the libidinal objects to be capital, power and domination rather than making a life rooted in care. It is heart-breaking.

I think that if we are going to transform shame, we have to transform the way we live into a culture that is rooted in and begins with care and not capital, disrupting neoliberal embodiments. If we start rooted in care, we orient around what is needed to live together and taking care of the environment that holds and provides for us. It is an ethical practice as opposed to raising people to take part in a system that harms us with these hierarchies of value and legacies of colonialism and extraction that are brutalizing and potentially taking this particular species out. The destruction in the name of profit as God is devastating when really sat with.

Re-imagine from the starting point of care
for each other and for the environment

RD: The core of a lot of the Black queer feminist thought (e.g. Dionne Brand, Saidiya Hartman, Prentis Hemphill, Sonja Renee Taylor, Christina Sharpe, Foluke Taylor, Gail Lewis) that I am engaged with asks the question: 'What does living look like if we imagine life otherwise?' Beyond the white, heteronormative binaries of patriarchy and capital, if we re-imagine from the starting point of care for each other and for the environment, it is a really different kind of orientation that I think is also an antidote to shame, this potential for becoming more community-oriented creatures rather than individuals with our phones in our hands groomed for shopping and practices of splitting and domination. Racial capitalism has done a great job of sowing the necessary divisions to maintain hierarchies of value that enough of us buy into these lies about what the actual problem is. However, we are living in another moment of disruption of that hegemony while facing the reality of what is happening with the environment.

JC: I agree, and I recall what you have said about shame and how it is a rejection of vulnerability; shame is the un-holding of vulnerability.

RD: Yes, vulnerability points to that edge of risk, we might be vulnerable to shame or the possibility of contact. I would add that shame is the embodied absence of holding, fragmentation, the absence of love within and the actual or projected absence of love without. It is also a naked sensitivity in the memory of scorn. It can also be experienced as a death wish in the face of what feels like an absolute hatred of our very being. 'I don't want to exist because it's unbearable here. I am hated, I need to disappear.' While inside shame we might come across the libidinal rage that says something like, 'I exist, I refuse your hatred of me, I will take you out.' I think part of the work of shame is to energetically connect with the hatred and anger, to infuse the body with these energies as a reclaiming of embodiment and our actual size; in many states of shame, we shrink. To feel into the anger and rage as an embodied practice can be an undoing of the protective physical contraction that exists in so many oppressed queer embodiments. To embrace vulnerability is to also take on the reality of our inter-dependency and that is attacked daily by the dominating forces.

JC: That's so true. I love how you describe shame as 'the absence of love within'. A couple of things I wanted to ask before we finish – as practitioners, we have our own shame and I'm wondering about how that might play out in the room if we're not aware of it and how we might unwittingly shame our clients and how we can recover from that?

How we unwittingly shame our clients and how we can recover

RD: I think we need to be relaxed about the realities of shame, the inevitability of enactments that will be infused with shame – which is ultimately a story of loss of connection, a disruption to belonging. It helps, I think, to hold it in mind as part of the territory of the work. The more I have really tended to my own history as a cisgendered, white gay man of Irish descent from a working-class background that was infused with violence and alcoholism, still bruised from all the homo love hatred (I don't use the term homophobia), the more able I am to sit with shame and be present with it, for it to unfold the stories contained within it: 'I felt so hated, I was so unseen within and beyond those who were directly raising me, this culture didn't welcome me.' The less defended I became about actually feeling the shame, the more I developed the capacities and understanding required to be with it, and the more it became a portal that returned me to humility and the realities of my past and current psychic arrangements. In turn, I became much more able and sensitized to navigate the maze of shame with my clients. So that which we feel shame about will get triggered in our work; it's how we relate to it that matters.

That which we feel shame about will get triggered in our work

RD: There will be shame and the client will feel shamed by us and we might even shame them, but we want to make it something we can both breathe with as well as talk into and about, to make it thinkable, survivable and liveable. As client, I need someone who can meet me in that state of shame, while in the aloneness of shame. Michael Eigen speaks of the client's self-hatred needing to be respected, the one who was hated as well as the one doing the hating seem to need a witness so that space and ease can arise. I have needed someone who would not attempt to alter what at the time feels to be an unalterable state of shame, of lovelessness; someone who could stay long enough for the alchemy of spirit, of presence to do its work.

I often meet practitioners who are really anxious about shaming the client. While we might want to take care, we also want to note what we are taking care of. Actively seeking to not shame a client can ultimately be a theft in service of the therapist's self-image. Shame work is fertile land and we recover when we can think and breathe and relate our way into and through it.

JC: Yeah, 'How did I shame you?'

RD: What a question, what an invitation to speak what might have been unspeakable, what Donnel B. Stern (2019) calls 'the infinity of the unsaid'. I imagine a simple offering to a queer client or group relating to shame(s): 'Tell us something that has so far gone unsaid here.'

Good enough therapeutic encounters make possible the relational processes of navigating the currents of shame: 'Take a breath into that and let it be here between us, let's find out what is to be found out.' So, we're not plotting to avoid it, we are plotting to be a breathing embodiment before it and within it, that can think and tolerate it, and go towards it, while also harbouring and noting the impulses to get away. Shame became one of my favourite subjects because it brings such freedom and love when encountered thoughtfully, that portal again.

JC: Yeah, and in terms of advice to therapists when working with shame, we need to attend to our own shame.

Therapist immersion in shame offers a container for clients to bring their own journeys with shame

RD: It is fundamental. My personal work with shame has been foundational and the most significant resource in my work as a therapist and my being in the world. Embracing the chronic nature of it is an ongoing act of freedom. Alongside the shame studies and practices are my studies and explorations with narcissism and white supremacy. For me, they are interwoven. In my work, I think my immersion in shame offers some kind of container for clients to bring their own journeys with shame. It becomes a very precious kind of work when shame is yielded into and returns the sensitivity of our nature back to us for a moment or more in time. There is a joy to that often, a painful tending that often leads to an openness. It is this return to openness and joy that makes shame work both worth it and essential for queer embodied souls.

CHAPTER 4

How do therapists unwittingly reinforce normativity?

Meg-John Barker

We are each formed by a complex relational matrix that starts from before the womb and guides us after birth throughout our lives. In the white supremacist cis hetero-patriarchy in which we live, we internalize the concomitant narratives about bodies, biologies and behaviours, whether they serve us or not. Therapeutic work, much of which is informed by these dominant socio-political ideologies, needs to be sensitive to this. How can therapists reflect on the values and biases we hold which may well inadvertently impact our client work? Meg-John Barker suggests ways to integrate these considerations into our practice.

We need to interrogate any idea of what a successful self or life is like

JANE CHANCE CZYZSELSKA: Often in therapy, we hear from clients that they are troubled either by their own and/or by others' internalized normative narratives. Can you say how you believe therapists unwittingly reinforce this normativity?

MEG-JOHN BARKER: I'm thinking about Igi Moon's (2008) work about how straight therapists use more negative emotional language to describe queer clients, and about ideas we may unwittingly draw on about what a successful life looks like. I love Sara Ahmed's (2010) ideas about becoming feminist killjoys and unhappy queers.

JC: I really like Sara's writing too. What do you think is useful for clients about those ideas?

MJ: I like the way it reframes the hetero-patriarchal culture as the problem, rather than those who struggle with it. Feminist killjoys and unhappy queers are helpful in pointing out the problems this culture poses for everyone, although we could question the fact that the emotional labour so often rests with them to do so. We need to utterly interrogate and dismantle any idea of what a successful self, or a successful life, is like. For example, we certainly need to question the idea that sex is necessary, that a love partnership of a particular type is essential, that it's good to have a family of a certain type, that making more and more money and buying bigger and bigger homes is a good thing.

JC: I love that you bring in writers like Sara Ahmed and Judith Butler from outside of the therapy gene pool into our therapeutic thinking and practice. It's important to look beyond the therapy texts to the wisdoms we can integrate from other traditions, such as feminism and philosophy – both of these have been influenced by psychoanalysis and vice versa.

MJ: Absolutely, and for me – as for Ahmed and Butler – the hetero-patriarchal norms around sex, gender and relationships, and the capitalist, colonialist mindset are all interwoven. I do hope that the current moment of Covid-19 and climate crisis might alert us to the dangers of the neoliberal capitalist mindset, both for our outer systems and for our inner ones. Systems based on these hierarchical binaries of normal/abnormal, success/failure, doing/being, etc. need to be called into question, as does any sense of ourselves as separate, atomized individuals whose focus should be on coupledom and nuclear families. As Butler (2006) is now pointing out, there is a violence inherent in seeing ourselves this way, rather than as inevitably interdependent.

JC: Agreed. We can reproduce these in our personal lives as well as with clients.

MJ: Yes, despite having thought and written about this stuff for years, I still notice myself falling back into normative ways of thinking and relating. It is a lifelong journey and requires systems and structures of support where others are trying to do it differently too, I think. That's why queer community – and other related communities – are so vital. As somebody who has been hurt a great deal by normativity, both when I was within it and now I am outside of it, I see it as something which really benefits nobody. A big part of my mission with therapists is to encourage them to attend to gender, sex and relationship styles with all clients, not just the overtly queer ones. Mental health struggles are strongly linked to gender, sex and relationships for straight, cis and monogamous folks at least as much as for queer folks, if not more so.

JC: I want to ask you more about how you have been hurt by different kinds of normativities, but can I first ask you about why it is that LGBTIQ+ people have higher rates of mental distress?

MJ: I would say it's a product of the everyday experience of being outside of normativity, and the impact of everything from micro-aggressions to hate crime which goes along with that. As research by Stonewall (Bachmann and Gooch, 2018) and others such as the PACE RaRE (Nuno Nodin *et al.*, 2015) study have consistently found, bi and trans people have worse mental health than lesbian and gay people, so it seems that the further 'outside' you are, the worse it gets. This is particularly the case for identities which are unintelligible within the current binaries, like bi, non-binary, asexual and aromantic identities and experiences.

JC: Right, that makes sense. And I guess the greater the number of intersections, the greater the likelihood of micro-aggressions and the toll on mental health?

MJ: Absolutely.

JC: And can you say more about how you've been hurt by normativity both inside and outside of it?

MJ: Basically, I was a pretty weird, queer kid, and being outcast at school and home meant I latched on to heteronormative love as the thing that would save me and being appropriately feminine and sexually desirable as the passport to that love. So, unlike many people who identified as queer from early on, I have some insight into what normative gender, sex and relationships are like from the inside. Not good is the answer. At least from my experience. Femininity comes with all the costs that we have been aware of since Simone de Beauvoir (1953) highlighted it about identifying yourself as 'for-others' rather than 'for-yourself'. Having a sexuality entirely based around pleasing others results in – at best – mediocre sex and – at worst – non-consensual sex and assault. And the norms of heteronormative, monogamous, exclusive, lifelong coupledom look disturbingly similar to depictions of co-dependent and coercive controlling relationships, and certainly were so in my experience. I feel I've spent my queerer thirties and forties undoing much of the damage internalized normativity did to me, piece by painful piece. You could say it was harder for me because I was 'really' queer, but I saw a lot of pain in those around me while I was in that more normative world too, and certainly saw that pain when I was a sex and relationship therapist working with mainly heteronormative young cis men and women.

JC: There are so many rules that we absorb as if through osmosis as we grow up in a white-cis-heteronormatively organized society and culture. It's hard not to bring them into our queer communities and our work.

You are queer enough

MJ: I guess I can speak personally to this also, as my move from normativity into increasingly queer communities has shown me just how painful new normativities can be. This is the crab bucket idea that I write about in *Rewriting the Rules* (2018). Terry Pratchett (2009) likened mainstream society to a bucket of crabs, where all the crabs feel safe staying in the bucket and try to pull any crab back in who tries to escape. I suggested that – if any crab does escape – they can't handle being a lone crab out on the beach, so they find a new crab bucket to join, which does precisely the same thing, often while ridiculing the crabs who are so oblivious in the original bucket. For example, the assumptions about how non-monogamy should work within polyamorous communities that I came across felt as restrictive to me – albeit in different ways – to monogamy. I'm also thinking about the normalizing of non-consensual sex/play under a veneer of 'safe, sane, consensual' within kink communities, which is as disturbing as the consent issues in hetero sex and is thankfully being written about more now. Also, I have certainly been hurt by some trans people's assumptions about what it means to be 'proper trans', as well as the 'queerer than thou' narratives in queer communities, and the lack of trauma-informed practice and sex-critical understandings within many conscious sexuality spaces. Now I've written a book on 'queer', I want to tell everyone, 'Yes, you are queer enough' because so many have experienced that 'queerer than thou'. Also, I really want sex/kink communities to think more carefully and critically around consent and trauma.

JC: This notion of 'not queer enough' is common. There's something about more generally not feeling good enough, which may be impacted through family dynamics growing up: queer kids 'disappointing' parents through their non-normative or other behaviours and/or having parents who aren't attuned enough to the child. This sense of lower self-worth gets reinforced by social messages about queers not being 'good enough' because we're not heterosexual or cis. Certainly, it doesn't seem a grand leap to believe that we are not (good) enough as queers, when from the home to the playground to the street to the workplace, this message is overtly and covertly present.

MJ: Absolutely. And, again, I don't think that heteronormative people escape from this either. Queers feel the shame of 'not good enough' because they know they have failed normativity. Straights often feel the shame of 'not good enough' because they are still trying to aspire to it but knowing – inside – that they don't really fit completely because nobody does. It reminds me of what Judith Butler (2006) says about gender and melancholy. There's pain and loss for cis people in disowning the parts of themselves which are differently gendered in order to perform their gender. Similarly, I suspect there is pain and loss for repressing aspects of the erotic in order to conform with the narrow restrictions of hetero sex. There could also be pain as a result of focusing solely on romantic – and perhaps parental – forms of love, rather than all the different kinds of love that are possible: self-love, friend-love, love of humanity, working-partnership bonds, etc.

JC: So true. I've been exploring shame for a while now, as part of my own personal work as well as in the service of my clients, and I agree with Robert Downes (Chapter 3), who talks about how this is a feeling state that we don't spend enough time with on most preliminary trainings.

MJ: I think that a huge issue in mental health – perhaps *the* huge issue – is shame. In a culture which constantly reinforces that us 'normal' versus them 'abnormal' division, there is huge shame around the ways we 'fail' at being manly men or feminine women, having 'proper' sex, and 'good' monogamous coupled lifelong love. A huge part of my work is to reveal that these normativities are constructed and hurting everyone. As I've said, many assumed straight people are actually quite far outside normativity, and many queer-identified people are still hurting themselves measuring themselves against these ideals about how to be masculine/feminine, and the kinds of sex and relationships they feel they should be having.

JC: I agree about the shame. It's such a big one. I think of how we can make a virtue out of not meeting heteronormative expectations and start to co-create different, more relevant value systems. I feel hopeful but it's an ongoing practice of self-care to dissolve the shame!

We are all queered by life

MJ: Oh yes, it was Halberstam's (2011) work on failing at normative life trajectories that got me thinking about how most – if not all – people are eventually queered by life. This occurred to me when I was doing therapist training around gender, sexual and relationship diversity (GSRD). I wanted to disrupt the us-and-them binary of me (a queer trainer) talking to (a mostly heteronormative) audience.

As I included activities around gender norms and intersections, it became clear that nobody in the room fitted within the masculine/feminine gender binary well, and that nobody's life had followed the straightforward normative ideal.

JC: I think this is really important. It's something I'd not thought of and is a really valuable awareness to have as a therapist.

MJ: I realized that we could see many life experiences as queering us from the heteronormative path. For example, many cancer treatments, menopause and retirement deeply challenge how people are read – and experience themselves – as men or women. As crip theorists have pointed out (McRuer, 2006), being disabled often results in people being seen as non-sexual and/or not a real man or woman. Class, race, faith, age and various other aspects intersect with gender and sexuality to mean that only a very specific – narrow – group of people really have access to the kinds of gendered expressions, sexual activities, relationships and families that are seen as 'normative', and even then, generally not for the whole of their lives. For example, I remember talking with one woman who was the fourth or fifth girl in her religious family. The disappointment of her not being a boy had marked her whole life. As Juno Roche (2019) points out, many cis people have such complex relationships to gender akin to what many trans people experience. And normativity sets everyone up to fail.

JC: It does, and yet there are some who benefit, perhaps in a status way, don't you think?

We need to move beyond binaries

MJ: Absolutely. We always need to be mindful of our positions on multiple intersecting axes of oppression, and the power and privileges it conveys to be part of the assumed norm. However, I think it is simultaneously important to hold the complexity that exists around the ways normativity impacts both those inside and those outside of it. I would add that Alex Iantaffi and I, in our writing on gender, have questioned the cis/trans binary, and the non-binary/binary, as well as the male/female binary (Barker and Iantaffi, 2019). I like the way the British theatre production *The Butch Monologues*, for example, brings people – cis and trans alike – together to share experiences of butchness (Bridgeman, 2015). We could, perhaps, do the same for experiences of chest surgery, hormone-taking, name-changing, gender expression shifting and various other things which many people – trans and cis – do at some point in their lives, and many – trans and cis – do not. This focus on shared experience could disrupt the current focus on identity in some usefully queer ways.

JC: I love this so much. So, when we look at lived experiences through a binary lens, we set up a 'them and us' understanding, a kind of 'me/not-me approach' which might not be helpful.

MJ: Agreed. And encouraging therapists, and everyone, to deeply reflect on their relationships to gender, sex and relationships, will – inevitably, I would say – reveal complexities and places where they deviate from the 'norm'. We can see that from statistics too. While LGBTIQ+ people tend to be called the 'minority', actually a majority of people report some attraction to the 'same gender', some kinky desires, a sense of being the 'other' gender, neither or both, and some form of, often secret, non-monogamy. Very few people occupy that assumed norm, and even those who do eventually fall out of it.

JC: Yes, that's so true.

MJ: The other problem of course is that because we are raised in a binary-obsessed culture, it's hard to de-programme from that. I notice how much I can adhere to binaries in so many aspects of my everyday life and work and I really have to work to be present to that. It's easy to fall into rigid binaries as queer folk too, isn't it?

JC: Absolutely, it is.

As queer therapists, we can't assume we have escaped normativity

MJ: Following on from this, I think it's important – as queer therapists and working with queer clients – not to assume we have escaped normativity. Bi folks can tell us a lot about the binaries in gay culture because so many have experiences of being excluded, assumed to be 'really' gay or straight by gay people, and the higher rate of domestic abuse among bi women in relationships with women has been linked to bi erasure.

JC: Yes, I can see how collecting information about bi women (and no doubt men) could be problematic because they may not be included in 'same-sex' statistics. I was shocked to learn quite a few years ago now, through the charity GALOP, that domestic abuse rates are the same among 'same-sex' folk as 'opposite-sex' folk. So, to erase bi people is to miss an important part of the picture of those who suffer and also perpetrate abuse. And that brings me on to the issue of consent, which feels so closely embedded in white cis-heterosexual cultural norms, yet as you have so rightly said, we barely even talk about it in therapy or therapy trainings and many of our clients come to us because of non-consent in the wider world. Can you say more about this?

We need to talk about consent

MJ: I think it's not talked about much anywhere, although hopefully post #metoo that may be shifting. American psychiatrist Judith Herman suggests that every wave of researchers/therapists who have revealed the extent of non-consent and trauma has been repressed. We see that in the way Freud's early understanding of the extent of child and adult sexual abuse was squashed (Herman, 2015). Then there were the dismissive responses to 'shell shock' – when military service is one of the key ways men are treated non-consensually and traumatized. And then a similar backlash after feminists raised awareness of the extent of domestic abuse.

JC: It's shocking to think about the various attempts over the decades that have suppressed a wider conversation about consent issues.

MJ: I think that facing the normalizing of non-consent that happens on every level in the world around us – wider culture, workplaces, family systems – is deeply threatening. It requires us all to sit with our inner survivors and inner perpetrators, just like really engaging with intersectionality and social justice requires us to sit with our inner oppressors and inner oppressed. It's massive work, and requires so much self-compassion and support, which is the very thing so many of us don't have as a result of trauma and non-consensual treatment.

JC: Yes, let's talk a bit about trauma.

MJ: I'm increasingly understanding that pretty much all mental health problems can be understood as responses to these kinds of traumas – past and present – in terms of the emotional toll they take and or the strategies we develop to survive them.

JC: How do you define a trauma? Is trauma relative or on a spectrum?

Marginalized individuals and groups carry additional shame and trauma

MJ: My understanding of trauma is that it's about having painful experiences which are beyond our capacity to process, and not held and heard by anyone else. I think it's utterly interwoven with both shame and non-consent. Most of what traumatizes us is non-consensual relating in one way or another: whether that's bullying at school; parents – in whatever way – treating us as something for them rather than helping us be for-ourselves; surviving abuse or assault; or being part of a marginalized group and facing collective oppression and injustice – knowing that our body, labour, knowledge or life – is valued less because of it.

JC: Right, I'm also thinking about how childhood neglect in its many manifestations can also cause trauma.

MJ: Yes, that's perhaps the main 'trauma' that I'm focused on in my blogging at the moment. It has been written about as developmental trauma, or complex PTSD, and also in the more psychoanalytic literature around shame as the impact of the 'dysregulating other' – that is, parents and others who could not mirror, contain or help regulate tough feelings in kids (Walker, 2018; Downes, Chapter 3). I'm personally using the language of trauma because that literature is so helpful to me, and because the neuroscience does seem to suggest that so much of what we struggle with in terms of mental health and relationship difficulties is about how trauma responses – fight, flight, freeze and fawn – operate in our bodies and brains.

JC: Yes, and as Janina Fisher (2017) explains, neuroscience has updated our understanding of what it means to remember trauma: we re-experience the feeling of being traumatized, but we don't always compute what events these are linked to; our bodies and emotions remember the past, but we have no words or images to accompany them.

MJ: Yes, Pete Walker (2018) talks about 'emotional flashbacks' where we have all the feelings but often no specific memory. However, as somebody who has always been very cautious around pathologizing diagnostic labels, I also want to recognize what the language of 'trauma' may close down as well as open up. Reading Alex Iantaffi's (2020) work on this, as well as other social justice-informed folks, I think we can say pretty much everyone experiences some historical and/or intergenerational trauma, and certainly all marginalization is a form of trauma. So, it's not about one minority of clients who 'have trauma'.

JC: True, and for some it's more difficult to talk about their non-consent-based trauma often because of the way people who are socialized and/or live as male are told that they can't show 'weakness' and of course when people, regardless of gender, are so traumatized that they have become fragmented.

MJ: Absolutely, I couldn't agree more. Also, men in relationships with men often feel unable to speak out about abuse and coercive control dynamics – for similar reasons that it's hard for men in relationships with women to do so.

Self-determined norms are necessary; normative norms for marginalized folks aren't

JC: Just coming back to normativity and consent: it's mind-blowing to think about how much it is built into, reinforced and reproduced in our daily lives and belief systems and structures. It is almost too overwhelming to comprehend how deeply it's a part of the fabric of our lives. But there is a difference between harmful normativity and the comfort of familiar personal/group norms. I think we all need our norms but, for many of us, they will be different to the mainstream norms, right?

MJ: I suppose my main thing would be that consent is key here. I still don't believe we consider that enough when our communities move to new norms. Wider normative culture is saturated in non-consent: treating ourselves non-consensually to 'be productive', relationships with friends and family based on duty and obligation, expecting people to remain the same in relationships rather than any sense of ongoing consent. I feel like queers and others outside normativity often bring such non-consent into their new norms. For example, norms around what is attractive in queer communities are often still ableist, racist, misogynist and fatphobic. Norms around how sex should happen often still pressurize people into following certain scripts. Norms around how relationships should work still often make people feel like they would have to lose their whole relationship – maybe even community – if their feelings or desires changed at all, for example. Consent just isn't possible under such conditions.

JC: I've been thinking that what was normal for many of us, or 'the norm' before the lockdowns of the Covid-19 pandemic, was familiar but not necessarily wholly conducive to a healthy life. Under the first lockdown in 2020, I noticed how much more time I and many people had for just being and thinking and how much we need that time to be able to process stuff within us and around us – to recover from the violences of normative life that you mentioned earlier. Time that, if it was possible, we could really use to examine things such as consent issues in our culture. Capitalism really benefits from keeping us busy and distracted, doesn't it?

MJ: Hell, yes! I think it's about taking this opportunity – albeit one with a terrific and terrible cost attached – to address our inner and outer systems. I think of it like the Tower card in the tarot – like we collectively, and often individually, have fallen apart, but we were built on such hugely shaky foundations, so it's time to build stronger foundations and grow from there. People talk about getting 'back to normal'. It's time to interrogate the whole idea of normal, the roots of that idea in capitalism and colonialism and eugenics, and to ensure that we never go back to it. The danger is that we simply try to recreate ourselves and our outer systems as they previously were.

CHAPTER 5

Lesbian erasure from Freud's lesbian patient to the present

Jane Chance Czyzselska

Jane Chance Czyzselska considers Freud's paper 'The psychogenesis of a case of homosexuality in a woman' (1920), and some subsequent critiques, to examine what we can learn about lesbian erasure in and out of the therapy room over the last one hundred years.

As a psychotherapist with lesbian personal and professional history, a family connection to Freud's lesbian patient and experience working with lesbian-identified clients as a practitioner, I would like to consider Freud's 1920 paper on his work with a lesbian patient as a site of the psychoanalytic pathology and erasure of lesbians. As with many of Freud's concepts considered useful today, such as the unconscious, some of his less helpful ideas, like those about lesbian sexuality, persist also. In this paper, Freud was trying to explain lesbians both to himself and to others, using language and concepts that came from a society that didn't and still doesn't want to recognize that lesbians exist. Today, lesbians are still often required to justify and defend their object desire and fear the consequences of self-revelation through ordinary acts, including public displays of affection, talking about a same-gender partner, booking a double bed in a hotel or a trip to one of the 43 countries in the world that criminalizes sex between women (Human Dignity Trust, 2021). And despite significant advances for lesbians in Britain – in legal status, representation and public profile – lesbian subjectivity is frequently overlooked, attacked, diminished, invisibilized and erased.

Structural manifestations of lesbian erasure

The term erasure as it pertains to lesbians has gained currency in the last ten or so years, used as it is by individuals and groups who have varied proximities to lesbian subjectivity. In my years as editor of the lesbian-centred publication *DIVA*, lesbian erasure cropped up almost daily in our editorial meetings: whether in the frequent killing-off of lesbian characters in popular mainstream TV shows, the insistence by representatives for lesbian or bisexual actors that we didn't mention their sexuality in interviews – even when they played lesbian or bi characters – or the ongoing omission of lesbians and bi women in most research. The list went on.

In our own profession of psychotherapy, some practitioners have been directly engaged in lesbian erasure, endeavouring to 'convert' their lesbian clients to heterosexuality. The UK government has recently committed to ending the practice of conversion therapy with lesbian, gay and bisexual clients in therapy but has stopped short of providing the same protections from this harmful practice for trans and non-binary people, some of whom will undoubtedly be lesbian. Some others in our profession claim, with concern, that there is an increase in the number of young people assigned female at birth who are eschewing lesbian identity in favour of trans masculinity. Not only does this reaction seem to confuse sexuality with gender, but it also feels like a sinister twist on what heterosexuals said to me and my lesbian contemporaries when they doubted, disbelieved and in turn diminished, shamed and made wrong our lesbian identities.

There are other ways that lesbian subjectivity is overlooked or made invisible in our profession: in many of our therapy trainings, all the non-heterosexual and non-cis identities under the LGBTIQ+ umbrella are addressed over just one or two optional third-year weekend modules, or texts for study, written mainly by heterosexuals, and assuming cis heterosexuality among fellow practitioners and clients. Worth noting also is the fact that people who describe themselves as lesbian sometimes have to hide, code-switch or play down their lesbian identity – if they are able to – for survival or simply for an easier few moments in a difficult day. This includes, but is not limited to, not correcting heterosexuals who assume you are also heterosexual, not speaking up at school or university, in therapy trainings or in the workplace about inequality/erasure, and dressing more normatively to fit in and avoid explicit and implicit discrimination.

Passing

This behaviour brings to mind Freud's lesbian patient who, in the years after her analysis with him, was able to 'pass' as heterosexual when she needed to, hiding her lesbian identity for survival at various times throughout her life: from the marriage she entered to enable her secret lesbian life, as she travelled the globe in search of a life and locations where same-sex love was – even if on the down-low – more possible than in her native Austria. 'Passing' is both an act and a term, present in most cultures, applied to marginalized individuals who appear to be one, or a combination, of the dominant social categories but who are in fact not. In the European context of the lesbian patient, these categories would have been – and incidentally still are – white, middle-class, able-bodied, Christian, heterosexual and/or cisgender. So, to pass as any of the above categories, whether intentional or not, can confer privilege or safety in contexts that might not be safe. For Freud's patient, who was Jewish-born and baptised as Catholic, passing in public as both Christian and heterosexual was a way to avoid anti-Semitism and lesbophobia. Passing for heterosexual and insisting – to both Freud and her father – that her lesbian desire had not been enacted was quite literally the patient's 'get out of jail free' card.

So, who was the un-named teenage patient rendered almost ghost-like by Freud, who so bewildered him that he decided to terminate analysis with her after four months? In the decades since the paper was first published, just over one hundred years ago, psychoanalysts and scholars alike have wondered who the patient was. I am no Freud scholar, and it may be that this case study is not the only one Freud wrote about a patient with no name or pseudonym, but the patient's 'voice' in the study is limited to just three words and – whether consciously or not – I believe this omission at the very least diminishes her lesbian personhood.

Moreover, it is unlikely Freud imagined that his patient would one day get to tell her own story. But in 2000 the mystery was solved when her life story was made public in the biography she collaborated on with authors Ines Rieder and Diana Voigt. When the three met in Vienna in the 1990s, they were unsure about whether to reveal her real name. There were no family members to upset but the former patient considered using a pseudonym to 'make her something special' (Rieder and Voigt, 2020, p. xii). Rieder wondered whether the patient was now suggesting a pseudonym to mask her old fear of lesbophobia. Under Austrian law, lesbianism was criminalized from the 1850s until 1971, so the former patient was 71 when sex between women finally became legal. Twenty-eight years later, aged 99, she died before they were able to agree on a pseudonym. So, in the first German edition, the authors decided on Sidonie Csillag. Sidonie was a popular girl's name at the time, and *csillag* is Hungarian for 'star'. The lesbian patient, whose given name was Margarethe 'Gretl' Csonka, was still in a sense hidden, but she was also finally the star of her own story in *The Story of Sidonie C.* Now she had a name, an identity and crucially a voice – a voice she used not only to reveal the fascinating details about her long and eventful life and many lovers, but also to condemn the famous doctor as 'a creep', 'a disgusting brute' (2020, p. 45) and 'a jerk' (2020, p. 356).

Freud's normativity

Today, relational psychotherapists and analysts might describe Freud's analytic approach – the unrelational, one-person psychology – as a factor in the 'failure' of his analysis with his patient. Contemporary relationality, in its queerest incarnation at least, requires the practitioner to consider their positionality to contextualize their perspective, and their lived experience in relation to that of their clients. For example, Freud's reading of the young lesbian patient in his consulting room was filtered through a matrix of lenses: middle-class, white, heterosexual, cisgender and male, which together reinforce a dominant world view and concomitant socio-political hierarchy. This list of characteristics has long been rendered the 'norm' from which everyone else deviates and against which everyone is measured. Lesser (1999, p. 1) claims that Freud's paper has since been neglected by the psychoanalytic profession – perhaps demonstrating one way that the profession has erased the existence of lesbian patients. Lesser (1999, p. 8) also notes O'Connor and Ryan's (1993) observation that the paper has nevertheless dominated analytic debates that pathologize lesbians. For instance, we read Freud's normative interpretation of the patient's physical appearance: her passion and her intellect are considered 'masculine' by the professor, showing the reader that he cannot see the lesbian patient outside of or beyond his misogynist, binary and hetero-centric perception of human character traits. Ahmed (2006, p. 77) also spots Freud's reductive perspective, noting that if the patient 'has "turned away" from men, then she has also turned into one'.

Squeezing Gretl/Sidonie's homosexuality into his Oedipal theory, Freud then dismisses her as infantile and narcissistic and concludes that her suicide attempt is a self-punishing expression of her mother-hatred and her desire to bear her father's child. It is this interpretation alone that satisfies Freud, rendering the analytic bond stillborn. D'Ercole (1999, p. 120) also believes that, in his analysis of the patient, Freud situates heterosexuality as the norm and 'ultimately subjugates all issues of the patient's identity to their function within the Oedipal Scenario'. For De Lauretis (1999, p. 39), Freud's understanding of the case is marred by his 'preoccupation with homosexuality' and his fixation on the Oedipus complex, 'the enabling fiction of his invention of psychoanalysis'.

Freud writes that he ended the analysis because he believed Gretl/Sidonie had no interest in being 'cured' of her lesbian desire, and it should be noted that he felt it would be impossible to do so. Somewhat frustrated, he accuses her of misandry, suggesting that their work should stop and that a female analyst should be sought. This notion that lesbians hold men in contempt is another heteronormative fiction frequently imposed on lesbians in which a critique of patriarchy is misread for individual antipathy. Indeed, as I mention in my conversation with Sabah Choudrey (Chapter 14) on therapy training, I too was branded 'anti-men' by some heterosexual trainees when I talked about the impact of internalized lesbophobia growing up in a hetero-patriarchal society. This positioning of me as problematic, rather than the social context being problematic, further diminished my experience as a lesbian. Although a queer tutor was able to respond empathically, my experience mirrors a wider societal lack of awareness and understanding of lesbian subjectivities.

As with most case studies, writers often end up revealing more about themselves, their values and beliefs, and the world they inhabit, than they do about their analysands, and in this case Freud is no exception. Being a Jew himself, Freud also deviated from the expected gentile 'norm'. Indeed, Gilman (1995) examines the various ways that Jews were feminized at the time, suggesting that Freud's internalized anti-Semitism underpinned his tendency to project his own sense of inferiority onto those in society also deemed inferior. At the time of the analysis, Austria's Jew-hatred was on the rise and Jewish men were viewed as effeminate, in part because of the practice of circumcision. Citing Gilman (1993), Lesser (1999, p. 2) reminds us that at the time Viennese slang for the clitoris was 'the Jew' and masturbation was 'playing with the Jew'. In her foreword to the English translation of the biography, psychoanalyst Jeanne Wolff-Bernstein suggests that Freud may have ended the work with Gretl/Sidonie because of his concerns about his own daughter Anna, who, then aged 22, showed no interest in men. Rieder does after all suggest that the doctor finds the lack of men in Anna's life 'disagreeable' (Rieder and Voigt, 2020, p. 54). Wolff-Bernstein also suggests the forced ending may have given Freud a way to reclaim a sense of power. Did he take on the daughter of the wealthy Hungarian banker to distract from his concerns about his own daughter and to further his acceptance into gentile – and genteel – society? Did he end the analysis because he felt further emasculated by his unapologetic and unyielding lesbian patient and, as both Lesser and Gilman suggest, project his own sense of castration into her? Anna did indeed turn out to be lesbian — her relationship with fellow psychoanalyst Dorothy Tiffany Burlingham spanned 50 years.

Despite these putative concerns, Freud does at least realize correctly that his patient is unapologetic about the direction of her desire, that she may also be a feminist and that he cannot collude with her father's wish to re-orient her or engage in what today would be considered a request for conversion therapy. Indeed, much has been written about Freud's belief that as infants we are all 'polymorphously perverse', meaning that babies project their desire indiscriminately. Further, he ascribes 'bisexuality' to emergent infantile desire – yet, as Angelides (2001) notes, psychoanalysis also has a history of erasing the bisexual adult 'in the present tense'. In other words, bisexuality is denigrated in adulthood. Freud was indeed vocal and public in his support of homosexual men, listing Plato, Michelangelo and Leonardo Da Vinci as fine examples. However, his elevation of the masculine in his comparison of the 'boy's far superior equipment' to the girls' inferior, 'atrophied' genitals (Freud, 1932, p. 126), his theory of female 'penis envy' and the immaturity of clitoral – and non-vaginal – orgasm all centre the white, cis, heterosexual male gaze and gender hierarchy of his day that continues today.

My queer ancestry

Nonetheless, I feel I owe a debt of gratitude to Freud for writing about Gretl/Sidonie. His is, as far as we know, the first ever psychoanalytic paper about a lesbian patient and, despite the specious therapeutic goal which seeks a reason or cause for her non-normative sexual orientation, it does at least put lesbians on the psychoanalytic map. The fact that lesbians were – and still are – relatively hidden in plain sight is clear from a reading of *The Story of Sidonie C*, which gives multiple examples of non-heterosexual liaisons between the women (and men) Gretl/Sidonie knows in Austria and the Czech Republic alone. And there is an even more personal reason for my gratitude. Were it not for his work with Gretl/Sidonie, the biography of her life might not have been written and she might not have got the chance to vouchsafe to her biographers the names and stories of her queer lovers. And particularly her first ever female lover, my paternal grandmother, Marianne.

I first learned about my grandmother's queerness in 2014 in Vienna, when I met Ines Rieder unexpectedly in Vienna's gay bookshop, Loewenherz, located on Berggasse, just a few doors down from what is now known as the Freud Museum, and where Gretl/Sidonie met the doctor for her daily analysis. As well as being a psychotherapy trainee, I was also the editor of the British magazine for LGBTIQ+ women and non-binary people, *DIVA*. I was on a press trip with my partner, to explore what the city offered to queer locals and visitors. We arrived on a freezing cold January evening, as the city's police were cordoning off the centre in advance of a far-right political rally that weekend. Our visit seemed to eerily echo something of Gretl/Sidonie's own brushes with the Nazis. In the cosy bookshop, among some of the city's queer activists, club promoters, performers, publishers and writers, Rieder and I chatted over coffee and sachertorte, and I learned that my paternal grandmother had been one of Gretl/Sidonie's lovers. The news was a revelation, not only to me but also to my father – then aged 89 – who was an infant when the secret affair began. Suddenly, I felt an unfamiliar embodied sense of recognition and validation.

I will never know how Marianne labelled herself or identified in relation to her sexuality, but I had discovered that I had queer ancestry. Knowing that I had a non-normative heritage sexuality-wise felt huge. As Ellis J. Johnson (Chapter 2) points out, there is something ungrounding about being 'the first' of a different or unwelcomed identity, either in society or in a family. And although I knew from the history books that there have always been lesbians, in my family I had, until the moment of discovering my grandmother's story, felt like the anomaly, unalike, someone whose identity had for a time to be hidden. Indeed, although my paternal grandmother happily consorted with women in the 1920s, in the 1990s I didn't dare tell my maternal grandmother I was gay. But by 2014, the mood had changed, and unlike Gretl/Sidonie's father, or Freud and his daughter, mine now shared in the joy of this knowledge with me. 'You come from a long line of lesbians, darling,' my father joked. 'If only!' I replied. In that moment, I recalled him telling me about his escape with my grandmother Marianne in 1939 from the brutal hatred of the Nazis which made many Jews feel ashamed about their cultural heritage. How much was the shame I felt about my homosexuality a legacy burden interwoven with anti-Semitism? Even if we had known about his mother's queer desire, would it have made it easier to come out and honour my lesbian identity? Is it possible that familial knowing and celebration of her sexuality alone could have dissolved my lesbian shame?

Certainly, in reading the passages about 24-year-old Marianne's sexual confidence with Gretl/Sidonie and another lover, I felt something within me relax. Shame and hiding were not present in those pages and reading what Gretl/Sidonie told her biographers about Marianne's excited longing for her, I sensed love as well as sexual desire in my grandmother's feeling for Freud's former patient. In Gretl/Sidonie's story, we learn that, although she visits my grandmother several times between 1926 and 1928, both women feel that their lovemaking is no more than an afternoon's affair. But when Marianne slips a pompom from her Pierrot costume into Gretl/Sidonie's handbag when saying goodbye, I wonder if we can read it as a queer love token or transitional object. Could my grandmother have loved or been in love with Gretl/Sidonie? On the page, my grandmother's personality was more fleshed out than it had been by my father, who had no knowledge of her hidden romantic and sexual life. How much had my own grandmother had to render invisible to make her life more comfortable and what impact might this have had on her self-esteem or her ability to live her life more freely? And what has been the impact on me? In the pages of *The Story of Sidonie C*, I learned that Marianne didn't much want to marry the older man who would become my grandfather and that the union was arranged by her parents. Had they known of her sexual proclivities? Were they marrying away the gay in her? Certainly, even if she had come out to her parents, Marianne didn't dare risk living more openly as Gretl/Sidonie did.

Lesbian critiques of psychoanalytic normativity

Indeed, Burch (1997, p. 40) reflects on the risk faced by lesbian daughters who come out to heterosexual parents, particularly those who experience this differentiation from 'compulsory heterosexuality' (Rich, 1980) 'not as separation but as severance' of the parent–child bond. In Burch (1997), Elise (2002), Roth (2004) and Yellin (2007), we see some of Freud's theories through relational lesbian psychoanalytic and psychodynamic lenses. Elise (2002) suggests an alternative to Freud's 'negative Oedipal resolution' – the term given to gay and lesbian adults who are unable to achieve the 'positive' resolution that he ascribes to heterosexual object desire. Referring to Freud's 'pre-Oedipal' and ergo infantile dyadic bond between mother and daughter, she suggests re-imagining the negative Oedipal to the 'primary maternal Oedipal situation' (Elise, 2002, p. 209), centring female homoerotic desire. Further, Elise contends that cultural/familial denial of the erotic relationship between the mother and her daughter underpins internalized lesbophobia. If the mother, and the culture, can experience and validate the mother–daughter homoerotic desire – subsequently validating the lesbian daughter's desire – her daughter may be more likely to grow up feeling she is an autonomous and agentic sexual subject.

We can see how this unrecognized or unregistered desire between mother and daughter plays out in the culture in the belittling of and inability to imagine how lesbians can be sexual together and in the often-fielded cis-het question, 'But what do you *do* in bed?' To counter this phallocentric dominance, Roth (2004) also attempts to restore lesbian sexual potency and agency in her paper 'Engorging the lesbian clitoris: Opposing the phallic cultural unconscious'. Yellin (2007) wonders whether the human tendency to inertia or a resistance to change – what Freud termed fixation – is what we today might call reification: 'the solidifying of an identity or a relational paradigm into a "thing", rigid, unchangeable, universally expectable in all circumstances' (2007, p. 34). She further invites us to invoke Butler's belief in the possibility to live gender and sexuality in a different way and the possibilities for lives lived otherwise. Yellin also wonders whether queer and relational psychoanalysis are up to the job, perhaps echoing Harris's (1999, p. 177) assertion that if psychoanalysis is to be fit for purpose, a theory is needed 'that recognises the social power of categories like gender and sexuality in both conscious and unconscious experience, but that can also account for the way in which these categories, at certain moments, lose salience and become more porous'.

Lesbians and trans masculinities

If categoric porosity and the complexities of gender, bodies and sexualities are to be acknowledged, what might such a theory be? Harris believes Benjamin's (1988) *The Bonds of Love* moves us in the right direction. Maybe it could also include a pinch of Freud (1932, p. 114) who, in one of his more radical moments stated, 'what constitutes masculinity or femininity is an unknown characteristic which anatomy cannot lay hold of'. Perhaps it could also be infused with what D'Ercole (1999, p. 127) imagines: 'a theory of sexuality devoid of gender and sex that is based on feelings, erotic and otherwise – feelings that are sustained and transformed in our ongoing relationships throughout our lives'. Clearly, we must make use of intersectional lenses such as race, class, trans and disability, and move beyond the pathologization of trans identities. We must also move beyond pitting trans against lesbian and gay subjectivities – as some are, both in and outside of our profession – in the belief that lesbians are being lost to trans masculinities and that trans-inclusive therapy is lesbophobic. I'd like to explore this subject – which causes great pain to those on either side – and consider what is being lost and to whom, and what is being gained.

It is posited that rising numbers of people who have identified as lesbian – regardless of age – are choosing to trade queer womanhood for non-binary and/or trans masc identities. This story of alleged lesbian erasure emerged in the 1990s in the UK and the US as there seemed to be an increase in people who had formerly identified as lesbian choosing to have chest surgery and/or take testosterone and articulate trans masculine identities. But this version of the story is told through a cis- and homonormative lens. In my client work, I sometimes suggest to trans and/or queer clients that we consider the issue that is causing trouble by looking at it through a trans or a queer lens rather than a cis-heteronormative one. When we see it from that perspective, as Amanda Middleton (Chapter 7) suggests, how might the problem change? Or is our way of seeing it – through internalizing the dominant ideologies – part of what is troubling us?

So, if we roll the lens to the trans and queer window to view this alleged occurrence of lesbian erasure, the story might be seen differently. Different in the sense that the label imposed on us by a system that categorizes people according to binary-gendered metrics no longer fits for some. Further, the expansion of both gender expression within the categories of woman/man and gender identity categories that exist beyond the binary is a positive and joyous thing that makes possible lives lived in greater self-alignment wherever one feels themselves to be on the gender continuum. For context, when many of us came out as lesbian, we faced disbelief and derision. Our sexual difference from 'the norm' was experienced as dangerous by the heterosexuals who diminished us, perhaps because it opened the door to a wider sexual landscape that they had not yet explored within themselves. If the person they had hitherto known to be straight pronounced themselves lesbian, what impact might it have on them if they too were not wholly comfortable in their assigned label? Could this fear of and objection to the emergence of more trans and gender-expansive folks that Harris, Benjamin and Young (Chapter 10) describe as the 'projection of unprocessed, disowned feelings' onto trans people be a repetition of this trope?

Furthermore, the concern about lesbian loss is not evidenced in the statistics. As this book went to press, a report found that the number of women aged 16-24 who identify as lesbian had risen from 3.1% in 2014 to 11.4%. This figure represents the highest number of lesbian-identified women since records began (Booth, 2022). Research by the Office of National Statistics (2020) found that the proportion of the UK population aged 16 and over identifying as lesbian, gay or bisexual increased from 1.6 per cent in 2014 to 2.2 per cent in 2018. In the same year, a UK government study on gender and sexuality (Government Equalities Office, 2018, p. 15) found that out of 108,100 respondents, 61 per cent identified as either gay or lesbian, 26 per cent identified as bisexual, 7 per cent identified as non-binary, 3 per cent were trans women and 3 per cent were trans men. We get a rough picture of the populations here, and drilling down further, the statistics also reveal that trans respondents were much less likely to identify as gay or lesbian (23 per cent) than cisgender respondents (68 per cent) but more likely to identify as bisexual (32 per cent) or pansexual (14 per cent), with 5 per cent identifying as queer.

Trans lesbian erasure

There is no record of the number of trans women who do identify as lesbian – we can see this as lesbian erasure too – and concern about losing lesbians to trans masculinity is not mirrored among gay males, who could be said to have 'lost' some of their number to trans feminine identities. Could this be because those who mourn this so-called lesbian loss see gender affirmation in the direction away from female masculinity and towards trans masculinity as reinforcing the patriarchal elevation of the masculine? Or even as the burying or rendering ghost-like of a former lesbian identity?

I use the word direction, in the Ahmedian sense of orientation (2006, p. 69), because I believe that gender and sexuality are imbued with movement rather than fixedness. My own personal experience and those of some clients over the years tells me that, for many of us, we will use the limited terms and frameworks available to us until something that fits better comes along. If I had been born 20 years ago, it is possible I would not have identified either as a woman or as a lesbian. Reflection on my gender and sexuality has made me realize how much my identity as a woman and as a lesbian was shaped by a binary, white, cis heterosexual ideology that privileges only two possible genders and concomitant sexualities – hetero and homo or bi, which also reinforces the binary. I was a gender non-conforming kid who was described by others as a tomboy, who eschewed skirts, dresses, dolls and the colour pink (as did my mother) and who wished, aged 11, that she could get rid of her budding breasts. But this kid also had no interest in football or the hurly burly of adolescent male culture, enjoyed both male and female friendship, reading, climbing trees and listening to the cross-dressing dandy popstar Adam Ant. I was a child who was told she was a girl, and then a lesbian. Of course, there will be some lesbians and heterosexual women who relate to these likes and dislikes, too, but when I was growing up in the 1970s, there was a paucity of imagination in the culture about who I was or could be.

Living in a gender-expansive-embracing world

Had I been a kid today, knowing what we do now, the adults and other kids around me might have made it possible to be known beyond the binary. Instead, I experimented with a spectrum of femme to masc gender expressions over the decades, and I sought therapy to explore my gender identity with experienced and brilliant cis heterosexual therapists who, despite being able to help me to explore many other significant troubles, couldn't facilitate exploration of my non-normative gender identity.

We explored how the gender binary teams up with misogyny to create the notion that it is weak or feminine to be vulnerable, and its masculine counterpart is inviolable strength. In detaching these qualities from the hierarchical gender binary, this expanded how I could be in the world, but I still had to be cis; being something else wasn't possible in the therapy space.

Undoubtedly, they too were limited by their lived experiences in relation to trans-ness, and what they learned or didn't learn in their therapy trainings. Over the years, the dominant categories have been stretched to accommodate binary homosexuality and binary trans identities. In more recent years, non-binary has emerged as a term that, it could be said, builds on the work that 'genderqueer' and 'gender-fluid' do. Gender identity, regardless of the body to which it relates, can therefore be fluid, and for some it is dependent on what their environment makes possible.

Indeed, Ahmed (2006) proposes that we draw on classical phenomenological thinking to develop a queer model of orientations, examining how directionality, space and time impact on and imbue bodies with meanings. Ahmed's 'queer phenomonology' gives a particular clarity to how the dominant culture's power dynamics manifest spatially between bodies. Queerness disrupts and creates anew not only these dynamics, says Ahmed, but also a politics of disorientation, as in oriented away from normative expectations, that liberates the bodies of those who are marginalized. Indeed, says Ahmed (2006, p. 102), 'To act on lesbian desire is a way of reorientating one's relation not just toward sexual others, but also to a world that has already "decided" how bodies should be orientated in the first place.' What's more, Ahmed notes, it takes time and work to inhabit a lesbian body in the face of hostility, and I would add courage, too. Similarly, it takes courage to move from a cis heterosexual or lesbian identity – whether butch or not – to a trans non-binary or trans masculine one. These reorientations, like ripples on the water, while being joyous in many ways for those who create them, can also provoke fear in others, threatened as they may feel by those who traverse from the known to the lesser-known categories.

Butler's (Gleeson, 2021) belief in the need to rethink the category of woman has been welcomed by many feminists, but this belief has also caused anger and fear among others. I believe this categoric expansion mirrors the evolution of the British feminist movements, from the suffragettes and suffragists to those who fought for equal pay, for the right not to be raped in marriage amongst other issues, and for the particular interests of lesbians, Black, Brown and other women of colour. Now, women – some of whom may or may not have penises, XY chromosomes or no uterus – are demanding the right to live as and be related to as women. This expansion of gender categories and gender expression is surely another step in the evolution of feminism and part of what Harris and D'Ercole are also suggesting?

Of course, as Ellis J. Johnson explains (Chapter 2), we cannot think about gender without thinking about race and all the ways of living and being that characterized pre-colonial cultures, where gender and bodies and sexualities were fluid and less fixed. We can see an example of this in the work of Oyěwùmi (1997), who explains there was no category 'woman' in pre-colonial Yoruba culture, challenging the fact of universal binary gender categorization. And as Bay De Veen posits in Chapter 16, there is a diasporic quality to lesbian subjectivities too, as I have outlined, describing the various ways in which we move or are moved towards and away from lesbian identities; sometimes hiding, sometimes being erased or made invisible, sometimes living as loudly as is possible.

CHAPTER 6

Meaning-making with queer clients

Charles Neal

In *The Cultural Politics of Emotion* (2014), Sara Ahmed argues that emotions are cultural practices and that bodies are given value through emotion and thus the bodies, as well as the individuals, become aligned with a popular ideology. Queer bodies are emotional sites that produce, reproduce and challenge popular beliefs concerning identity. Psychotherapist and author Charles Neal reflects here on meaning-making for therapists and their queer clients.

We are polymorphously perverse and we are fabulous!

CHARLES NEAL: There is just as powerful a pressure today to adopt specific sexual and gender identities as, for example, there was in the 1950s, such that 'maleness' and 'femaleness' remain heavily policed by our educational, medical and familial environments, as does heterosexuality. The relatively recent addition of trans as an identity in certain industrial metropolitan societies is an interesting and important development for making change happen, as well as a key part of a burgeoning new taxonomy. Few of the inner experiences, behaviours, manifestations or cultures represented are 'new', of course, many having long been lived in other places and times, and frequently not named as distinct, or other.

JANE CHANCE CZYZSELSKA: Yes, trans and non-binary people, just as lesbian, gay, bi, queer and intersex people, have always existed regardless of today's labels.

CN: Yes, and recently ABC News Network listed 58 genders; the list is always developing so choosing an identity has become more complex than ever. Freud flagged this up using the term 'polymorphous' for our earliest sexuality.[1] The search for an identity – and the conflicts and arguments which rage over such issues – from the ever-expanding range today is interesting: might we expect in the future to transcend gender and categories of sexuality?

JC: When you say earliest, you mean as infants? Freud, despite his acknowledgement of, and attempt to study, homosexuality, was limited by a nineteenth-century cis-heteronormative lens and believed that attaining a 'stable' – as in fixed – gender and sexual identity was the mark of successful psychoanalysis.

CN: That's right. Naturally, Freud was limited by the contexts in which he lived and had been trained: bourgeois nineteenth-century Vienna; medical models of the psyche and body; wealthy clients with neuroses; working from the pathological to posit norms about human development; attempting later to force the art of psychology into being acceptable as a 'science'. However, his earliest work, the ground-breaking 'Three essays on the theory of sexuality' (1905), in particular was a huge contribution to distinguishing sexuality from gender and pleasure-seeking drives from reproductive ones, as well as in proposing that all sexualities are on a continuum.

JC: I've been reading a paper on bisexuality by Rapoport (2009) in which she takes issue with the tendency in psychoanalytic thought to conflate biology, sexual orientation and gender identity and portray bisexual desire as impossible and hysteric. What do you make of that?

The living world is a continuum in each and every one of its aspects

CN: I'm very taken with Rapoport's critique not only of Freudians and their companions but also of modern queer therapists or theorists who continue to erase bisexuality as a unique 'real-life' sexuality, not as coming between one binary and another, nor as blending two (as the Freudians have), nor arising from the gender of the partner. Part of the problem is the origin of the term: obviously 'bi' already points to two! When first used in biology, it referred to intersex individuals. Some queer theorists still take it to mean either/or, or both/and. Rapoport (2009) says the concept is both outdated and valuable for how much it exposes of the deep-rootedness of binary thinking. Kinsey (1948, p. 639) himself, while only referring to bisexuality as sexual behaviours, explains:

> The world is not to be divided into sheep and goats. Not all things are black nor all things white. It is a fundamental of taxonomy that nature rarely deals with discrete categories. Only the human mind invents categories and tries to force facts into separated pigeon-holes. The living world is a continuum in each and every one of its aspects. The sooner we learn this concerning human sexual behaviour the sooner we shall reach a sound understanding of the realities of sex.

JC: I'm wondering about the value of the term 'polymorphously perverse' now!

CN: OK, me too! Let's drop the antiquated idea of 'perverse' but 'polymorphous' means 'having, assuming, or occurring in various forms, characters, or styles', and that is us!

JC: It is! And I like how Rapoport (2009) cites Layton (2000), who challenges the idea of universal pre-Oedipal bisexuality, namely, that mental attitudes and behaviours are categorized as either feminine or masculine, and that paternal is always synonymous with masculine and maternal is synonymous with feminine. Layton also challenges the idea that cis-hetero-based concepts of personhood and identity can help us to make sense of unconscious motivations for non-sexual activities. This really speaks to me! How about you?

CN: Absolutely. Again, bisexuality is erased. Identifying as bisexual need not imply that the object of desire is either one gender or another, neither does it mean the individual lives within a hetero/homo sexual binary. The usefulness of the term 'queer' was supposed to be as a label refusing all norms and no attraction to genders at all. Melissa

Caro Lancho (2015) has written fascinating explanations of this in her analysis of misrepresentations of bisexuality in Netflix's *Orange Is the New Black* and the BBC's *Torchwood* series.

Freud's 'Letter to an American mother' (1951) showed his early openness about homosexual sexual expression but he later muddied all that clarity with pseudo-scientific stuff about penis envy. I agree his ideas got more rigid and, what we would today call, sexist and heteronormative over the few years left to him. Although he clearly described sexuality developing independently from a desire to mate, he still viewed variation as 'perverse', meaning a deviation from the norm. Freud also viewed sexuality as fluid and not fixed, that it developed over the course of an individual's life. In light of his own 30 years of revisions and a century of critical analysis, it's interesting that Freud himself acknowledged his work was contradictory and ever-changing in perspective, conceding that the result was that 'it may often have happened that what was old and what was more recent did not admit of being merged into an entirely uncontradictory whole' (1923e, p. 141).

JC: He was a bit of a slippery fish old Freud, wasn't he? He distinguished sexuality from gender in 1905 but in his 1920 paper on the lesbian patient and in a lecture on femininity (1932) he seems to conflate sex, gender and sexuality.

CN: What interests me greatly, as someone originally trained in socio- and psycholinguistics, is our enduring need for naming and labelling one another and ourselves. This is the first task of languaging, of course, the sorting out of our world through nouns and descriptors in order to feel we control it. Once we can get the names of chairs and dogs right, despite their shared leg count, we're on our way to gaining power over this confusing world. A huge difficulty arises, however, because human beings are not things, not static but fluid, continually in process. Sorting transgender people from genderqueer, pangender or gender-fluid ones brings us right back to polymorphous complexity. We learn labels for defining who we are, but for whom? Often, we do not fully recognize our self in the label. The terms have been useful historically perhaps, but part of having agency might be to reject terms which don't quite fit us. Can any word be precisely right for oneself? Sexuality and identity are frequently concerns that play with categorization.

JC: Right, and there are no two genderqueer or pansexual people alike, so becoming confident in one's identity, on one's own terms, is an important process.

Psychotherapy is in danger from labelling in its own ways

CN: Yes, very much so. Psychotherapy is in danger from labelling in its own ways: in attempting to be scientific, we can come to categorize processes in people's lives as diagnostic categories or things – hyper-vigilant, psychotic, schizoid, bipolar – and, naturally, some clients who seek comfort from being labelled are satisfied by this. Similarly, it can feel like a relief in one's personal life to find a name for what we are: lesbian, vegan, multi-allergic, dyslexic. This immediately connects with notions of inclusion and exclusion, belonging and otherness. Once I've accepted my label, I know which group I belong to and can distinguish those who do not belong to the same group as 'other'. This tribal legacy helps us to know who is 'one of us' and who is not – and may therefore count as an outsider, an alien or even an enemy. We seek out those who seem as much like ourselves as we can find and distance ourselves from those who are not like us.

JC: Right, and that can have positive and negative wider consequences, I guess. Like the importance of finding community with other LGBTIQ folk but then only hanging out with other white queers.

CN: Absolutely. We hang out everywhere with those we feel secure and comfortable with – be it a club, a pub, Facebook, on Twitter, at university or in therapy training groups. And therapists need to work hard not to fall into easy communion with clients without scrupulously examining the meanings and individuated experiences of, say, being a 'top', being polyamorous or being asexual. We cannot assume commonality of experience and must hear from the client what meanings they attach to these terms, how they are personally experiencing these identities in their daily lives, how being a lesbian is actually lived.

Language and thought are in constant flux

CN: Language – and, therefore, thought – is also in constant flux: terms change meaning, too. Marriage, for example, for several centuries defined a union between a man and a woman and this is no longer generally so – except in Catholic contexts. In the 1940s, the dictionary defined lesbianism as 'the sin of Sapphism'! In the seventeenth century, 'gay' meant prostitute; at other times, it meant cheerful and fun. I have always been interested in who controls language and definition. I wish to encourage clients to be in control of their own.

JC: Yes!

CN: Because we are mammals and designed to live together in groups, we have always lived in tribes for our safety and survival. Two key mechanisms by which tribes maintain integrity and police their memberships are shaming and ostracism. Today's battles over whether trans women can be counted as 'real' women, and the great threat perceived by some non-trans women if they are, give us examples of these primary dynamics.

JC: Yes, when trans women are perceived and othered through a cis lens they are treated as less-than, and also as a threat to non-trans women. This reminds me of how gay men were accused by homophobes of being predatory paedophiles in the 1970s. It ends up in pathology, which is not based in fact, and is unfair and hateful. It is also a missed opportunity for support and solidarity. Trans and gender non-conforming people experience shaming, violence and vilification pretty much daily, and it is unacceptable. As it is when it happens to non-trans women, and as it is when it's racialized. I love Roche's (2019) approach, which is to jettison the binary, cis-framed 'debate' about trans identity and instead simply be trans.

Difference is a plus, not a threat

CN: That's important. If none of us is 'other', none of us can be made wrong; we all find ourselves in contexts where we are othered and when that happens, we are being seen, however covertly, as 'wrong'. Although as individuals we are different in life experience, attitudes, beliefs, psyche and even biology – to say nothing of our gender and sex make-ups – tribes always attempt to limit these differences in their appeal to sameness as requirements for belonging. This is as much a truth about modalities in psychotherapy as it is elsewhere. Just as clients can benefit over their therapeutic journey from finding peers or 'community', so can therapists in their various schools, allegiances and associations. We need to know the effects of such 'belonging' on the development of wider choices and learning, on our growth and on the development of our understanding. For example, is being a practising existential therapist closing me off from experiencing family constellations work? Is my client's identifying as a cisgendered or gay male inhibiting investigation of their undiscovered queerness or heterosexuality?

JC: I think what you're saying is that we need to reflect carefully on how and with what and whom we align ourselves?

CN: Yes, and for me, psychotherapy must remain a queer activity in itself – transgressive, pioneering, as it was originally, especially in relation to sex and gender. We mustn't forget that therapy has contradictory dimensions: ground-breaking and creative at times, often boundary pushing, it also has a bourgeois retrogressive history: expensive, luxurious, elitist, white. Who is in charge of explanation, analysis, meaning-making? Definition is critical to the exercise of power.

JC: Yes, the whiteness is really problematic, both in its assumptions about who gets to be a therapist, as well as who the recipients of therapy are, and also in what has been left out – that is, the experiences and impact of structural racism. Despite the massive contribution to the field by Jewish psychologists and therapists, many like Freud and his Jewish peers experienced virulent, hateful anti-Semitism. But they also benefited from being male and having access to, and being a part of, a white middle class.

CN: While claiming a focus on individuation, psychology has often aligned itself with sameness and control. Behaviourism's pact with repressive military-industrial power systems during and after the Second World War is an example, as are the decades of pathologizing sex and gender variation which still toxify much theory and practice in psychology and therapy today. We owe it to clients, when they come to us for assistance in meaning-making, to remain curious, opening, learning alongside them, co-creative.

JC: I'm also interested in Goldener's (1991, p. 249) argument that an internally consistent gender identity is neither possible nor desirable because it assumes and reifies a unified psychic world. This also really speaks to me.

CN: Having spent the whole of my working life in therapy arguing along similar lines, I too am excited by Goldener challenging the assumption that a consistent gender identity is possible – or even desirable. A consistent gender identity assumes and reifies a unified psychic world and the 'fixing' of what is naturally fluid, the ossifying of the much more fascinating continual movement of real bodies living real lives. All identities are narratives, fictions if you will, including gender identities: our belief in them makes both them and us feel real. There is no difference between a gender and a transgender; both are equally real and – in a sense, therefore – equally fictitious. Genders and sexualities are in reality a series of actions, of embodiments, of becomings.

JC: Well, Judith Butler (2006) talked about that in *Gender Trouble*, didn't they? That repeated learned, gendered, embodied behaviours are part of how we enact and encode gendered 'difference' and crucially in a white, ableist, cis hetero-patriarchy status. Also, Alok Vaid Menon (Theil, 2021) explains the colonial underpinnings of this.

CN: Yes, and I'd like to connect these ideas to an understanding of what's behind much of this distortion: fear of difference. We see it forcefully highlighted today in underlying issues beneath racial hatred, misogyny and attacks on those who breach sexual boundaries or widely held norms. We see this fear in the raging culture wars distracting us in capitalist cultures from much more important issues of inequality, power, exploitation and corruption. Currently, trans people are a main target in this regard because their very existence challenges heteronormative, binary power models. The violence that is erupting in all these sites indicates that difference – even the holding of a different view – is a huge challenge to existing power structures.

JC: I agree there's an element of fear in this, and also perhaps envy? Perhaps othered groups have had projected onto them the parts or characteristics that those in more socially dominant groups fear to express themselves.

CN: Yes, that is certainly true. In psychotherapeutic terms – splitting or polarizing. All bullying, in my experience, is also rooted in envy: conscious or, more usually, subconscious as well as in splitting off unwanted aspects of oneself and projecting them onto the 'other'.

As therapists, we must address our own fears, envy and biases

CN: I've written about the requirement to perform gender and sexuality in ways delineated by those who have held the most power in order to maintain unequal power relations (Neal, 2013). From cataloguing our differences and asserting oppositions and binaries (gay/straight, male/female, trans/cis, able/disabled, BAME/white), we move to making hierarchies of status: some are best, some worst, some are right, some wrong. Difference threatens the coherence of the tribe and who its 'bosses' are: the body politic splits off, dissociates and projects its shadows onto those who dare to transgress. Psychotherapy and psychology still lag behind, unsure how to embrace diversity.

JC: It's true. Some psychotherapists separate politics from the personal, which I believe can be harmful to clients because lived experiences and differences – from the therapist – can wind up being pathologized, personalized or minimized and, again, othered. To me, it's like the Gramscian notion of hegemonic thought (Gramsci *et al.*, 2005), in that unequal power relations are reproduced as if they are natural and not created by design. And as a feminist I believe that the personal is inherently bound up with the political. All these considerations are important to me in the therapy room.

CN: Me too! My work and my politics have never been divisible. Celebrating difference is at the heart of both. Working therapeutically with conflict and pain in relationships, the focus often narrows to how one person is different from another or how they've 'changed' and thus become less loveable or acceptable in other ways. Sometimes what was different or novel about the other/s was the source of original excitement; finding out more was the adventure. Now the conflict is over which person's experience is 'right'. The main task is to bring differences into the open with curiosity and acceptance and, if achievable, even celebration. It's also crucial to locate all our relationships – clients with each other and ours with clients – within socio-political, ecological, familial and religious contexts that take account of oppression and intersectionalities.

JC: Difference and diversity has been proven time and again, particularly in studies of the workplace and in innovation, to be advantageous. Yet it is often feared. Lorde (2007, p. 115) cautioned against the 'institutionalised rejection of difference', saying:

> We have all been programmed to respond to the human differences between us with fear and loathing and to handle that difference in one of three ways: ignore it and if that is not possible, copy it if we think it is dominant or destroy it if we think it is subordinate.

I think our field minimizes, fears and diminishes difference, and this can sometimes retraumatize clients in the therapy room.

Black Lives Matter shows us the importance of listening to the lived experience of others

CN: I wholly agree, Jane. We must allow clients, and others, to define and redefine themselves – sometimes even with regard to being known as clients – and accept ownership of their difference, not attempt to absorb, change or diminish that. It is deeply loving for a person to divulge as much of their uniqueness of thought, feeling and experience as they are able at the time and equally loving for another person to fully accept, with or without full understanding, that this is how it is for that person, however difficult that is. The Black Lives Matter movement shows us the importance of listening to the lived experience of other people and educating ourselves as fully as we can about that – and, by the way, in our own historic and present part in that. The UK Labour Party's failure to hear the experiences of their own Jewish members has caused hugely damaging rifts between the two groups. #MeToo is a powerful warning to listen to and believe what horrors are being accumulated and colluded with behind the scenes. Kipling Williams' *et al.* (2005) work on profound long-term damage to participation and relational skills caused by being ostracized or ignored has considerable implications on a societal scale in relation to marginalized and excluded people.

JC: How do you mean?

CN: Well, in how possible it might feel to be able to take part in relationships and/or have a role to play in wider society. Helping clients to celebrate and develop their own differences, uniqueness, individuality and integrity is a huge part of the healing task of therapy, be it with clients in relationships, with individuals or with groups. Our first developmental task in early infancy is attachment, based on trust, which we need to have experienced, and the second is individuation without loss of esteem or rejection, which we also need to experience. In good therapy, these two challenges are often relived, oftentimes attaining greater resolution.

Sex is really just another form of energy

CN: We have touched on the importance of co-creating meaning – and identity – with our clients on the basis of their own experience and of how societal splitting off through fear and envy can lead to 'othering'.

The next important strand of our work with clients concerns integration, moving away from the splitting of body from mind – or, more accurately, brain – mind from spirit, desire from energy, sex from the rest of our lives, our bodies from the life of this planet and even therapist from client.

JC: Yes!

CN: This probably occupies LGBTIQ+ therapists more than others because of the implicit, unvoiced heteronormative assumptions in our culture and their impact on clients and ourselves. It seems to me crucial for us to acknowledge firstly that we are bodies together in a room. Or, I suppose, more usually since Covid-19 took us over, online, but still bodies in rooms. Psychology has tended to prioritize thought over actions, mentality over felt experience. Our body is the site of all our drives, as well as the site of mind – whether we narrowly focus on the brain or appreciate that all our cells contribute to a wider kind of 'mind'. The body is also the site of desire, of sexual and relational drives, including our own relationship with our bodied self.

Janet's initial writings (1903) – preceding Freud – on somatic psychology focused on the mind–body interface, the relationship between our physical matter and our energy and the interaction of our body structures with our thoughts and actions. His work was developed by Ferenczi (1949), who stressed that clients need to be co-participants in therapy and emphasized the huge part 'empathic reciprocity' plays in successful therapy. The 'second generation' analyst Wilhelm Reich (1925, 1933) extended the idea of sex as central to the life of the body and its repression or distortion as the cause of neuroses.

Bringing awareness to the felt body is important for affect regulation and integration

CN: This work massively influenced Janov (1970), Perls (Perls *et al.*, 1951), Lowen (1958, 1975) and the various subsequent developments of body – or somatic – psychotherapy. The primary relationship addressed in somatic psychology is the person's relation to, and empathy with, their own felt body, based on a belief that bringing sufficient awareness to this will cause healing. We must imagine the significance of this approach for those whose bodies have been politicized and attacked, denigrated, enslaved, injured and even destroyed by those whose hold on power enables this.

JC: Yes, I think for some - though not all - clients, drawing their awareness to their felt sense can be an important part of affect regulation and integration of the body and mind.

CN: Indeed. Joyce McDougall's (1989) *Theatres of the Body* was an amazing psychoanalytic breakthrough in admitting the body – and its ailments – into the work of psychoanalysis. Stanley Keleman's (1989b) innovative and much understudied contribution, through his formative paradigm, shows that we can each learn volitional self-influence of instinctual and emotional expression to manage dilemmas of daily living and thereby make personal choices that create a more satisfying future.

JC: Can you explain why this is especially important for queers and other marginalized groups?

CN: This is especially important for those from marginalized or oppressed groups because of the alienation and oppression of our bodies and desires. Through internalized oppression, queer clients can dislike or discount their own desires and sexual behaviours, or even their bodies, which are, after all, the site of these experiences. If they can come to experience their own power and control over expression, containment and intensity, for example, they can become freer from the assumptions, expectations and demands of mainstream culture.

JC: I'm struggling to see how the particular excitement of having sex might be equivalent to the excitement even a political queer might feel about politics, or am I taking this too literally?

CN: I don't know about this either, and I'm not sure where it comes from, but I certainly have sometimes experienced in political solidarity something akin to the orgasmic! In all of this work, sexual feelings and behaviours are located within energetic dimensions of the body as it is lived, influenced necessarily by biology, environment, genetics and culture. Our sexual selves are not in any way distinct from other forms of energy: love, money, work, politics; all are seen as metaphors for the growth and expression or repression of energies. As Gestaltists point out, our patterns are our patterns and that's what we must confront, accept and work with to change or grow in satisfying ways.

JC: Hm, interesting. How would you say this plays out with people whose sex drives change over time, particularly those who are affected by menopause?

CN: Well, I guess even our patterns of changing will be repeated as we grow – we may be a risk taker, or a gradualist taking steps, considering during each pause; we may be someone in whom frustration or yearning builds up to sudden action; or a planner; or impulsive. We all live through phases of heightened and lowered drives or focus on different 'objects' of desire or live through periods when desire and sex seem irrelevant for a time and foreground at another time. Everything that lives is in constant flux; all energies can be blocked or unblocked by changing circumstances. When we learn that our experience can be very powerfully made volitional, we equip ourselves for living more of our own life and less that which is prescribed for us by others.

JC: I see. Can you give me other examples?

CN: A person who has lived in a heterosexual partnership for decades can find same-sex attraction foregrounded in the present. Another who has responded to their experience by living asexually might shift towards experimenting with role-playing. A trans woman might enjoy retaining their previous sexuality for some time and then change to a different identification. Someone who previously relished penetration may change direction and find more pleasure now in other ways.

One of the main drivers for a therapeutic journey will be wanting change

CN: Clients of mine have grown into their inner queer or dominatrix, celibate, female or male, sometimes when these changes have been their original motives for therapy, and sometimes surprising themselves and me. Certainly, a main driver for a therapeutic journey will be wanting change; this is not always *away from as much as it is back towards* a discounted aspect of the self, an othered part.

JC: OK, I understand.

CN: How we are with sex in our lives will be how we are with money, time, love and other forms of energy. Sex and sexuality is not fixed but fluid, in process, changing over time and circumstance. All energies are finite so, as we age, they change, and we must adapt in response to be healthy. We see this currently on a macro level with the imminent dangers of the climate and biodiversity emergency: change or stagnate, even perish. So, with our personal somatic geography: rigidify, refuse change or fluidity and contort one's true self; arm oneself against inevitable reorganization and we counteract our own growth, have heart attacks, develop life-threatening illnesses or simply wither away from the fullness of what might have been our life.

JC: Can you give a clinical example in relation to sex and sexual expression?

CN: We do know that some erogenous areas can be exchanged for others; that sexual behaviours can be extended, developed, learned and, therefore, that erotic change is possible; that people change objects of attraction, means of stimulus and expression, or charge. I imagine we can learn much from those who have been wounded or lost abilities due to illness, surgery or accident. They too have to re-negotiate with their changed bodies and people they engage with, re-imagine excitement and reward, nurture and excitation. We have so much more to learn.

In conclusion, I feel we are, in many ways, fortunate to live in times of momentous social, political, medical, technological – and hence linguistic and identity – changes. To best serve our clients, we therapists must choose whether we place ourselves in the vanguard of these developments, moving forward to embrace complexity – as some psychologists and therapists always have done – or have our feet jammed against the doorframe, obstinately refusing to go ahead into the next, yet to be discovered, space or adventure.

Note

1. Freud's 'polymorphous perversity' referred to his theory that, in the first five years or so of life, objects and modes of sexual satisfaction are multifarious, directed at every object that might provide pleasure, not having learned what is outside the socially acceptable (and thus 'perverse') until repression kicks in.

CHAPTER 7

Queer sex and relationships

Amanda Middleton

A s queer people, we are defined by the people we love, desire and have sex with. We are often viewed or view ourselves through a white, cis, hetero-patriarchal lens that is not capacious enough to hold us in all the ways that we manifest. Systemic, sex and relationships psychotherapist Amanda Middleton reflects here on how we can navigate queer relationships with the clients who present in the therapy room.

The template of heteronormativity wrongfoots us in our attempt to understand how we relate to each other

JANE CHANCE CZYZSELSKA: What are some of the assumptions about sex, romance and intimacy in relationships that queer clients come up against?

AMANDA MIDDLETON: That being a healthy, successful human is attached to how we do or don't do our relationships. Then there's the relationship pyramid, which – like the gender pyramid – positions certain types of relationships further up the hierarchy than others. So, the assumption is that to be 'successful' and 'healthy' – concepts that tyrannize us – we must be in long-term, stable, often legally recognized, monogamous relationships where two people are just the right sense of being gendered in relation to each other and also maintain the right sense of distance from, and closeness to, each other. I'll talk about distance more in a bit. In the therapy room, all this shows up in questions about commitment, compatibility, enmeshment or where people are up to in the escalator model of relationships.

JC: By escalator, you mean there is an assumption that both parties agree they are moving smoothly through expected – heteronormative – stages of a relationship story?

AM: Yes! This model powerfully creates an evaluative mechanism, through which we grade our relationships, and in turn ourselves. People might question how often they have sex, whether they live together or not and whether that makes their relationship OK or not, and what happens between them in terms of patterns of communication and if this means they are somehow 'doing' the relationship wrong. It might be that someone thinks 'we have to communicate in this way or have this level of intensity in our intimacy in order to be seen as being in a "good" or "healthy" relationship'. I think queer folks often use the template of heteronormativity to understand how we relate to each other and it's a massive misstep.

JC: Yes, that's so true.

AM: And that's where I think we bump up against this sense that we don't fit into the template, but we still measure ourselves by it. The tension of rejecting hetero and cis norms and yet appraising ourselves with them simultaneously. And it's so insidious: the heterosexual couple and the nuclear family form are constructed out of assumptions about biology, the binary system of gender and then gender roles. This is the holy triad of the nuclear family form. And then we can end up thinking that the closer we are to that, the more legitimate we are; conversely, the further away, the more likely we are to see our relationships as being problematic in some way. What happens then is that we lose all other significant ways of relating and understanding what it is between us in queer love, queer relationships and queer sex. What other markers of success or wonderfulness might be a better frame than so-called 'health'?

JC: Yes, 'healthy' according to who?

AM: Right, so we miss all of that. Often when I work with couples, part of what we try to do is to figure out, 'OK, how much are you evaluating yourself by normative systems? If we use other ideas and systems to understand what's happening for you, how does the problem change, maybe even dissolve or disappear?' It can be that our problems are constructed by and imposed upon us by our oppressors, with little relevance to the lives we are living.

JC: And I guess we all internalize those cis-heteronormative oppressors too.

AM: Yes, so then we reflect on how these systems have got into your head as the mechanisms for evaluation? And instead, we might also rate relationships on their intensity to us, the way they make our heart feel, how much we're growing within them and whether they are world-changing in their form, even world-shaping when we are in love and in desire with people. Queer people excel at relationship resilience, at strong connections, at these world-changing and world-shaping relationships, and here I'm referencing the queer theory notion of disrupting and resisting normativity.

Chrono-normativity and how queer relationships disrupt and bring difference to the world

AM: I'm really interested in the relationship between normativity and time and what that does to our relationships. Chrono-normativity is the way in which our experiences follow patterns over time in conformist and normative frameworks. For example, the idea that you are supposed to have sex for the first time at around about a certain 'acceptable' age; you're supposed to buy a house, get married, have a career in a certain order. At particular life stages, certain behaviours, tasks and ways of being are seen as acceptable and others are not.

JC: How so?

AM: I think it's important to talk about how the regulation of time regulates not only our relationships, as in what 'stage' they should be at when, but also the number of partners we're supposed to have at any one time or in a lifetime, or at certain times in our life. I think this is one of the most undervalued parts of queer existence, that we're often shaking up and living in ways that are not necessarily recognized or legitimized by the expected regulations of space, time and multiplicity. The challenge for therapists is not pathologizing those relationships and those ways of relating and having sex and being alongside each other. So much of psychological theory is based on chrono-normative assumptions which are tethered to the white, western, heterosexual couple as the place of health and normativity that everything else is measured from. So, the further you fall from that, the more problematic you are and, therefore, the more likely it is that a straight therapist is going to see you as problematic. Even if the therapist isn't explicit about it, a pathologizing energy can be in the room, getting between you both. I think it's a danger in the therapeutic relationship, especially when you're working with non-normative queer couples, poly and non-monogamous folk and those with other ways of relating.

JC: That's really unfortunate when that happens, isn't it? I know I've experienced that with a straight therapist. I think a lot of queer people internalize the heteronormative/homophobic notion that there's something wrong with them. And when the, as you say, chrono-normative narrative of 'I've got to this age, and I still haven't met the right person' collides with that, often questions can arise like 'Why can't I find someone or trust my own judgement about people?' How do we work with these belief systems? It's not even that the back-to-back, short-term relationships are inherently bad – they may be mainly good; they may have created loads of fun and growth while they lasted – but in the end there is often a feeling of being incompatible or of feeling a 'failure' in a relationship that undermines all of what it offered. It's also important not to fall into the binary thinking of long-term mono relationships or marriage as the pinnacle of relationship success and learning to value relationships differently.

The power of homonormativity

AM: We shouldn't dismiss why people are keen on and move towards homonormativity because it is incredibly powerful to be legitimized in a world which delegitimizes you. Also why are we creating this binary of conformist and radical queer relationships depending on where you are in the relationship pyramid? I do think there's a marked difference in lived experience the further up you are of that relationship pyramid. There is something in being a married gay or lesbian couple: you are seen as stable, safe and less disruptive, and that's useful in terms of accessing space in the world. But notching it up as less valuable than queer buys into this notion of radical versus conformist: I think all queer relationships are radical – they are all constantly disrupting, they are all bringing difference and they are all world-shaping in a myriad of ways.

JC: Definitely, good point.

AM: And how do we own the disruptiveness we inherit through being ourselves and acknowledge that there's no way of getting it 'right' without tying our self to the concept of 'wrong'? Wrong as measured by those hetero-patriarchal standards equates wrong with failure and with unhealthy. Relationships either work out or they don't. There's a lot more to it of course, but what I'm interested in is the sets of stories we have about them; what meaning do we inherit about ourselves when they do or don't work out? In queer relationships in particular, if they don't work out, we can feel more of a sense of failure because we have this double experience of being seen as less legitimate by the world because of who we love and then when our love fails it's a double blow. That's big for queer people to navigate. For instance, in the way that problems with sex (too much, too little, the wrong kind, etc.) can be experienced as more serious for queer couples. Our sexuality and ways of having sex are the way we've been defined by the world. So to struggle with that can create a bigger ache and sorrow for a queer couple than it can for couples who aren't defined by their sex lives.

Rethinking 'lesbian bed death' and the power of women's love relationships

JC: As you say that, I am thinking about the so-called spectre haunting long-term lesbian couples: lesbian bed death. Perhaps what you're saying here speaks to a sense of failure when there is a reduction in sexual activity over time?

AM: The comparing of lesbian and queer women's sexuality to straight people's is highly problematic. It means we are measured by standards that might not be relevant or useful. The concept of lesbian bed death came from studies that measured rates of shared genital contact in different types of relationships, and that found lesbian women were least likely to be having this type of sex that straight couples and gay male couples have (Nicholas, 2004). These studies didn't think to ask about different types of sex, to define sex differently, to enquire about broader sensuous or erotic themes and activities, or to even explore the meaning of sex for couples. So where, in the past, a woman wanting to have sex with a woman was problematized, now not wanting to have sex has also been problematized! Sex is reduced to genital contact, reductive of the penis-in-vagina model. I think we have far too narrow and prescriptive notions about what counts as sex, how it 'should' happen in a relationship and the rates at which it is 'normal' to have sex. Clients will often come in worrying about how little sex they are having, bringing with them the theory of lesbian bed death or other unhelpful ideas such as fusion, merging and co-dependence in relationships as possible reasons. I challenge the idea that intimacy and closeness are problematic to sex, and that our sex lives need to be measured against common heterosexist standards. The ways queer women have sex with each other are endless, and very rarely fit with what can be measured in research.

JC: Are you saying queer couples can often feel less queer the less sex they're having? Obviously having a lesbian or gay identity is more expansive than the sex we have, but in a heteronormative society, we have inherited a label that focuses on the sex as the thing that makes us different to straight folks.

AM: Yes, legitimizing our queer identities through being sexual is something that we might do to feel strong as we discover and know ourselves. We are defined by the outside world through our sexuality and gender expression. The two things that can give us power, I think, are knowing ourselves as sexual beings and being outside of normativity and the way that normativity instructs our selfhood. I think that if we have troubles in a relationship because we think we're not having sex in the right way or the right amount or too much with other people, or whatever it is that people bring, we are more likely to think 'how will other people think of us?' because we have grown up thinking and worrying about what people will think of us. That is, of course, if we've known ourselves as queer children. If we haven't known ourselves as queer children and we come out as adults – maybe it's a surprise even to ourselves – then what the hell other people are going to think is huge too, so we are more likely to be thinking, to be internalizing this gaze or Foucault's (1977) notion of the panopticon: 'What will other people think if I'm gay but I'm not practising that gayness sexually right now?' or 'How will my queerness be understood if I am not sexual, right now or ever?'

JC: Ah yes, the panopticon – social media is a bit like that these days too, even queer social media. The pressure to show how queer you are can be intense.

AM: Queer social media can be so focused on the aesthetics of queerness and assertions of a queer sexuality that is visual rather than felt.

Moving away from being a 'good gay'

AM: So often when I work with women who are not as sexual as they'd like to be or they haven't been sexual for some time, we talk about the degradation of companionship between women by broader society, and the idea that that is less successful, or a less good type of relating or being. This belief can enter the couple and eat away at their sense of confidence and strength of their identity and who they are in the world. For gay male couples who have an experience of non-monogamy, be it consensual or non-ethical non-monogamy, and are then working towards monogamy, there's this idea that this is somehow a wound or interruption to their story of being a 'good gay' or a 'good gay couple'. This can start to eat away at confidence and the couple's sense of being valid or legitimate. They lose sight of how glorious and world-changing their relationship is, regardless of whether they are sexually exclusive or not. Does that make sense?

JC: Yes, it does. I'm also thinking about – maybe particularly for gay men but it's not only gay men – when gay sex has been pathologized within the family as it is in wider society, there can be a journey into hypersexuality. Sometimes this ends up, depending on the person, in them taking risks, perhaps to defiantly punish the disapproving parents and also the gay part of themselves.

AM: I'm not sure I would say it's always just punishing. It's also an intensive reclaiming or an undoing or going to the opposite side of the pendulum; an important carving out of new space in relation to the pathology they have endured. Again, I'm interested in the set of stories and the meaning we inhabit about that. I think that gay men have always been pioneers at the intersection of drugs and sex and lots of straight people, and also some lesbians and queer women use drugs and sex in similar ways. There are of course risks too, as we can see in the communities that are then impacted so greatly by chemsex. How much do people think that they have to do that? Again, this 'good' versus 'bad' gay concept shows up often. As soon as we hit good vs bad, we hit binaries and we hit hierarchies of normativity. I think it's the job of the therapist to notice what's not being described in someone's description of themselves and how what's absent relates to ideas of normativity/deficit.

Learning from the systemic approach

AM: In systemic training, we are taught to look for resilience and strength in relationships and couples. We think alongside the clients as to how their stories might be being constructed and understood by the wider normative culture, and how this can blind them to seeing the strength and personal power in their queerness.

JC: I was going to ask you about what those of us who have trained as individual counsellors or psychotherapists could learn from systemic therapists and what we might miss. We may think about the family constellation when we're working with a client but what can systemic thinking add to our practice as individual therapists? No person is an island. Everyone is affected by their family constellation, cultures and relationships as well.

AM: Yes, so what might we miss if we don't hold in mind this family systemic frame and also culturally? I think it depends on how you think about the self. There are so many ways to work systemically. There's this idea that we fill the room with people; we are never just sitting in the room with the client but also with people who are interwoven in their lives and stories that make up the self of that person, as well as the systems of power and institutions that are around that person. We move away from individualistic notions of the self. One of the things I often say in therapy is, 'Let's think for a minute if we can blame society for what's happening rather than you blaming yourself.' I suppose that's one of the systemic biases: it's not what's wrong with you or your immediate family of origin but what's happening within the context in which you find yourself that's creating this set of dilemmas. In short, the problem is the problem; the person is not the problem.

JC: Great, so you bring the political relationship into the self?

AM: Yes, and often it can feel like a great relief to understand that it's not us, our personhood, but it's the systems we find ourselves swimming in that are creating these problems. Sometimes we land on socialization squared.

JC: Ooh, what's that – socialization squared?

AM: So, the idea is that whatever gender norms you are socialized into, once you enter a relationship with others socialized similarly, then those gendered components will be amplified. So that might be caretaking or competition, for example. And again, we can think about the societal systems and gender stories that have created this.

I think it's incredibly empowering for clients to know that they don't need to change within themselves necessarily, but rather think and respond differently to the discourse and the stories they are swimming in and that are shaping them.

JC: I hadn't heard of socialization squared but that makes sense.

AM: Yes. Another example of this is how turn-taking is done. Often in couples assigned female at birth (AFAB), I see people making loads of room for each other, which is great, but individual needs can get lost within that. In some of the cis gay men's relationships I've encountered, they might hesitate to make enough room for the couple in their lives. This might be because they have been socialized to think more about individual needs than relational ones.

JC: I was thinking about how poly relationships have been pathologized by some in our field who hold the long-term monogamous relationship as the holy grail. Can you recommend good reading that understands and de-pathologizes it? What do you say to poly clients who might have internalized that stuff too?

AM: I might explain attachment theory and then critique it. The basic idea is taught through a white western frame, and the heteronormative nuclear family form with all its trappings around gender roles and gender norms. So we end up with this idea that the best type of relating is the monogamous kind. It doesn't account for so many other ways of relating across the world, so many other ways of relating where the monogamous couples and families of origin are not the most central thing in someone's expression of selfhood or knowing of themselves. There is this assumption that the family-of-origin story is the most important story in who they are. For queer people, it's often cultural attachments, families of choice, community knowing, attachments to ideas and important people, to queer ancestors and queer moments that shape who we are.

JC: There are attachments that go beyond the family-of-origin styles identified by Bowlby, Main and Fonagy, (Wallin, 2007). The Black American psychotherapist Resmaa Menakem and other Indigenous and queer practitioners speak of cultural attachment also (Menakem, 2017).

Being poly could be seen as over-achieving in terms of attachment

AM: Yes, much indigenous knowledge has held space for the self as shaped and nourished from beyond the immediate family. Broader notions of kinship, ancestors and connection to spirit are important alternatives to attachment theory. And as Judy Yellin says, poly could be a way that people work out different attachment paradigms in different relationships (Yellin, personal communication). We end up working them through with multiple family forms. Being poly could even be seen as over-achieving in terms of attachment. Those who pathologize poly relationships perhaps don't see the benefits and see it only as a deviation from a norm. My experience of poly people is that so much is being done to work out ways of relating that are more satisfying and more world-changing. They are trying to undo the constriction of monogamy. Let's not forget: monogamy was invented when life expectancy was around 40!

JC: Oh, I didn't think about that!

AM: So how does our greater lifespan impact on our relationships? I also think people miss the fact that there's a lot of – of course, it's not termed poly – but families where parents have split, creating multi-parent families. This is across all genders and sexualities. We don't consider this lived experience of multiplicity as a resource because ideas of mono-relating are culturally preferable. So, these multi-parent families contribute to a generation of knowledge and people are doing something similar in sexual relationships too.

JC: Yes, that's really true and a good way of looking at it.

AM: But because it's focused on sex, it's devalued. So, while we might be impressed by a client's negotiation of their parenting responsibilities between their exes, current partners and all the children, these same negotiations, thinking and arranging, in poly relationships, are about sexual partners, so we won't value it in the same way. It's knowledge-generating around sex and relationships, but because sex – particularly 'deviant' queer or non-normative sex – is devalued, a therapist is more likely to pathologize this network. If therapists see poly clients as on a mission for knowledge-generation, for overachieving in attachment stories, how might these conversations be different?

JC: Yes, they really do need to be different and generative, as you say. I've had clients who approached me saying, 'I need to know you're not going to pathologize me for this, as others have,' which is concerning.

AM: For me, it's really important to know the history of psychiatry, psychology and the healing professions in dealings with people of diverse genders, sexualities and sex practices. There is such a history of harm and misunderstanding, of social control. This is particularly acute now for trans people. This history is about power and pathologization and a degradation of selfhood and lived experience. It's about the further marginalizing and stigmatizing of communities and people. The declassification of homosexuality from the DSM comes from the activism of gay men and women saying, 'I am as legitimate as you. I refuse to see myself the way you see me, and further than that, I refuse to see myself as wrong.' Therapists, myself included, must think about how to ensure we aren't doing harm to clients, harm that comes directly from our ideas and theories and their impact on marginalized genders, sexualities and forms of relationship. There's a real risk right now of therapists repeating harmful patterns from the past. Currently, many trans people still have to justify their existence, their gender, and seek acceptance from helping professionals in order to access basic healthcare needs. We, even as trans-inclusive/affirmative/celebratory therapists, are part of the system that requires this. The power inherent in this relationship repeats the notion that helping professions, like psychology and psychiatry, have some kind of expertise over clients' lives, some right to define and describe how trans experience should be. This gatekeeping and notion of expertise is always going to be at the cost of trans people, and that is simply not right. There are some very harmful stories and practices that are perpetuated in our field about trans people. I see this too in the field's relationship to clients who practise kink. The relics of deviance, perversion and paraphilias still permeate theory and practice in psychotherapy today and that has a detrimental effect on people's well-being in everyday life.

All couples are managing stories of sameness and difference

AM: I think all couples are managing stories of sameness and difference. In heterosexual couples, there are these huge cultural scripts about difference: the stereotypes of he goes to football; she likes shopping and a night out with the girls – these are resources that are permission-giving. In the straight world, there are unnoticed patterns and rituals in how relationships are managed and how they are supported. Often for queer or same-sex couples, there are not so many cultural resources around to draw on. We find ourselves with fewer scripts, fewer rituals to help us negotiate our similarities and our differences.

JC: So, just to clarify, are you saying that cultural scripts shape how we understand and manage similarities and differences in our relationships?

AM: Yes, these often unnoticed 'rules' or patterns about how to be in a relationship are responding to how we can manage similarities and differences. These can map onto how similarities and differences get reduced to gender stories in the straight world. There's a normative critique of queerness, where anything that seems to be the same or similar between us is problematic. For example, we end up talking about enmeshment, 'the urge to merge', and all of the jokes about gay men and lesbians dressing the same or having the same haircut. How people are managing their sameness is denigrated by the wider world. Sameness is such an important balm for us as queer people – being an outsider and often feeling as if we don't belong. To then find a person to experience sameness with is a great healing. It's a buffer against homophobia; it's a buffer against transphobia; it's saying that our sameness is powerful in this moment. We are undoing those stories of not belonging.

JC: Yeah.

AM: I think the power of sameness often gets missed. Conversely, if people experience themselves as 'too different' from each other, they can then think they are not compatible. And this gets in the way of picturing a future, which then messes with the couple in the present. The acceleration of matchmaking and dating apps has amplified the notion of compatibility in relationships. Compatibility then becomes another constant mechanism of evaluation. Compatibility stories usually map onto how similar and different we are and what this means for relationship success. The 'right' amount of similarity and difference that makes for a successful relationship is based on a standard created by an opposite-gendered cis couple. So, struggles with being too different or too the same get localized to the individual and the couple, rather than pinpointed to the meta stories of gender, heterosexuality, etc. that we inhabit. This also connects to the wider social and cultural locations we inhabit.

JC: I'm thinking about couple relationships where perhaps one person is trans and one is cis and if you add race and class difference into the mix, these will need to be processed and digested within the couple. We are not schooled in navigating these structural differences, either in life or in most therapy trainings.

AM: Yes, and if we were to set up the therapy training school of our dreams, this kind of consideration would be on the curriculum – how to work with multiple differences and similarities across social and cultural locations in couples' lives; how intersectionality can work as a therapeutic device; knowing your history and thinking about how the history of pathologization shows up in the therapy room, how it shows up in your work and how you relate to that across the therapeutic relationship. And the second thing would be to undo our expectations and assumptions of family and couples and relationships in the way that they are tethered to this white, western, nuclear family form. Instead, seeing intimacy and family in the way that queer people do because I think it's just a matter of training your perspective, rather than using the gold standard of measurement, which is heterosexual and heteronormative family forms. Choose a different stick to measure your knowledge and you'll see something entirely different. Take the borderlands and bring them to the centre. This is well talked about by Falicov (1995), who explains how we can take the knowledge that we see as peripheral and centre it in our therapeutic approach. What happens between us and the client is radically different if we work from the borderlands position rather than the normative position.

JC: I really love that idea. It's really beautiful and really important. I was wondering about whether you wanted to come back to the assumptions about cis gay men and intimacy as an issue that arises in the therapy room.

Assumptions about cis gay men and intimacy

AM: I wonder how the stories of masculinity get in the way of what you want and who you want to be. Often with gay men couples, I will see this competitiveness and we lose the couple, the relationship. Often, we end up thinking, 'What does he need or what do I need?' rather than, 'What do we need or what is best for our relationship in this moment?' I think the 'What's best for me and what's best for him, and how do we compromise?' approach is such a dull story of relationships. Of course, we need to negotiate, but if we think about our relationships in terms of compromise, they become less satisfying, and we don't want to have them. More exciting, I think, is 'What are we creating together? What is this precious space between us? How is it helping us grow? How is it interrupted by big stories and forces in our world? How do we create something which is beyond and of us? What do we want from our togetherness?' I think for gay men there are so many stories about masculinity which are problematic and then, on top of that, there are stories about transgressing masculinity as a gay man that get in between this precious thing, this precious togetherness that someone is trying to create with somebody else.

JC: So, are you saying that the normative story that impacts on gay men's realization of intimacy is 'real men don't get intimate with each other'?

AM: There is so much that impacts on gay men's intimacy, and much of it is connected to masculinity not offering enough permission for closeness, for mutuality, for vulnerability. If we think about how gay men were socialized as children – obviously it's not always the same – but how does that get in the way of relating, of intimacy? What is welcomed and what is not welcomed in the relationship? For gay men who want to be non-monogamous, what are their scripts about intimacy, masculinity and sexuality? Some gay men might want to be monogamous because it ensures their relationship is closer to 'normal', and they can then be higher up the relationship hierarchy pyramid we talked about earlier. There are these ideas about how they inhabit the relationship, how close or distant they need to be to feel OK. That's huge for some gay men to be negotiating, and it's an awful lot to see, feel and experience and to communicate to a partner. For example, saying, 'I had a funny moment when you were super feminine in the kitchen dancing the other night, and I don't know if it's because campness makes me less attracted to you or because I am dealing with some internalized misogyny or femmephobia or both, but I would like to talk about it with you. Are you up for that?' How often are we able to be that articulate? How often do we welcome this vulnerability, this honesty, as part of day-to-day life in a couple?

JC: Yes! And I'm thinking about Jessica Benjamin (2017) and mutual recognition and intersubjective relating. I don't know how much you know about her and this idea of 'doer and done-to' and how couples may fall into that along intersectional and/or relational dynamics.

AM: How are power stories inhabited in the couple? What might make one person feel more victimized or done-to and less seen than the other? How does racism, ableism, classism and cis-centrism shape the lived realities of the couple? And using an intersectional lens, how does that change across contexts? I like to think with couples about how we are talking about and working with the lived realities of power in the couple. It might be worth referencing the social graces tool here, which is a systemic tool authored by John Burnham (2018). It proposes a lovely long list of the 'social graces', which are markers of difference and power in the way we inhabit ourselves and which shape family life. It stands for gender, geography, race, religion, appearance, (dis)ability, culture, class, education, spirituality and sexuality. It's a long, yet never exhaustive list, and I think it's a bit of a step before intersectional thinking, but it does allow us to see what's in this relationship and how it shapes interaction: what affordances and constraints emerge for each person?

JC: I wanted to also talk about queer and/or trans clients who have cis straight therapists and who may have to do a lot of explaining about what it's like to live as an othered individual, couple or thruple. With straight therapists, I've sometimes had to explain what goes through my head when I want to hold hands with my partner because I assume they won't know about the attrition of accumulated heteronormative micro-aggressions. Is there any way, apart from working with queer and/or QTIPOC therapists, that we can bridge that gap?

AM: I think it's really tricky. When I teach, I have this slide that reflects on the dilemma around cultural competency for therapists because any kind of competency or affirmative practice creates another set of normativities and, therefore, we lose other people within the community. We fail to account for their stories and experiences. So, if we know the stories about the fear of holding hands or coming out or those things, we create another set of norms. If we train straight therapists to know certain cultural competencies around queer norms, we do a disservice to other parts of our community and other folk among us who live in different ways to that.

Cultural competencies: don't treat everybody the same

AM: So, I often think that therapists take up three different positions: the idea that our theories and our tools are good enough for everybody.

JC: Go on.

AM: I think there is a strong belief in some parts of the field that, 'If I treat everybody the same and as long as I'm empathetic and understanding, therapeutic change will happen,' and I find that dangerous as it's likely that therapists will be replicating existing power structures and dominant discourses to shape the therapeutic relationship. This can further marginalize people. Or some therapists might think, 'I need to be a bit queer-affirmative/have some cultural knowledge/do a short CPD course that will make me better.' They might join this to their existing tools. This risks the creation of new normativities that the therapist then uses as a lens to see the client through. Therapy becomes a process of evaluating how close the client is to their existing knowledge, rather than creating new knowledges with the client.

JC: Right.

AM: In social constructionist therapy, we might use a 'not knowing' position (Anderson and Goolishian, 1992) to avoid the trappings of these big, expected stories. Instead, we co-create knowledge with the client, seeking to create a shared world in the therapeutic conversation. I think that's a useful position, but the client might find themselves feeling the labour of co-creation. We must be careful not to put the client into the role of educator. We know that marginalized people end up having to teach their therapists and that is a drain and a pain. It is about inhabiting these different positions and asking whether it's good enough in the moment. I want a therapist who understands that the constant scalp-burn from bleaching my hair as a young queer person is a right-of-passage. I want a therapist who's going to be thinking about the constant managing of risk a queer person is having to do by just existing in public spaces.

JC: Or a client of colour is doing just to exist, or a trans or intersex person.

AM: Exactly! I want a therapist who is thinking about belonging before I do, misogyny before I do, fatphobia before I do, so I don't have to say it. That might be a queer therapist, but it also might be a straight therapist depending on their intersections, knowledge and models of practice. I don't know if that answers it. There is a dilemma around how a queer cultural competency model or a queer-affirmative model would serve our communities. I want therapists to step into this dilemma and be reflexive about who they are and why that matters. After all, who we are is all we have as therapists.

CHAPTER 8

Trans desire and embodiment

Jake Yearsley and Beck Thom

Despite the passing of the trans-inclusive 2010 Equality Act, we are witnessing a cultural war against trans and gender-expansive individuals. This hostile and unloving environment impacts negatively on trans embodiment. Psychosexual therapist Jake Yearsley and certified sexological bodyworker (CSB) Beck Thom share their insights on working with trans clients' desire and embodiment.

Hearing our clients into existence

JANE CHANCE CZYZSELSKA: I would like to start by asking what kinds of things trans and gender-expansive clients ask for help with in relation to sexuality and desire and the embodiment of their gendered selves.

JAKE YEARSLEY: I firstly want to acknowledge the use of your term gender-expansive. My understanding is that this is a relatively new term that is used to broaden definitions of gender outside socially constructed gender norms. It feels like a more affirming and inclusive description, which anyone can occupy. In my responses, I will use the terms trans/non-binary as most of my clients tend to identify with those labels. Trans/non-binary are umbrella terms and represent a marginalized and often oppressed social group where in this context the term provides group solidarity. Clients ask for help with themes of dating, desirability, body image, disassociated states, gender dysphoria, issues of transition, relationship concerns, relationship styles outside of mono-normativity, sexual identities/behaviours outside of cis/heteronormativity, navigating an intersectional identity, whether POC, neurodivergent identities or disabled bodies, trauma, abuse, oppression and shame. This all may sound rather negative and risks pathologizing, but there are celebratory stories within these themes. Listening to our clients' stories, we allow for those negative and positive emotions; we hear our clients into existence; we can begin to do the healing work. We will likely be working with change and uncertainty. So, as a therapist, that is always for me one of the first reflexive challenges I need to address in myself. Where am I un/comfortable with change and uncertainty?

BECK THOM: I am an unusual practitioner! People approaching me know that I am a certified sexological bodyworker (CSB) and somatic sex educator (SSE) whose work centres queer/trans embodiment, sexuality and pleasure. I work with individuals, relationships and groups. My workshops are notorious for their experiential and explicit nature! I work on a spectrum from talk to touch, and all my work is one-directional touch, from me to client.

People want a place where they have permission to centre and focus on their body, sex and pleasure. They are attracted to my queer- and trans-centred approach where they do not need to censor themselves, fear judgement or be compelled to educate a cis practitioner.

Sharon Wheeler's ScarWork is a way of working with scars that stands alone or combined with SSE. If, as Van der Kolk (2014) says, 'the body keeps the score', then contact with scars can elicit stories and memories that can be re-experienced and expressed in new ways. Many trans people who have had gender-affirming surgery are dealing with layers of trauma, medical trauma and disconnection from sensation, including pleasure, or needing a ritual to celebrate and connect. Receiving gentle, non-invasive touch in a therapeutic space can be transformative, physically and emotionally. Trans clients often carry complex combinations of experiences – trauma, neurodiversity, minority stress, sensory needs, incongruence/dysphoria/euphoria, relationship and attachment needs, anxiety and a generally upregulated nervous system. They deal with the daily experience of transphobia and a hostile climate of cultural wars. Other intersecting identities, such as also living in a fat body, being intersex, disabled or a person of colour, or a trans woman – facing the specific experience of trans misogyny – are important. These, not any personal flaws or failings, can give rise to a generalized feeling that the body is an unsafe place, a battleground both 'out there' and 'in here', and that the realm of sex, touch, intimacy and pleasure is incredibly stressful, scary or traumatic. People often bring this very present, powerful discomfort to our consultation. In my first contact with a client, we are working out our Venn diagrams – what I offer as an SSE, what the person feels they need and what the crossover is in the middle. That middle segment will help inform our work plan. SSE is the umbrella term, but CSBs have been specifically trained to offer hands-on, intimate bodywork. This can include genital mapping, genital and anal massage and internal work, always wearing gloves.

Anatomy is not limited to what we might see in an anatomy textbook

BT: A core concept in my work is a 'gender-freeing and gender-affirming' approach to the body, and particularly to intimate and heavily gendered parts, such as the chest/breasts and genitals. People are often delighted to hear that we will embrace their energy and psychic genitals! My view of anatomy is not limited to what we might see in an anatomy textbook. People can be in their authentic expression; tucking or wearing binders and packers during our work together.

JC: These are really rich answers, showing that – of course – although some themes are recurrent, no two trans or gender-expansive clients are the same. Can you talk about some of the kinds of changes that might occur in a client who is going through physical (surgical/hormonal) interventions and how practitioners can think about working with them?

BT: My starting place is which changes are a concern to my client and what clients need from me. This is not universal; I do not make assumptions or define their problem or advise solutions. I like Lucie Fielding's (2021) term 'ethical curiosity' in contrast to how trans people are often treated, including by helping professionals, about the client's needs and story. I tend to translate apparent needs into a practice. If a client is talking a lot about a big change, such as hormones changing their genitals, I might suggest we do the Genital Interview. This is ten questions I address to the genitals, and the client replies, giving the genitals a voice. The questions cover how they like to be named – and their pronouns – how they like to be looked at, how they like to be touched and other aspects of the life of your genitals, their story, to help us get to know them more intimately. It can be meditative, immersive, deep, or more casual and informative.

Some trans men and masculine clients on testosterone supplementation report intensifying and escalating sexual arousal, desire and motivation, which can be disorientating. It is common to have concerns about desires and fantasies and use of porn that seem contrary to their feminist and egalitarian values. There can be conflicted feelings about what it means to become or be a man, and masculinity, in a society rife with toxic masculinity. Existing relationships and shifting sexual orientation can also be flashpoints. Clients benefit from being heard empathically, normalized, and some erotic education on sexual fantasy and core erotic themes; across the board of all genders and sexualities, fantasies and kinks revolving around non-consent or eroticizing oppressive dynamics are very common. This challenging work is enhanced by brave, intimate peer-sharing in workshops.

Traditionally, focus has been on the physical and not psychological and emotional changes of a trans person

JY: Through the medical model lens of trans healthcare, there has traditionally been a focus on the physical changes without attention to the psychological and emotional changes of a trans person. Therapy can create that space for those reflections. Physical changes through medical interventions can be experienced as both positive and negative. Helpful conversations around this are reassuring for clients to know they can have space to express their possibly contradictory emotions. Clients may feel expectations from others – usually cis people – that they 'should' feel happy in their choice of hormones and or surgery. If they express negative feelings after surgery/hormones, this may reinforce a shame narrative that they made a bad, or wrong, choice. In reality, undergoing surgery or hormone treatment is always going to be a choice that has both benefits and losses. In my experience for nearly all clients, if physical interventions are wanted and needed, the main goal is to feel more comfortable in the body. However, there may be other intentions that we need to acknowledge without judgement. Clients may be focused on the gains they will get from hormones and surgery, but they may not have considered the feelings of loss. It is wise to acknowledge this and see if it is something a client needs to address or not. One loss that may be a concern is the impact on sexual sensation after genital surgery. After this kind of surgery, nerves are distributed slightly differently and bodies may respond differently. This is an opportunity to work more somatically, and/or to signpost clients to work with queer knowledgeable certified sexologists. I remind clients that most of us have only learnt sex through a heteronormative view of 'doing' sex instead of a 'being' sex. With a more holistic view of sex, we can discover the multiple ways to experience an embodied erotic, sexual self that can be both arousing and pleasurable. As hormones and surgery hold many implications of change, I strongly advise therapists to gain as much up-to-date medical knowledge on trans surgeries and hormonal effects.

JC: Yes, the more we can learn about the process that many trans and gender-expansive clients have to go through, the better the support we can offer. What are some of the kinds of issues that can arise in a client who is not going through physical (surgical/hormonal) interventions and how can practitioners think about working with this?

JY: For some clients, the choice of hormones/surgery is not always about whether they want it or not, but about the hormones/surgery being inaccessible to them financially, for health reasons or for reasons of safety. There may be many other different reasons clients choose not to have hormones or surgery and this may not be a choice a client makes willingly. For example, a client with a cultural/religious background where trans identities are either unacceptable or illegal can face severe consequences if they were to make physical changes.

The choice is always with the client

JY: Choice for hormones and surgery is always with the client. We need to be mindful of our judgements with clients' choices and remember that just because a client chooses not to have surgery or take hormones, that doesn't mean that they may not make a different choice later. Sometimes it may be years later. Our role is to support our clients in making those choices at the time we are with them. Surgery is not a holy grail to finding self and, therefore, not a necessity to the confirmation of a trans/non-binary identity. Issues for these clients are that they will likely feel the oppression of cis normativity and have difficulties feeling recognized for who they are. Access to public spaces, especially toilets, will be problematic and misgendering could be a common experience if the client does not 'pass' within binary gender expectations. Misgendering can run throughout a client's entire day, such as the workplace, education, family and friends. This often leaves a person feeling powerless, socially anxious, avoidant, depressed, angry, disassociated and passively conforming. Conversations that can be useful for clients will evolve around deconstructing what it means to be with a gendered body that doesn't fit societal norms. We may wish to consider dismantling these norms for clients as an act of breaking cis normativity and a micro affirmation for our clients – that is, we recognize the power hierarchy of gender imbalance throughout our culture. This thereby makes the societal structures the problem and not the client. Encouraging clients to surround themselves with affirming people, and/or members of the queer community where their gender is recognized and celebrated, can help alleviate shame and feelings of isolation.

Ask trans clients how they know when they feel gender euphoria

JY: If clients have chosen not to have surgery, for whatever reason, exploring how they wish to experience their gender in other ways can be empowering. One way I may wish to do this is by addressing gender euphoria moments using a more somatic approach. I may ask questions such as, 'How do you know when you feel gender euphoria? What situations does it occur in?', eliciting from the client information as to how it makes them feel and what sensations they experience. Re-imagining this experience through visualization can be a useful anchor and grounding strategy to bring them back to good feelings of who they are and act as a reminder that they can recreate this experience – as if it was a real one – in their reality. It may also be supportive for clients to have the space to talk about feelings of dysphoria. However, from my experience, clients don't usually care to talk about dysphoria, but just need it acknowledged and not necessarily picked apart. I would suggest that therapists be careful here when working with clients that have unprocessed trauma and who are unable to co- or self-regulate. Those clients first need to know internal safety, to have the ability to ground and come back to regulated states. Therapists taking this approach would benefit from the knowledge gained from the newer neuroscience/psychology models of working with trauma, such as polyvagal theory.

All trans/non-binary clients' journeys are individual and subjective

JY: It is important to remember that all trans/non-binary clients' lives are individual and subjective. There is definitely not one narrative or any one experience. However, there may of course be similar themes and issues. We need to ask and listen to our clients' stories and let them tell us their experience. It is fundamental we believe them and not try to interpret our version of transness onto them, even if we are well meaning.

BT: I agree. The global perspective is that, throughout history and across our planet, trans people exist and the vast majority do not have access to these physical changes. It does not make them any less trans. Some trans men and women and some non-binary people choose not to have surgery and/or hormones even if it is available to them. For many more, access is very restricted or made impossible by their social circumstances, health or other factors. Some trans people who are also intersex may live in bodies that have some degree of gender ambiguity, and may have experienced non-consensual medical interventions, with the resulting experience of navigating our binary world. Because the mainstream world is reading people's genders based on body type and presentation, navigating the world is fraught – like bathrooms. For many trans clients, a major concern is being misread and misgendered in sexual and dating situations. We are aware of the 'male gaze', but trans people fear or experience the 'cis gaze' from partners who are unaware, unethically curious or entrenched in their gendered assumptions.

Many may think, 'I am taking my clothes off with this person, and they are going to see my body, and I am frozen and distracted by the thought that they are not seeing who I really am.' This fear and reality can inhibit people from seeking opportunities for intimacy. Quintimacy workshops are spaces where trans people do deep, intimate and conscious work together, in a trauma-informed, consent-based, trans-centred space. This counters so much erasure and promotes a sense of agency and empowerment – I *can* be seen for who I am, *and* I deserve to be!

JC: Absolutely! Would you say there are some dos and don'ts of practising with trans and gender-expansive people around sex and embodiment?

Let go of the narrative about being 'born in the wrong body'

BT: I'd say, let go of the simplistic narrative about being 'born in the wrong body' or hating the body and unequivocally wanting to change it. Do not assume that the aim of transition or our work as professionals is any 'outcome' at all. We are not trying to make trans people and trans sex exactly like cis people and cis sex. As in the Genital Interview, start with a beginner's mind and make no assumptions about how the person identifies or the language they want to use for their gender and their body. Make sure you are informed of our active queer and trans community and communicate this to your client when appropriate. Don't operate a privatized, silo model of therapy that views the person only as an individual and not as a potential member of a rich community. Refer to practitioners and organizations that create positive, affirming and sex-positive spaces for trans people – for example, Trans Bare All, Quintasensual and Quintimacy. Be careful with the concept of gender socialization. Defining someone by the idea they were 'socialized male' to explain assigned male people taking up a lot of space or acting entitled, or 'socialized female' to explain assigned female people struggling to know and hold their own boundaries can seem to make sense at first glance but needs unpicking. These claims are imposed on the trans community, and sometimes they feature in trans people's stories about themselves. Many harmful trans exclusionary arguments that justify attacking and excluding particularly trans women are founded on socialization. I like Price's (2018) commentary on this – that gender socialization is complicated, and each person has their own unique gender socialization and that 'socialization never ends'. If someone is trans and has trans experience through their childhood, then they were 'socialized trans' (Tanenbaum, 2020).

Ask clients what their preferred pronouns are when first meeting them

JY: I'd say, ask clients what their preferred pronouns are when first meeting them or on intake forms, then use this. Be OK with making mistakes. Mistakes can happen with pronouns when we are not used to something different. It's the intention behind the mistake that gets picked up. Don't use pronouns as a way for power play. Just saying sorry is fine. If you discuss the client's body, begin with neutral language and then ask what words the client prefers to use. Clients may not wish to discuss their bodies at all, but to open up the conversation gently, ask questions such as, 'How do you feel towards your body?' Encourage affirming words that the client feels OK or good about using when discussing their gendered body. Don't individualize clients' issues just because they are trans. Acknowledge the cultural narrative of cis/het privilege and remind clients they are not the problem. Be aware of which therapeutic models are more supportive of working with trans clients. The person-centred, existential, psychosynthesis, systemic models all have good feedback. Be mindful that some models of therapy are less supportive. In particular, the psychoanalytical theories can come up against a lot of criticism. Purely focusing the issues of someone's trans identity on their childhood histories can be experienced as pathologizing and is potentially reductionist. Be aware that traditional therapy models originate from patriarchy and may not always be so useful and affirming. Looking at social theories such as queer theory, feminism, post-modernism, trans theory are encouraged as they acknowledge a trans lived experience. Encourage clients to seek support through community, whether online groups, face-to-face support groups, going to events/workshops, having discussions on surgery within the community or finding online blogs and videos that are supportive and positive.

JC: Yes, connecting with community is so vital. So, what kind of individual and collective practices have you found useful when working with clients somatically/sexologically and/or psychotherapeutically?

BT: I really appreciate you mentioning collective practices because my pathway into doing this work was the UK's queer sexuality/spirituality festival scene. That is where I met my first CSB! I facilitate Quintimacy weekends to be co-created spaces where everyone brings support and 'erotic peership'. There is something radically queer about bringing queer sex out of the bedrooms and into community spaces – that has a queer lineage from sex clubs, bath houses and cottages. It flies in the face of shame and secrecy. There is an added layer for a trans person with a trans body, to be *seen* in a space where queer and trans bodies are the norm. Attendees use words like empowered, transformed, truly seen and heard, and gender euphoric. Betty Martin's Wheel of Consent underpins all my work. Embodied consent is finding the 'yes' and 'no' in our own bodies' signals. It starts with noticing what happens when you hear the suggestion of lemon juice on your tongue, or a finger up your nose! The Bossy Massage is one of Betty Martin's best creations. It is a structure where nothing happens unless you ask for it. It works on the principles of one-way touch, impeccable clarity about who the touch is for, and short episodes of touch. No tolerating and/or dissociating! Practices like Body Show and Tell and Genital/Chest/Anal Interview can be combined into one practice. Show and tell offers useful emotional, somatic and relational experiences. It welcomes packers or energy genitals and can represent a reclaiming of the body and self from the medical system, the gender clinics and the cis-normative culture in which they have no choice but to exist, and which featured in sexual history. This reclaim may include naming body parts, experiencing pleasure where previously there was pain, trauma and abuse, and speaking out loud, 'This is how my genitals like to be looked at and touched.' Some trans people enjoy touch, movement and sexual techniques that are congruent with their felt gender; sex educator Jamie Joy, referenced by Fielding (2021), calls this 'Bobbing and Swirling'. For example, a trans feminine person may get pleasure and gender euphoria from her erectile tissue – usually read as a penis – being treated and touched as a clitoris. Cultivating this approach is validating and something that can be practised with sexual partners.

We are surrounded by cis-normative images and role models

BT: We are surrounded by cis-normative images and role models in everyday life. I try to avoid using images of cis anatomy and items like vulva cushions are used with care. People who have had genitals surgically created often have a complex relationship with the outcome. Getting to know the new genitals can take us down many different paths. Our culture encourages all of us to experience our bodies from the outside through the judgement and standards of others. I can invite us into a space where *all* genitals are experienced from the inside – interoception – and how they are experienced in relation to the space around them – proprioception – rather than from the point of view of the external gaze. The questions I might ask are, 'What about how they feel? What happens when you breathe into them? Let's be here and now with *your* new vagina – how do you experience her? Tell me about your relationship with your erectile tissue and nerve endings which are here, alive, now in this room. Is there something I cannot see with my eyes, your energy genitals?' Genital Mapping is a great practice to explore what sensations and nerve endings we can find. I take a gender-freeing approach to our biological bodies. I share my fun analysis of pan-gender ejaculation to recognize that all body configurations have a prostate with equivalent functions, fluids, pleasure and release.

JY: My ways of working are a combination of my individual models and the collective models that have grown within the GSRD community. I have found the work of Meg-John Barker and Alex Iantaffi (2018) excellent. Meg-John and Alex have offered a very different approach to writing, where the books encourage the reader to ask questions after each topic, through gentle exploration. Meg-John also offers a unique style of visual and written zines to support trans/non-binary people. I often use these books and zines to support the exploration of the client's relationship to gender and sexuality. As a psychosexual therapist, I work towards deconstructing cis-normative sexualities and de-medicalizing psychosexual narratives. I do this by taking the approach of de-centring away from functionality and performance-based genitals and orgasms, following a view that sex is more than your genitals. I follow models and concepts from writers such as Lucie Fielding (2021), Kate Bornstein (Bornstein and Bergman, 2010), Barbara Carrellas (2012, 2017) and Cabby Laffy (2013) that de-centre away from genitals. I find this approach really beneficial for gender-expansive and trans clients.

Discuss the physiology and purpose of disassociation so clients feel more in control of these states

JY: Some homework exercises I can offer work similarly to sexological bodyworkers, but the client does this work in their own time, and not in the therapy room. These can include getting to know your own body, likes/dislikes, etc. – what feels good, what doesn't. I also offer written exercises on desire, writing sexual fantasies and genital exploration. Homework – or a different term – is discussed in sessions as and when the client feels comfortable to do so. I work with client consent and client collaboration. Rather than hand out an exercise on paper – the traditional medical psychosexual way of working – we discuss the exercise and adapt it, if required, to what will work best for the client. Or the client can say no to the exercise. As a psychosexual therapist, one of my roles is psychoeducation. So instead of offering cis het genital images, I have recreated trans genital images as an educational talking point. Clients will have varying levels of comfort connecting with their gendered body. So, it is important to have discussions on levels of disassociation a client may have when connecting to their genitals before offering a client a somatic exercise. Working with gender euphoria exercises through visualization or other methods may allow a client to go deeper to connecting to their genitals in an embodied way. However, it is rare to bring clients to this place of a fully embodied connection through talking therapies. This is where Beck's work of embodied sexology (Thom, 2022) can create a powerful shift. With any somatic exercises I offer to clients, it is essential that the client has a good sense of internal safety, so they can bring themselves back online if a triggered state of dissociation occurs. Not all clients wish for or can follow these exercises. Discussing the physiology of disassociation and its purpose can be helpful for clients to feel more in control and less shameful of those states. For clients ready and willing to work more with their physical gendered body and/or genital connection, I have adapted traditional sensate focus exercises for trans/non-binary people and prefer to use terms such as my beautiful trans body, sensory touch, erotic touch and nurturing exercises. Here there is an opportunity to work collaboratively to support clients to find their own language for their gendered body that is affirming. It is an opportunity to re-discover, reclaim and re-learn new ways into connection to redefine one's genitals, as one's own, proud and beautiful. I'm reminded of the words of Juno Roche in *Trans Power* (2019, p.22) when they say, 'I explore my body now as I would a work of art, its surface populated with divergent ideas that allow me to wander and dissolve into comfort to discover my meaning.'

JC: Yes, I think their work is invaluable; they revolutionize how we can re-imagine/re-configure our bodies. Can you comment on the usefulness of therapists working alongside body practitioners and group workshops where people can explore stuff in more physical and collective ways?

BT: Listening to Jake's responses reinforces to me how mutually complementary the work of talk-based therapists and somatic practitioners is. I work with clients who also see a counsellor, and sometimes I suggest that the client seeks out counselling as an alternative, or alongside, when perhaps the client has a high level of active trauma, or they need help with decision-making, as Jake describes. SSE is a here-and-now and body first modality. For many trans people (but not all), being asked to focus on the interior of the body's experience, the sensations, the breath, or to touch their own body, is difficult, which can then lead to compounded feelings of inadequacy that, 'I can't even do the therapy right.'

I'm all about workarounds, ongoing consent, explicit permission-giving and a real curiosity about the huge range of possibilities for experiencing and expressing their erotic selves and pleasure. The client remaining in control and in choice is key, as is the trauma-informed concept of titration – a drop of an experience at a time, so as not to overwhelm. Sessions are more person-centred and dysphoria-aware than some mindfulness or mainstream embodied classes or sessions clients may have previously experienced. For example, a body scan will ask the client, 'Where is your attention drawn to in your body?', rather than instructing the client to focus on potentially tricky areas.

If something is trauma-informed, then it is also gender dysphoria-informed

BT: Treleaven's (2018) ideas around trauma-sensitive mindfulness are so relevant here. To me, if something claims to be trauma-informed and is not gender dysphoria-informed, then something is missing. I believe that the aspects of gender incongruence or dysphoria that arise from being misread and misgendered, responded to with fear, disgust and transprejudice, are embedded with traumatic feelings. Sometimes we are doing some edgy work, and it can be very reassuring to me that a client has a supportive, therapeutic relationship with a talk therapist to process what comes up.

JY: I value the work of queer-identified or knowledgeable sexologists, tantric healers and the kink community, where relevant and useful for the client as a way to find meaningful and affirming experiences of sexuality and gender. Events such as Quintimacy, queer festivals, small group gatherings and workshops that are specified for trans/non-binary/queer-identified people can be experienced as very rewarding. If clients are interested in these avenues, I would ask them to do their research to ensure they are safe spaces first and foremost. Have they come as a recommendation from others in the queer/trans community? We can explore clients' desires, intentions and expectations from these events in sessions to better support their choices to attend or have these experiences.

JC: This is all so useful and makes a lot of sense to me. Thank you! Finally, as two practitioners working with trans people around sex from contrasting ways of working, what considerations do you feel are important around your professional roles, ethics and boundaries?

For certified sexological bodyworkers, all touch is one-directional from practitioner to client

BT: CSBs have a professional code of conduct and the three main pillars of that are: all touch is one-directional from practitioner to client; the CSB is fully clothed; and gloves are worn for genital or anal touch. We follow similar guidance to counsellors about becoming personally involved with clients. I recognize my limitations. My service would not be appropriate for someone who was in active crisis and I cannot provide an emergency response. I am not a qualified counsellor or psychotherapist, although I have a therapeutic social work background and training. I facilitate human experiences and offer the tools to reflect on them. I support multiplicity; I encourage sharing and exploring a range of routes to wholeness. I trust the client to find their own way. My intention is to resist any sense of possession over my client or the outcome of the work. I do not attempt to foster bonding or a long-term attachment relationship, or a dependency on our sessions. There is something about learning the tools and practising intimacy skills to enable the client to go out and enhance their relationships or start dating, or to enjoy solo pleasure. I want a client to experience safety, but for this safety to be owned by them, so it is transferable beyond our sessions. I am a facilitator of intimacy skills, not a means to experiencing erotic intimacy. After practising consent and other skills with me, a great place to graduate to is a Quintimacy or similar workshop. Just like a counsellor or psychotherapist, I have professional and legal responsibilities on hearing about sexual behaviours that cause harm to others. I recognize that there are situations and problems that are beyond the scope of an SSE. However, due to being in this world of 'erotic outlaws' (Jesse, 2021), my ethics around sex are less based on rule-based ethics and more interested in principles of harm, restorative justice and understanding the global context of sex negativity, sexual violence, rape culture and the pathologizing and marginalizing of certain communities. The phenomenon of a 'sex addiction' label/diagnosis is an example of where I resist individualizing, pathologizing and sex negativity and seek a more compassionate response. I am insured to offer sexological bodywork, including intimate touch. CSBs can choose to register with a professional body, such as the Association of Somatic and Integrative Sexologists (ASIS) or the Association of Certified Sexological Bodyworkers (ACSB). I have regular mentoring and supervision, as well as my own counselling. I take seriously the need for my own self-care and self-stewarding. This enables me to hold space for others against a challenging and often hostile, sex-negative backdrop and while managing the complexity of working and being a member of a small community. Conversion therapy is on a spectrum, and it is an ethical responsibility not to collude with clients' requests to 'convert' them. Sometimes clients do not have any frame of reference other than the one given to them by an oppressive system which marginalizes anything but cis het normative sexuality. I intend to find ways of offering them more liberatory possibilities. Given that I cannot represent all trans experience, and I am not taking an 'expert' position, workshops are great places to witness others' diverse journeys, and trans peers can be both role models and sources of inspiration to each other.

JY: I am an integrative psychosexual therapist and trained with a holistic approach to psychosexual health from a course run by Cabby Laffy, who invented the concept of the homeodynamic model of sexual well-being. I have also trained in many of Pink Therapy's GSRD courses over the years. As a trans person, therapist and teacher of GSRD, I do not practise conversion therapy and actively support the UK ban on conversion therapy. Although it is currently being debated as to what conversion therapy actually means, the key consideration is that, whatever it is called, nobody has the right or ability to change another person's gender or sexuality. I do not provide sexual or erotic touch to clients, although we may talk about sex and the erotic in sessions, and I can offer exercises that involve sexual touch for clients to take home.

Erotic privilege

JY: Under the College of Sexual and Relationship Therapists (COSRT) guidelines, one of the governing bodies I am registered with, I am not allowed to actively support clients in procuring bodywork that involves touch, or sexual surrogacy. I find COSRT's viewpoint somewhat old-fashioned and heteronormative as it conflicts with my GSRD and somatic approach of psychosexual therapy. I also find it disappointing as sexological bodywork and group events, whether kink spaces or queer erotic events, are so important and valuable for GSRD clients seeking support psychosexually. Positive spaces for trans/non-binary people to experience a safe, embodied, erotic, sexual self are very rare. Withholding that information just reinforces the erotic privilege (Fielding, 2021, p. 17) that idealized, white, cis, het, able-bodied people take for granted and that trans/non-binary people, including those with intersecting identities, are having to work so hard to alleviate the shame of not having. Although I can't direct a client to work with a certified sexological bodyworker, I will offer resources from viable and ethical sources and support clients to make their own decisions by discussing with them consent, risk, ethics and safety. This is not procurement, but a responsible and informed approach.

CHAPTER 9

Working with queer sex workers

Karen Pollock

There have always been queer sex workers and, as Karen Pollock argues, all sex workers 'queer' not only sex but also heteronormativity by transgressing norms and selling sex. Because sex work is stigmatized and often criminalized, those who are engaged in such work are often pathologized both by clinicians in the medical and the counselling professions and by the wider world. Here, Pollock reflects on some considerations when working with individuals who are or who have been sex workers.

JANE CHANCE CZYZSELSKA: Sex workers have a long history of being denigrated not only in wider society but also in our profession, so it's important to me to have this chapter on queer sex workers. It's important to note that some sex workers are women, some are men and some are non-binary. Some are cis and some are trans. I've come across therapists who believe that sex workers have somehow 'gone down the wrong path' and that a successful outcome of their therapy could include a decision to leave sex work. I find this approach problematic for a range of reasons and, although for some clients, leaving sex work may be something they want to talk about, for many others it won't be, and for the therapist to assume it is, could be harmful to the client. So, I wonder if this is a good place to start our conversation.

Sex work has to be as relevant or irrelevant as the client finds it to be

KAREN POLLOCK: I think that's a really good place to start. When you work with sex workers, their work has to be as relevant or irrelevant as the client finds it to be. This is where I think there are huge parallels to queerness – in that you only talk about queerness with a client if they want to talk about it. I would argue, without imposing identities, that it's almost impossible not to be a queer sex worker, especially if you are AFAB because the very act of transgressing norms and selling sex means you are queering heteronormativity, but let's dump that over there because that's probably too controversial.

JC: Say more.

KP: Let's use GSRD, because if you're a sex worker who's a straight woman, married to a man, you are GSRD because you are subverting the norms by which we believe relationships should happen.

JC: True.

KP: So, for some people, the work will come into the sessions. For some people, their sex work will be irrelevant. For some people, they will want to change their job and for others they will not and will wonder why you want to know about it. Just as we – as clients – try to get into the heads of our cis het therapists, our queerness is as important or as irrelevant as we make it in the session. And that nuance is really important. Therapists often want to talk loads about it, saying, 'Oh, I treat everyone the same' and I think, 'Please don't because then you're ignoring things like transphobia or minority stress.'

JC: Yes.

KP: That has to be the starting point for anyone working with a sex worker. You do not determine whether the sex work comes into the room. You make the space for it to come in. And that's multidirectional. What I mean is, there can be an element of, 'Whoo hoo, I'm queer and affirmative and sex positive,' but that might not be the right approach at all. I have to make clear here I'm sex critical, not sex positive.

Consider sex criticality

JC: Can you explain what sex critical is?

KP: You could say it's what sex positivity should have been and perhaps is in some people's heads, but it accepts that sex isn't for everyone – not everyone finds sex pleasant; not everyone wants sex; sex can be a negative in some people's lives.

JC: Yes.

KP: To look at the totality of how everyone experiences sex and say, 'If that is your experience of it, I accept it and I'm not going to impose a "whoo hoo". You hear some therapists say something like, 'It's perfectly natural to want sex.' Not if you're asexual it's not. So, are they saying asexual people are unnatural?

JC: Yeah, I get it.

KP: I understand there is more nuanced sex positivity out there but the big broad-brush famous names are very much, 'It's natural, it's wonderful.' I wrote this big blog, 'Stop shaming people for faking orgasms' (Pollock, 2019a), which very much came from sex work experience. Just fake the orgasm! If it gets the sex over quicker – and I'm not saying sex is bad, but for some people faking orgasms is a valid choice. Why do we keep saying that women must tell men if they're having bad sex? So, sex critical is much more like, 'Don't assume everyone wants, needs, enjoys, has sex.' And I fully accept that many people who describe themselves as sex positive believe that too. I believe that there's nothing wrong with being asexual and not wanting sex, but the more nuanced voices aren't always the voices that are being heard.

JC: Yeah.

Does anyone else have a job they're expected to love all the time?

KP: So some sex workers will hate their job, and some will love their job. There is an element within the queer community that only sees, 'Oh, you're making such an empowered choice.' They want to affirm someone's choice to be a sex worker. That has to go out of the window as much as, 'Oh my god, you poor victim; were you abused as a child?' And that's the nuance within the work again: it's as important or as unimportant as the client wants it to be. This is an area where I would say an affirmative stance could be damaging if you are not listening to what you're being told because in a society which oppresses certain bodies and races, certain ethnicities, some people's experience of sex work is very negative, and they need a space to work out how they stop doing it or to deal with the fact that they don't have any choice. Some people's experience of sex work is positive, and the majority say, 'It's my job. Does anyone else have a job they're expected to love all the time?'

JC: Right, yes.

KP: And so, yeah, that idea that we can't have a bad day at the office – and this is what might be too hard for some people – a bad day at the office for a sex worker if they're a full-service sex worker can be anything up to and including rape. It's incredibly common. Can you sit with someone who's been raped in the course of their job and not say, 'Well, I think you need to change jobs'?

JC: Mm.

KP: Because that is really hard to do.

JC: Yeah.

KP: Sometimes we go too far into 'it's just another job'. Lots of it is, and therapists who have been sex workers in a previous incarnation have probably learnt 90 per cent of how to do admin as a therapist from being a sex worker. It's the same bloody job except they get paid less as a therapist.

JC: I've heard that too!

Just another job but with a specific set of stigmas and risks

KP: Also, a lot of the people skills and 90 per cent of how to read a room you can get just from doing the job – so they're very similar, and I'm talking here about full service. If you're doing camming or porn work, phone or different forms of not-in-person sex work, there's much less risk. But with full service, yes, lots of it is the same work as anyone else is used to in a service sector job. However, because of stigma and risk and the way our society is constructed, there is one huge risk that you and I do not face when we meet a client. And that is that sex workers are sexually intimate with someone who is usually bigger than them; and if the client rapes or sexually assaults them, they will have great trouble getting any support or help from the authorities. I've gone very dark very quickly, it's interesting.

JC: Go on.

KP: If you or I were raped by a client as psychotherapists, we would expect to be at least believed when we made a police report. I'm basing that on the fact that we are both white, we're both reasonably femme-presenting and we needn't tell the police about any other identities that we don't want to. We would be the middle-class professionals who a terrible thing had happened to. If that happened to a sex worker, they would probably be blamed. So, it's like holding two almost contradictory beliefs in your hand. One is that this is just another job: treat it like another job, give the space to the client to talk about what they need to talk about regarding the job, just as you would if they were a hairdresser. And two, it's a job with a specific set of stigmas, risks and mental health impacts. It's not the most dangerous job in the world by any means but the intersection of being trans and doing sex work, for example, means it looks much more dangerous than it is. If you look on Sex Workers Memorial Day and Trans Day of Remembrance, a lot of the same names are on that list. So here we're saying it's a job, but it's a job with a really specific set of risks if you're AFAB, and different risks if you're assigned male at birth (AMAB), I have to say.

JC: Do you want to say something about those risks if you're AMAB?

KP: I can only really speak to the US/UK/Australian/Canadian experience. The stigma is generally less within the gay, cis, male community, so the risks are less and the chances of being a victim of crime are less. Largely, the community – the gay, cis, male community – is more accepting of sex workers and it's not unusual for a cis gay man to have sex work experience in his background and almost shrug it off to his peers and colleagues.

JC: Oh right, OK.

KP: So it's just less risky if you are a white, cis man; there's more community acceptance and more likelihood of community support if something happened. However, this is also a very privileged viewpoint, and it is not without risk, because you are still a sex worker in a world that largely doesn't respect sex workers. If you're, say, an Indian or African male sex worker, it may be harder to find someone to turn to because of homophobia. At least there are projects – usually from HIV charities – for AFAB people so any universal experience is impossible, I realize. But everything I'm saying is caveated with the fact that this is the largely privileged, western, white, north European/Australian experience.

Racism, transphobia and sex work

JC: Yes, sex workers of colour have even less support and less likelihood of justice if they are raped.

KP: Everything goes back to those intersecting axes of oppression, which is why we have to be very careful when we talk about risks and harms. For example, if I reported a rape, I would be treated far better than many because my race is top of the tree: I am not a migrant, I am not visibly trans. I don't have to fear being put in some bloody prison camp by the government because my passport wasn't the kind they liked.

JC: Yeah. Some people say that pro-domming can be safer than doing full-service work. What's your view on that?

The whorearchy

KP: Oh, the whorearchy! There is a site called Tits and Sass. It's written by sex workers, for sex workers, and it's really informative about the whorearchy, the hierarchies of respectability and acceptability that exist even within sex work communities. Something that is very apparent in people's minds on the ground, and I would say in general literature as well, is that pro-domming is at the top. You're almost acceptable; you're maybe a little bit wild but people would take you home to meet mother. Street working would be at the bottom and then you get this strange thing called escorting, where people make up their own minds about what the hell they think that is. Pro-domming, to a degree, is safer but we need to always be very aware of the whorearchy and be very aware of that idea, 'Oh well, you don't actually have sex with them so you're OK.' A dear friend of mine died four years ago this month. She was a pro-domme who was very badly beaten up by one of her clients and killed herself.

JC: Oh my god. I'm so sorry.

KP: We really miss her now. She was the leading sex worker activist in the country. But you're still alone in a room with someone. I think, to go back to therapists, they need to be very aware of the whorearchy and the cultural norms and assumptions that they cannot help but have. You know, just as we all have internalized racism, transphobia and biphobia and all those cultural messages about what an identity means, we can only start to unpick them if we acknowledge it; people will also have internalized what they think a sex worker does, what it means and what that says about the person's sexuality, sense of self and life experiences. Part of that internalized narrative will be that the pro-domme is more respectable. The reality is that there are very few pro-dommes who just pro-domme – you have to be really well established and top of the tree. It's not unusual to have a secret adult work profile where they just do full-service, but the respectable face is in the kink because the kink community has been better and accepted some forms of sex work, so it's a community where you are more able to be a pro-domme or a pro-sub.

JC: I hadn't heard of the term whorearchy before but I'm aware of the hierarchy that you describe.

KP: The whorearchy would say the brothel worker was below the escort, and that's the cultural narrative. It's kind of like working for Improving Access to Psychological Therapies (IAPT) or being in private practice. I could not work for IAPT – seeing eight clients a day, coming by Talking Matters, boom boom – but you get a wage each month, you get your office supplied and you don't have to do any promotion. In fact, it's a great analogy: IAPT are the brothel keepers of the NHS! But we don't judge, or we shouldn't judge, the counsellor who says I can't run my own business; I'm going to get a job with Talking Matters. However, we do judge the sex worker who does that kind of high volume, very tiring brothel work. And we still have this idea of the independent escort: they're clearly OK, they know their own mind, but the brothel worker must be being forced. Is the IAPT therapist forced? They can't say which client they see next. They are forced to give their emotional labour to the next person even if it's someone they don't want to work with, whereas an email comes to me and I might think, 'Actually no, I don't think I want to work with you' and you send a nice polite reply saying, 'Sorry, I'm full.'

I wanted to go back to something. I mentioned child abuse. There is no evidence that being abused as a child means you become a sex worker. The anti-sex work academic and campaigner Melissa Farley has published and released several studies claiming there is a correlation between the two (Farley, 2003).

Busting some myths about sex work and sex workers

KP: Let me bust a few myths here, particularly about the idea that all sex workers begin as exploited children, and that sex workers are unable to consent due to being exploited, or that victims of childhood sexual abuse go on to become sex workers as they re-enact their trauma.

This last one, I think, gives some therapists an 'aha' moment as they seek to understand why someone might 'demean' themselves by selling sex. A lot of the myths around this come from the work of psychologist Melissa Farley (2003), who based her paper on research and interviews with under-age runaways who were living on the streets and selling sex to survive. Her work has since been robustly challenged (Bennachie, 2010). She was trying to argue that childhood sexual abuse (CSA) meant that you had messed-up attitudes towards sex, an external locus of evaluation and an inability to make good, healthy choices. The reasons that those are awful things to believe about survivors of CSA are many, but we start with the fact that she was interviewing under-16s who were runaways. They were selling sex because they were runaways and we know from other research that, by and large, children run away from home because of abuse at home, whether it's physical, sexual or emotional.

JC: Mm, yes.

KP: So that's the big study she cited, but being abused as a child does not stop you making healthy, rational choices as an adult, and one of those choices can be to be an adult sex worker. Being abused as a child does not mean you are unable to have bodily autonomy and it doesn't mean you can't decide, 'The abuse has damaged my mental health. I need a low-intensity, high-paid job so I can go to therapy twice a week. Oh yeah, sex work; that will work for me.' And being abused as a child doesn't mean you can't be kinky or queer or any of these other things. I'm trying to show that linking CSA and 'bad choices' as an adult is just sickening, as is putting sex work in as one of those bad choices. Again, it's worth repeating that there is no correlation between sex work and CSA but statistically some sex workers will have been abused as a child because a significant minority of children are sexually abused (Office for National Statistics, 2019). Saying that you are not allowed to make a choice that other people have made because, 'I think your childhood abuse has somehow damaged you' is a place no therapist should ever be.

JC: Yeah.

KP: So, sometimes you will hear that someone has been abused as a child and – again, holding those two contradictory positions – sometimes they will not have been sex workers, they will have been abused children. Rotherham, in South Yorkshire, the location of one of the largest child sexual exploitation scandals in UK history, is a classic example we have to talk about here. Those girls were dismissed over and over again because the police said, 'No, you are prostitutes,' and it took a long time and a lot of really careful work by a charity saying, 'No, they are 14-year-old girls being abused.' Sometimes someone will come to you and say, 'I was a sex worker,' and I'll think, 'I don't judge you for that but actually you weren't, you were 15 years old and being horrifically abused.' The comparison here is domestic violence (DV). The training I got in DV is that the person has to see it for themselves – we can give them resources like the wheel of power and control or ask them questions like, 'How do you feel when he shouts at you for talking to your friends?' But if we go too quickly to, 'It sounds like you're in an abusive situation,' we run the risk of trauma-bonding our client and the abuser and pushing them together. If we hear something and think, 'Actually, you were under 18; I'm not sure this was consensual sex work but you've framed it in your head that it was,' you need to very carefully unpick and allow the client to figure things out. Again, you need to hold two contradictory ideas until the client reaches it because some under-18s are doing consensual survival sex work because they need to bloody eat. No one is pimping them or exploiting them; they just – especially in the queer community – have had to leave home, and there is money to be made. I feel like I'm telling you that, for everything, there is an equal and opposite reaction. Apologies but that's just the case. There will be – this is not a real person – a trans guy, 17 years old, thrown out of his home by his parents, sofa-surfing; he realizes that a few guys on Grindr have offered him money in the past – contacts; £50 will get him through to the weekend. Is he an exploited child? Legally and technically, yes. Is he making choices constrained by his circumstances, exercising bodily autonomy and probably improving his life situation in the process? Yes. Then you have a 15-year-old queer person whose boyfriend tells them that they will be having sex with these other people but it's to pay the bills and they don't have any choice. They may say they are choosing to do it because they love their boyfriend, but it's very different in terms of there is almost always an equal and opposite reaction.

JC: Yes, true.

KP: That said, the statistics show that the majority of sex workers in the UK are over the age of 21, AFAB, educated at least up to the age of 18 and have very high job satisfaction. I feel I have to say that because I've been talking about the negatives because that's where people get into territory that can be harmful: by either seeing too much or not seeing that the average person is far more likely to be selling sex because rents are high, wages are shit and/or they enjoy the sex.

JC: And it can fit around whatever their lifestyle is, or needs are, as you said, mental or physical health needs.

KP: There are a hell of a lot of disabled sex workers out there.

JC: Yeah.

KP: If you can make the same amount of money in a couple of mornings' work as you can in an entire week's work when you have chronic fatigue or mental health problems, why the hell wouldn't you?

JC: Although I know some who didn't, most sex workers I know have largely enjoyed their work. What they don't enjoy, understandably, is when they have to deal with arseholes, feeling scared about safety and renting space from unscrupulous landlords.

Sex is work, so it says nothing about gender or sexual identity

KP: That's all stuff that proper decriminalization could fix, you know. You'd never, in any service industry, get rid of all the arseholes. If you ask any pub worker if they're looking forward to going to work on a Friday and it's cold and wet and people are not going to be socially distancing and drinking too much, they'd probably say no too. Sex work is no different.

There is something I wanted to quickly return to around the enjoying the sex side. It's really important to remember when working with sex workers that the sex is work, so it says nothing about gender or sexual identity. Huge assumptions can be made. The most money is to be made from having sex with cis heterosexual men. So, it's kind of like you can work in McDonald's and be a vegetarian, you know! It doesn't mean someone isn't sure either. And one thing that can come up is with people who were sure of their queer identity pre-sex work and who are struggling if they enjoy the sex at work. So, orgasms can feel very complex and problematic, especially if you identify as only being attracted to women and you're orgasming with male clients. Sometimes some people just don't want to have orgasms with clients of any sexuality or gender but it's not necessarily around the fact that it's a client; it's around the fact that the gender isn't the kind of person they are normally attracted to. This is where the queer side of what you're writing about comes in to play: being very firm in your behaviour with clients does not confer your identity outside of work. Don't project that onto any clients that are struggling. And don't do conversion therapy: 'Oh. You said you're a lesbian but you're having sex with men!' Yeah, it's her job! It can be useful to have some psychoeducation to just understand how bodies work. I haven't had to do it very often, but a few people find it quite reassuring to learn that we don't actually physically control how this happens and there's nothing to be ashamed of in enjoying your job. If you orgasm at work, you've had a good day at work, kind of. I'm not saying it's a huge thing, but it has come up and I could see how, if someone had a very fixed identity of not being attracted to men, it can throw you quite a bit.

JC: Yes, I can see that too.

Sex work and the minority stress model

KP: I wrote a paper on sex work and minority stress (Pollock, 2019b) because I really strongly believe that the majority of the mental health of sex workers, rather like queer people, can be put under a minority stress model. And then we have to consider: are we getting a double whammy of minority stress in the way that a queer person of colour does? You have different communities that are excluding you, so there is some evidence about the mental health of sex workers that isn't great, but again we live in a whorephobic society that shames and judges and, if you are queer as well, it all adds up. That's why it's really important that there's stuff out there like this book and community support. The difference between now and 15 years ago is that the queer community now is really openly sex worker-affirmative, and this is a considerable boon. We know that community links are the way we tackle minority stress.

JC: I remember in the early 1990s I knew a few queer women who were sex workers who did the booths in Soho, London. I went to Tuppy Owens' Outsiders club for sex workers and people with disabilities. There has always been a lot of crossover between sex work and queers, and the people in the kink crowd were always accepting of it. The folks from the Rebel Dykes, many of whom were involved with lesbian BDSM club Chain Reaction etc., were always accepting. Maybe it was a minority acceptance at the time?

Sex workers have been at the forefront of every sexual liberation struggle

KP: I think sex workers have been at the forefront of every sexual liberation struggle. I have no guilt that I concentrate largely on the AFAB experience because it's far more transgressive for someone AFAB to do but if you break that norm, if you basically spit in the eye of patriarchy and say, 'This is my body and I'm making money from it,' you've already done a liberation struggle, you know? It's really interesting and I really strongly believe that one of the mis-steps feminism took in the UK was to become anti-sex worker during the Wages for Housework movement. Feminism was campaigning to say the emotional and physical labour of women should be financially compensated. A huge part of the prejudice against sex work, at least by AFAB people, is the idea we should do this for free. Again, there are huge parallels to counselling, something that has often been expected to be provided without financial recompense because women/AFAB people should be doing it anyway.

Useful terminology and organizations

JC: Yes, true. I was thinking also that it would be useful for therapists to learn about terminology. Are there any other terms you think therapists should be aware of? There are obviously organizations like the English Collective of Prostitutes (ECP), which many sex worker clients are likely to already know about.

KP: Regarding terminology, I think the most useful is to read sex worker sites and be aware that language varies, particularly between countries. There's the Sex Worker Advocacy and Resistance Movement (SWARM) and National Ugly Mugs. There's a really good paper on the stigma faced by sex work researchers – say, someone well-meaning but ill-informed and they advertise they are working with sex workers: they will get stigmatized by association (Hammond and Kingston, 2014). I am also writing a unit for Pink Therapy on working with sex workers, which will include a helpful glossary and resource sheet.

JC: All those resources are great, and the course sounds much needed. Thank you.

CHAPTER 10

Don't panic! Queering the child

Paul Harris, Anthea Benjamin and Neil Young

Welcome

When I looked in your eyes and gazed
I saw you
Not as I wanted you to be
But as you revealed yourself to me
I wished for you
To remember always
Who you are
Where you have come from
How perfect you are.
Your gaze spans all worlds and pulls me in
Newly arrived – wriggling to be in your skin
You hold the memory of time before time
A living blessing
I closed my eyes and I wished for you
I wished for me and I wished for you again
To remember always
Who you are
Where you have come from
How perfect you are.

Harris (2021)

This chapter is the product of a rich dialogue between three queer elders and psychotherapists, Paul Harris, Anthea Benjamin and Neil Young, about the current situation for queer children in the UK, with a detailed focus on one school's culture.

We had regular, online discussions over six months – with time in between meetings to reflect, research and write. In this chapter, we provide analysis, make necessary challenges and map out a child-centred framework for change that we hope will inspire readers. We have drawn strength and insight from our embodied queer and childhood experiences, as well as key anti-racist, intersectional and historical perspectives. At the heart of our writing – organized into a case study that threads through and supports our narrative – is the experience of one queer, Black, working-class girl, who sparks her school system, including its therapeutic practitioners, into holding her as deeply as any newborn child of a queer, human family could wish for. To you, Ayo, and to queer children across the globe – future queer elders – we are humbled in your presence.

'Queer' is used throughout this chapter as an approximate, respectful short-hand for primarily western lesbian, gay, bisexual, trans, queer, questioning, asexual and intersex (LGBTQQAI+), as well as other historic and perpetually emergent sexual and/or gender minority identities – such as gender non-conforming, non-binary, pansexual and the growing, detailed language reflecting degrees of romantic and/or sexual attraction – as they hold embodied, felt meaning for children and their allied support networks.

Aside from the authors' names, all other people identified in this chapter have been given pseudonyms. The case study material has been altered to protect the identity of the child and has been approved for use by the child's parent, the head of school and the clinical lead of the therapeutic service involved.

> *When I looked in your eyes and gazed*
> *I saw you*
> *Not as I wanted you to be*
> *But as you revealed yourself to me ...*

For decades in the UK, we have been undergoing a transformative shift in how many of us feel about, embody and react to our sexuality and gender identities. Increasingly, this change is being voiced by children and young people growing up and into a culture that has fewer shame and hate-based reactions to queer identities, especially to lesbians and gay men. Thanks is largely due to grassroots activism and the courage of millions of people to come out about their sexuality and/or gender identities; or, arguably, to let people into this part of their lives (Espinoza, 2013). In short, individual, family and community attachments – love in ordinary terms – have increasingly been able to weather and celebrate these emerging queer differences, which are overwhelmingly taking place within heterosexual, cisgender families.

Case study, part 1

Ayo is a nine-year-old Black, working-class, female child who has recently disclosed, in confidence, to a trusted teacher that she is pansexual and intends to tell her mother. The teacher shares this information with Ayo's classroom teacher, who phones Ayo's mum, concerned that this is a potential safeguarding issue, and that Ayo might experience unwanted attention or bullying if she came out at school. This call takes place against a background of tension between school and home, with Ayo's behaviour at school – and her relationship with her peers – being questioned. By contacting Ayo's mother directly, her teacher hopes to prevent further concerns, strengthen the school's relationship with the family and offer support to Ayo. As it happens, Ayo's mother is concerned about her daughter's current gender and/or sexual identities being disclosed without consent, contacting Zoe, the school's Counselling Services Manager, to share that she feels her child's trust and confidentiality have been breached.

Globally, these life-changing and life-saving societal changes in attitude towards queer identities have been emerging for at least a generation, and not just in affluent western countries. For example, acceptance of homosexuality over the past 20 years has risen by double digits in the UK, Canada and the US, as well as in countries in the global south, including Argentina, Mexico, Japan, Kenya, the Philippines and South Africa (Poushter and Kent, 2020, p. 4).

One result is that we are seeing large numbers of children and young people who are continuing to search for the language, behaviours, desires and experiences that will help them develop into the unique human beings they are. Currently, this movement in the UK – by and large, a collective of individual children with the support of their caretakers, families and wider allies – remains subject to a historic and evolving, many-tentacled moral panic. In its current extreme forms, this can mobilize online and real-world mobs to whip up hostility, prejudice and fear about children just becoming who they are, through widely mediated lies, personal attacks and the projection of unprocessed, disowned feelings – such as shame, hate, fear, grief, anger, disgust and envy – onto and into queer children and those who love them.

This moral panic is driven by more regressive, Victorian values; a semi-conscious drive to promote the inalienable right to abuse children and claim rights of determination over queer children's lives. Anti-queer hatred in the UK is not new: over the centuries, queer folk have faced execution, criminalization and torture at the hands of state-funded psychiatric 'professionals' (including castration, drug-induced sickness and electric shock treatments), as well as being imprisoned, stigmatized and attacked in their homes and on the streets – just for being themselves.

The current anti-queer backlash mirrors similar pushback against other progressive social movements, including feminism, anti-racism and disability rights. While there is now more legal and cultural support for queer lives, in recent years hate crimes against LGBT people have soared (Jones, 3 September 2021). UK press and social media attacks on LGBT people, activists and organizations, especially trans children – foolishly amplified by politicians, celebrities and uncivil organizations – have become 'the gateway drug' to rebuilding anti-LGBT feeling for political ends (Jones, 17 October 2021), with the queer child as acceptable, collateral damage.

The birth of the heteronormative, cisgender, un-queer 'child'

The idealized, heteronormative 'child' remains a long-standing, primarily western, societal norm which – even before conception, consciously or otherwise – is imposed on babies who are assumed to be binary-gendered and heterosexual, with an in-built developmental drive to 'grow up' through childhood and adolescence into a desirable adult world of 'marriage, work, reproduction and the loss of childishness' (Stockton, 2009, p. 4). Given the long-standing hatred and fear of queer people, it is no wonder that the existence of queer children has traditionally been denied, treated as unbearable pollution of sex and gender roles, and even positioned as a recruitment cult led by mad, bad and/or sad queer adult paedophiles and rapists – usually gay men and increasingly trans women – who threaten the very future of childhood itself with their (perceived or actual) queer phalluses.

Underneath these projected, disowned feelings and traumatic othering is an attempt by adults to silence children, who are often assumed to be too young, confused or hard-to-believe when they come out. Non-binary children – who may represent the greatest proportion of queer-identifying children – also have an identity without legal or social recognition (Goldberg and Kuvalanka, 2018, in Bower-Brown *et al.*, 2021, p. 15). In short, queer children and their allies – despite recent progress – are still struggling to be seen, heard and respected.

I wished for you
To remember always
Who you are

Case study, part 2

Ayo's mother speaks to Zoe to share her concerns about the school outing Ayo to her as pansexual, without Ayo's consent. They agree that Zoe will talk to senior management about the school recognizing it should not have disclosed such personal information – which could have put Ayo at risk if her mother and/or family were unsupportive or actively hostile to queerness – and how its reaction pathologized and sexualized Ayo's identity and feelings without any attempt to hold, explore and celebrate them.

Ayo's mother has a disability; it may be that her experience of being othered – with its consequential silencing and dehumanization – enabled her to advocate for Ayo within a system that might also render her daughter invisible and potentially unsafe. While Zoe and Ayo's mother spoke on Zoom, Ayo was also present and as such her queer identity was sensitively acknowledged and welcomed at an individual and systemic level.

Loving acceptance, immediate and over time, from caregivers and families of choice (Mills-Koonce *et al.*, 2018, p. 637), wider family, communities, schools, professionals and peers may well be the critical factor in helping to shield queer children from the worst impacts of pathological, traumatic hatred, which – once internalized – can then be expressed in poor mental health, low self-esteem, self-harm and murder of self. Evidence suggests that if parents and caregivers of queer children are negative or openly hostile about their children's identities, this will make them vulnerable to bullying and exploitation in other parts of their lives (Clark *et al.*, 2021, p. 1); in short, parents who don't honour their child's queerness may rupture their child's internalized attachment.

Even when bolstered by love at home, in the face of a heteronormative, cisgender world that remains largely unseen and unchallenged by adults, professionals and institutions, many queer children inevitably seek peer- and sibling-type support outside of their family, community and school. Research shows that 40 per cent of school pupils are not taught anything about LGBT issues and that, perhaps unsurprisingly, for most queer children (96 per cent), the internet is their go-to for exploring their gender and sexual identities (Stonewall, 2017, p. 6). Children increasingly have access to social media (Ofcom, 2021, p. 25) and are curating their consumption – using profiles, digital platforms, messaging apps, blogs, gaming and video calls – to interact with friends, explore queer identities and create and/or share their own content.

We do not romanticize social media, online gaming and other digital spaces which are poorly regulated and can be a source of bullying, hate speech and sexualized attention from predatory young people and adults, as well as addiction, reduced sleep quality and poor mental health (Craig *et al.*, 2021, p. 1). Too much time spent online may also leave children less comfortable about connecting with friends, nature and opportunities outside their home. Nonetheless, it is important to acknowledge the power of online spaces as 'informal learning environments' for queer children (Fox and Ralston, 2016, in ibid., p. 2). The relative safety and anonymity of the online world allows children to experiment with labels, personas and disclosure about their gender and sexual identities, while finding friends, organizations and resources to nourish their emergent queerness. As Clay Holmes-Brown (2021) puts it, social media allows queer children to 'create mini-communities' of 'child-centred, accelerated learning' in which they can 'get what they want in a quicker, more targeted way'.

It is adults, particularly parents, carers, wider family and professionals working with children and young people, who have the power to challenge heteronormative beliefs and facilitate change for the children they love and work with. Queer young people want their stated names and pronouns respected; the creation of gay–straight alliances and gender-neutral facilities; inclusive curricula; access to LGBT+ youth groups and gender identity services; and the implementation of queer-inclusive policies and staff training (LGBT Manifesto, 2020).

We might also begin by asking ourselves questions: What is our relationship with our own bodies, as sexual and gendered beings, and how do we bring this into our relationships with children who are exploring their own unique selves and need our containment, love and support? What stereotypical beliefs about being 'male' and 'female' have we swallowed and how might we project these onto others, especially children in our care?

Where you have come from
How perfect you are.
Your gaze spans all worlds and pulls me in

At this point, we must acknowledge the impact of British, and wider European, colonialism. Vaid-Menon (2021) demonstrates how contemporary attitudes to gender and sexuality have been fundamentally shaped by brutal racist and misogynistic beliefs and behaviour, including colonialists seeking out and murdering gender-diverse people and imposing a strict gender binary on Black and Indigenous people and people of colour, as well as within their own societies. Historic collective fantasies of who is, and what makes, a 'real' man or woman reinforce a secondary 'us and them' binary culture, whereby trans folk – and especially gender-diverse children – become dangerous, gender traitors undermining the 'natural' gendered order, rather than individuals modelling authenticity, showing us all a way to our unique gender identities (ibid.). As Vaid-Menon observes, 'many of us don't know who we are outside of who we've been told we should be … [we need to] stop living someone else's fantasy of who we should be and actually get intimate with who we actually are' (ibid.).

Against this overarching backdrop, queer children are arguably the uncrowned leaders of an exciting transitional movement, educating themselves and others about an emergent kaleidoscope of unique gender and sexual identities.

Interviews with frontline service providers reinforce this analysis: more children are being open at a younger age, especially about their gender identities, and parents/carers and families are increasingly willing to listen, learn and advocate; to trust and allow exploration as a process – not a phase with a 'return to normality' – while saying 'we believe you and love you' (Furley, 2021). Project workers describe children identifying as gender variant from six years old, perhaps reflecting the importance of gender to early childhood life, and coming out as non-heterosexual from around 12 – early adolescence, with its often-rapid physical, cognitive and emotional changes, including puberty.

But there remain concerns: schools and other agencies continue to 'out' children without their consent, which can put children at risk (Bastian, 2021); anti-LGBT prejudice remains persistent; and parents and professionals often treat trans identification as a mental illness in children (Mordanti, 2021). Instead, there should be recognition that as professionals they may need more information, processing time and therapeutic support.

More broadly, we are also seeing increasing awareness and activism about the climate emergency, especially among the young, who will literally inherit the earth. For queer children and their allies, watching adult staff fret about which toilets, clothes and pronouns they will 'allow' gender-diverse children to have at school misses the point that ignoring environmental change and disrespecting queer children's development may both have catastrophic impacts. Over a quarter of trans teenagers (27 per cent) have tried to kill themselves, while nine in ten have thought about it (Metro Charity, 2014).

Clearly, children who are engaged and experimenting with this relatively new language about gender and sexual identity are often negotiating how to challenge adult reactions, including emotional, physical and sexual violence from those whose 'job' includes a duty of care for their emotional 'development' and future lives. Transition does take time – and there is often grief for caregivers who may have had normative hopes for their offspring – but these feelings should not end up being dealt with solely by queer children.

Many queer adults knew they were queer when they were very young. Yet while some older children are becoming 'competent agents' (Tilsen,

2013, p. 3) for change on gender and sexuality issues, they need adults with power to advocate for the institutional and individual changes needed for them to be safe, happy and healthy. Adults who care about and work with children could helpfully interrogate their own prejudices, design more inclusive services and open up spaces in which any child could safely share and process their thoughts, feelings, experiences and fantasies about queerness. This should not be a toolkit but a 'process of reflection, education and action' (ibid., p. 108) – one we would argue is lifelong work.

Case study, part 3

Zoe is a white British, pansexual-identified woman in her thirties, with responsibility for in-house therapy services at the school, including the clinical work of several qualified and trainee child psychotherapists. Before Zoe speaks to Ayo's mother, she has supervision with Paul (Harris) about her concerns for Ayo and how best to respond to issues of gender and sexual diversity within the school. Paul, who has known Zoe throughout her therapy training, is curious about her personal perspective and how she has been impacted, rather than immediately sharing his view as a queer, white-identified male.

Zoe found herself questioning her counter-transferential response given her own pansexual identity: she questioned whether it was valid to challenge the systemic response to Ayo. Zoe remained uncomfortable about the school's reaction to Ayo's disclosure and its failure to hold, let alone celebrate, Ayo's attempt to express how she might wish to embody and explore her desire for intimacy with her peer group. Ayo's courageous and open-hearted expression of identity prompted a fearful reaction from the school system that indicated a deeper level of unconscious prejudice towards diverse gender and sexual identities as experienced by children, including – in this case – a reactionary, sexualized assumption about Ayo's use of the word 'pansexual' to describe herself.

Newly arrived – wriggling to be in your skin
You hold the memory of time before time
A living blessing

As a group of integrative arts psychotherapists, child psychotherapists and supervisors, our practice is founded upon a theoretical framework that seeks to integrate psychoanalytic/psychodynamic concepts such as transference and counter-transference alongside humanistic, relational and existential modalities – each of which is firmly grounded in somatic (neo-Reichian) and trauma-informed principles. In addition, our work recognizes the importance of the arts and creative process as a potent and integral force in the process of healing and growth.

We know, from our own training and personal therapy, the importance of working with, and safely holding, experiences of embodied shame. The legacy of unregulated fear and shame states, where children have developed in environments that fail to mirror the totality of their emergent identities, is a significant issue where gender and sexuality are concerned.

Understanding of gender within western cultural frameworks is limited to a binary positioning of male and female within a heteronormative framework (Moon, 2008). This operates through mechanisms of power perpetuated through daily acts, in the othering of minority groups that are located outside dominant cultures. Butler (2006) challenges the 'truths' of gender, sexuality and the body as sexuality and gender is a socio-cultural construction that intersects with the body. The mass continuation of a heteronormative ideal and linking this with good morals creates perverse splitting, denial and projection, which continue to create significant harm.

When Winnicott describes the 'psyche as dwelling in soma' (1949), he is describing a developmental achievement which emerges out of the intersubjective field, which is contingent upon the infant having been held simultaneously by the parent as a physical, emotional and cognitive 'whole' to the degree that the child comes to experience themselves as an individual capable of thinking about their feelings as they experience them in body.

When the environment has not been adequately holding for infants, children and young people, it takes a conscious community of grown-ups to create the conditions of safety that allow the possibility of healing and integration. This notion lends itself to Bion's concept of the container-contained (1962), which offers some practical insight into the culture and process that would characterize a healthy community, such as a school, where reflective practice and accountability are prioritized.

We aim in our therapeutic work with children to hold them in mind, from a stance that is unapologetically queer and that celebrates the uniqueness of each individual coming into being. Panksepp's seminal writing on lust as one of the seven intrinsic neural pathways within the mammalian brain has bolstered our thinking enormously (1998). He shares a deeply compassionate and realistic vision, based on the emergent findings of affective neuroscience, that recognizes an infinite array of gender and sexual identities within nature and that challenges the perennial, binary vision of a cisgender, heteronormative world within which children grow.

At the heart of our practice is a belief that, as biological organisms, we each have the right to embody desire, to explore and to celebrate our libidinal relatedness, without fear or prejudice. As Porges (2017) clearly argued as part of his polyvagal theory, safety as the deepest expression of our autonomic nervous system is the neuro-physiological foundation of the social engagement system and the prerequisite state for human beings to be able to learn and grow together as part of a healthy community.

We are keen to acknowledge, as Freud (1923) did, that the first ego is indeed a body ego and that inter-corporeal states are the foundation of latter stage intersubjectivity and the verbal narratives of self and other that might convey the fullest sense of who we feel ourselves to be. Furthermore, the work of Colwyn Trevarthen (2001) encourages us to hold the queer infant foremost in mind when working to counter the pervasive, toxic effects of shame, which is such a common lived experience for children, queer and non-queer. Trevarthen has written so beautifully about the co-creation of positive affective states as an essential part of the parent–infant dyad, including pride – a psycho-biological state which we view as synonymous with a sense of safety, belonging, aliveness and relatedness within the bodymind of the developing infant and the very foundations of an authentic self. Unregulated shame states, in the absence of the former, are likely to constitute a disorganizing force in the bodyminds of children, for whom parts of self must remain hidden or split off, particularly for those with multiple intersectionality identities.

Case study, part 4

While Zoe contemplates how to support expressions of queerness among pupils at the school and how to facilitate a thoughtful, celebratory institutional response, Paul has reached out to his peers – Neil and Anthea – for additional support about his role and responsibilities.

Over the next few months, the supervisory focus is on processes of school-based change, broadened now to incorporate the Black Lives Matter movement and its focus on the ongoing, institutional racism within UK society, and the need for immediate and long-term reparatory action. Following the experience with Ayo, Zoe has spent a considerable amount of time reflecting upon how equality, diversity and inclusion (EDI) work in school might address the historic and current prejudice experienced by the children that she and her colleagues serve.

As a starting point, Zoe invited all trainee and qualified therapists across the 15 schools served by the charity organization she works for to meet. The intention was for the unique identities and experiences of the therapy team to be considered from an intersectional perspective, allowing for a critical dialogue to unfold about how experiences of discrimination can be challenged within the therapeutic team and subsequently across the whole school community.

I closed my eyes and I wished for you
I wished for me, and I wished for you again

Intersectionality is an analytic tool to support our understanding of complexity in people and the human experience. We are used to seeing the world through binary thinking; an intersectional approach invites us to view the world as it really is, by embracing a both/and frame. This can be particularly helpful in understanding social inequality and the organization of power as being beyond race-only or gender-only lenses, examining their interconnections. Therefore, intersectionality is the inquiry into the interaction between various identity categories and considering the role of interlocking systems of power. Power relations show up in all relationships, as in who is advantaged or disadvantaged within systems and social relationships. Within these, some members of society who are marginalized (i.e. those who are not members of the dominant cultural norm) encounter different treatment regarding the rules that apply to them. In thinking about the case study with Ayo, this led to some thinking about part of the anxiety being located in a stereotype of Black/children of colour being more sexualized. Crenshaw (1989) argues that an intersectional approach identifies how related intersectional identities such as race, gender and class overlap to create inequality on multiple levels, and this is important to address in the issue of school discipline and risk.

As a society, we have systemically failed Black/children of colour, queer, non-binary and trans children as part of their early development – a reality which is further compounded by the relative absence of queer professionals in the field of child mental health. This is amplified for Black/children of colour who identify as queer as they have to hold the triple load of racist projection, stereotypes of hypersexuality and becoming sexualized much younger than children from other ethnic identities. The need for contextual understanding (Firmin, 2020) when working with children and young people with emerging identities is essential and needs to be reflected in professional trainings so that Black, people of colour and queer people feel welcomed and safe.

All too often, queer people training to be child psychotherapists have to carry the projection of disowned perversion, as normative assumptions about non-heterosexual, non-cisgendered identities are inappropriately linked to child sexual abuse. If such historic anti-queer prejudice continues to go unchallenged, consciously or otherwise, within the psychoanalytic and humanistic traditions, they will continue to reproduce the symbolic and clinical reality whereby queer adults remain untrusted as a safe container for the infant. To challenge this is to challenge the cisgendered, heteronormative assumptions of the maternal archetype and motherhood itself – a notion that has been met with a subtle yet pernicious level of resistance within the current models of training, where outdated and harmful paradigms can hold fast.

Postcolonial theory and normative narratives reflecting on race and the centring of whiteness and Euro-centric thinking are useful in understanding the ways in which childhood has been colonized through western frameworks. Young-Bruehl (2012) argues that children are subject to social, cultural and political constructions and othering, as are many groups who face prejudice. Her thinking about 'Childism' (a form of prejudice towards children) is an important framework for understanding the use of power in relation to children, particularly in considering their identity rights. This illustrates the socio-cultural and socio-political construction of childhood identities that underpin western relationships between adults and children. Additionally, it provides a critical framework for non-heterosexual/homosexual binaries, which have been erased through colonizing practices. Therefore, it is important to incorporate social constructionist lenses to better understand how we operate within the world, and how this becomes replicated throughout organizational systems. Our argument is a reflection on how we can better pay attention to practices of power and assumptions through self-reflexivity with children and organizations who serve them.

Brazilian educator Freire's *Pedagogy of the Oppressed* (1970) examines how education can disempower or empower. Freire uses terms such as 'oppression' and 'oppressed' and speaks to the need for oppressed people to call for social justice, particularly within education establishments. An increased critical consciousness in education facilitates the support of children from minority groups, including those who are queer, so they can be heard and responded to. This way difference can really be validated, rather than being negatively labelled or suppressed.

W.E.B. Du Bois (1903/1994, p. 2) wrote about 'double consciousness', which is a sense of always looking at oneself as a person through the eyes of others, as someone in a white world and therefore creating a constructed self to fit in. This level of displacement is damaging where the self can become a stranger as the world's projections become internalized as a false self. This would be even more problematic for a child who is Black and exploring their emergent pansexual identity, and the projective processes within the interlocking identities in this child.

Case study, part 5

It was decided that the therapy team should divide up into work groups to deepen exploration and dialogue about key intersectional identities, including race, class, differing abilities, gender and sexuality. Each subgroup would then report back to the overall team to share their experience and dialogue. This work is ongoing, informed by the need for safety as a priority throughout the organization – from individual pupils through to senior management – to encourage embedded cultural change as an institution with responsibility to the whole school community and beyond.

In getting started, the therapist group will prioritize four key areas: recruitment, induction and training (to address a lack of diversity within the staff team); supervision and reflective practice groups (in addition to clinical management and supervision, to maintain safe spaces and to deepen the dialogue); ensuring therapeutic spaces and materials are inclusive and representative of the entire school community; and an extended inter-professional work group (where other key staff members within and between schools are encouraged to participate and to push for change beyond therapeutic spaces – to classrooms, the playground, home and the wider community).

To remember always
Who you are

Challenging conceptual frameworks and assumptions that underlie the practice of therapy and organizational systems is at best challenging and at worst soul destroying for marginalized/othered practitioners. It can also create enormous amounts of emotional labour alongside the troubled psyches we support in our own bodyminds. We are all situated within a cultural context of normative processes which upholds ideas about conventional ways of seeing children and children's bodies. Children, like adults, can make sense of their own subjective experiences but often need support in making sense of these experiences. Our ability to engage children in meaning-making about their emerging identity through this process is important, rather than seeing them as passive/powerless victims of socialization.

Sara Ahmed (2004) talks about shame being a key component of moral development and central to normative cultural understandings about sex. Ahmed discusses 'the social contract' and how shame is used to assimilate one into society's normative positioning as acceptable (2004, p. 107). This communicates the preference of certain identities – race, ethnicity, social class, gender, sexuality and/or disability – in terms of acceptability and being included over others. This hierarchy of difference reflects organizations' comfort/discomfort, tolerance/intolerance and their level of commitment to children who identify as 'other'. In this sense, power is operating through shaping children's experiences within the organizational context and socialization process they encounter. Therefore, we need to look at how organizations can adapt and create more self-understanding and self-regulating environments which are capable of self-reflection.

Where you have come from
How perfect you are.

Social constructivism holds the view that knowledge is a human product that is socially and culturally constructed as opposed to discovered. Therefore, reality is constructed not discovered through human activity, so that societies together invent the norms of the world. An important way of making sense of how these norms become replicated is in understanding how organizations work and how children are held within these systems. Organizations often operate as closed systems, which have set values and beliefs that certain members align themselves with. The members who don't or can't align with these values can end up being either marginalized or pushed out. Therefore, the work of every organization is how they can evolve and adapt to the changing culture around them which will positively reflect the diversity of members. Schools are a microcosm of the wider society and tend to perpetuate conservative ideals around children's sexuality and education, and they are especially sensitive to the transgression of the community's dominant moral values in this area (Simon and Whitfield, 2000).

Affirmative practice requires reflexivity in thinking about and acknowledging difference and how we are all positioned within a gendered, heteronormative world which fundamentally shapes our perceptions and behaviour. The paradox of applying this thinking to children's emerging identities is that it becomes caught in an innocence–perversion divide, which both reinforces and replicates prejudice against queer or non-binary identities. The cultural projections that focus on trying to hold onto children's innocence by enforcing heteronormative ideals disempowers children from finding their own sense of identity in an authentic and organic way.

There is a growing need to sit with and hold complexity in children's emerging identities and to enable them to express this process without shame. Creating safe spaces within organizations for children to explore their intersectional identities such as race, gender and sexuality is needed more than ever. As a culture, we are not skilled at staying with complexity as we lack resilience to stay with discomfort as norms are challenged. This is particularly true of organizational structures such as school environments, which are given the responsibilities of 'raising children with an appropriate moral code'. This 'moral code' needs to be interrogated, particularly asking who decides what it is and who is discriminated against by it. Disrupting these power discourses is key for inclusive practice to enable children to have a time and space to make sense of their own authentic identities.

Interlocking systems of oppressions operating within systems influence the questions we ask about lived experiences. The anxiety provoked by difference often shuts down thinking (Bateman and Fonagy, 2016). Yet our ability to enable mentalizing ensures we can partner with children and young people in making sense of their lived experience embedded in oppressive structures. Negative discourse about difference, such as being in the wrong body or loving someone with the same/binary gender, leaves young people vulnerable to becoming traumatized because of the pervasive effects of oppression on individuals with marginalized socio-cultural identities. Oppression is a form of trauma which is experienced most fully by the body due to the powerful projective processes that become located in othered bodies. How do we understand the emotional resource required to navigate oppression and the theories that reinforce these oppressive narratives?

It would seem imperative that psychotherapeutic theory and practice, if it is to challenge and counter the potential harm done to children within educational settings and beyond, embrace the reality of 'queerness' as an innate part of the development of self. It should acknowledge that this experience exists as a fully embodied reality worthy of celebration, along with other core intersectional identities that have long been neglected within institutionalized systems of prejudice. Only then, at the deepest level of our collective and conscious endeavour, will we truly begin to hold space for emergent queer identities in childhood and help to build a future where queer children have an inalienable right to exist, thrive and contribute.

CHAPTER 11

Working with trans children and young people in therapy

Kris Black and Igi Moon

At the Bowlby Centre's conference on gender and attachment in 2021, Igi Moon described the clinical landscape for trans young people and shone a spotlight on the harm inflicted on trans and gender-expansive children when adults use the child to configure the world for us. Here, Igi and Kris Black, a child and adolescent counsellor, integrative arts psychotherapist and clinical supervisor, discuss this and other pressing matters for the field.

JANE CHANCE CZYZSELSKA: Hello, Kris, Igi. I wonder if you can start by giving us a sense of what the situation is like for trans and gender non-conforming young people now.

KRIS BLACK: Worldwide, I think young trans people's lives are increasingly being made harder by transphobia. I am really aware of the degree to which – particularly under lockdown in the UK – they are being made homeless by their own families, struggling within the context of education and are now under attack by attempts to change legislation that affords rights to protest, or to be afforded proper state benefits, or even the rights to live here and seek asylum. I kind of feel it's a privilege being older, to be honest.

JC: Can you say more?

KB: Well, I grew up in the 1960s and, whereas being trans wasn't something that I was able to embrace wholly until I was much older, I don't think it's easy for young people right now. I have a pretty good picture of what's happening to young trans people given I work with them and supervise across different sectors. I'm also aware that our profession itself is not necessarily taking these truths on holistically and wholly.

JC: Can you say what you think our profession should be doing or doing more of to support young trans and gender-expansive clients?

We need practitioners who are trained to work with trans young people without judgement or prejudice

KB: Unconditional positive regard would be a start, instead of pathologizing trans young people out of ignorance – or arrogance. I think young people are struggling with a lot of life-threatening issues and they don't necessarily have resources being allocated to them in the way that they should be. We need practitioners who are trained to work with trans young people without judgement or prejudice, better training on how difference and diversity among trans and gender non-conforming youth manifests and a broader acceptance that it is not our job to judge the person sitting in front of us or to impose our own ideology onto the client just because they are adolescents or younger. Trans young people do not need judgement; they often need to be assisted with surviving the trauma that arises from being trans in a world that is trans-intolerant. Many practitioners are, quite simply, not trained adequately to work with the trauma of transphobia, or intersecting trauma affecting young trans POC, or any other intersectional issue for that matter, or to understand and respond appropriately to the myriad of issues young people may present with.

Understand the diverse ways that gender and gender non-conformity show up in young people

KB: I think it would be a major milestone if counselling and training organizations started to understand the many diverse ways that gender and gender non-conformity show up in young people, and the ways that prejudice, discrimination and the complexities of our transference show up towards marginalized young people. Some practitioners seem to me to be far too obsessed with fixing rather than listening. With genitalia rather than compassion. With confusing sexuality issues and gender issues. Many are far too influenced by histrionic news media agendas rather than listening to and learning from experienced clinicians who have been working well with and within the LGBTQIA+ community for decades.

The main resources being ignored out there are the need for specific trans-led services for young people that provide free and low-cost counselling and psychotherapy. Charities that are working successfully within the trans and LGB communities often do so within a context that is non-pathologizing – usually on a shoestring budget. That's what I understand to be the picture. Within our profession, there are certainly people who are trying to understand trans and gender non-conforming young people's issues. However, there are often therapists who see it as a phase and as age-specific, thus invisibilizing the many trans people who are over the age of 35, and some of us who are over the age of 55. So it's not just a young thing and it's not a culturally specific thing. I think across the board trans young people are finding their lives difficult and they are not necessarily being met with the empathy that they deserve when they come into counselling and therapy practices.

JC: What's causing this lack of empathy, do you think?

KB: I think it's coming from a media bombardment of anti-trans sentiment, and I think it's hitting home everywhere. Over lockdown, housing organizations that work with LGBT youth reported a huge increase in homelessness among young people who were not able to turn to their families of origin for support. That's where I'd like to start. Thinking about how resource-poor trans youth are – the basics: shelter, food, access to education, access to good mental health support, access to safety and access to work, creativity, survival, community and justice.

IGI MOON: I actually agree. I think at one level it seems quite depressing and we know that at a structural level there is a massive push going on from some within the government, and certain people in all the political parties, who detest anything to do with trans. I have been told that the gender clinics have been advised to stand away from Stonewall.

JC: I didn't realize that! What are the implications for therapists working with trans kids as a result?

IM: The message that gives, if you're a young person and you want to align yourself with Stonewall's work in education, is that Stonewall isn't to be trusted or worth the money. It's disgusting rhetoric that's being used to make sure that people stand away from Stonewall. Organizations that used to want to be seen as champions, like Ofcom (McManus, 2021), have done it – it's not good for organizations to do that because that message filters down to the academies and to schools and to young people that any support for LGBT is unacceptable in some way.

KB: And it also filters down to families and ordinary individuals on the street, like being trans is somehow to be suspect.

IM: Transphobia is so potent now and the words being used to attack trans people I think leave a lot of young people feeling incredibly insecure and I don't think our profession really knows what to do – I'll come to that in a minute – but we've got, as adults, to start firing back at some point. The thing is, when you do try to do that, you are aware that some organizations are going to come at you and it's actually quite monstrous after a while. I can't speak for anybody else, but I am now 60, and having to fight to establish equality has been going on since I was 20 at least. That was when I chose to get involved in fighting against the politics of hate because that is what we are faced with really, a politics of 'we hate your life'.

KB: Absolutely.

IM: So at one level I will do anything I possibly can to protect young people and to let them have a life that they need to lead in order to be free.

JC: What does that look like in your consulting room?

IM: I recently heard about someone's 14-year-old AFAB client who has met an AMAB other young person who is 13 and they see themselves as a little couple but the person who was AFAB is now saying, 'I think we both need to explore our gender and our sexuality because I feel that, although I am attracted to you, I'm also attracted to girls and I like to think I'm more non-binary.' And the person who was AMAB has also said, 'I'm going to look into what that means and say for now I'm non-binary.' Now these are just kids, and I don't know what they know about being non-binary, but the fact is one is 13 and one is 14 and it is part of their language from somewhere.

Young people have access to language and meanings about gender that weren't in place a few years ago

IM: So, although all those gender-critical people and those who want two genders, one male and one female, and who believe everything is based on biological sex (which, let's face it, is just another story about bodies) can try and trample and kill us off, the fact is that we can't destroy the young people who want to live their life. And what that might mean in 2022 is that these young people have access to language and to meanings that were not in place just a few years ago and it doesn't matter what the people in government do, you're not going to, unless you actually decide to destroy children – which to some degree part of what they're doing is about that – you're not going to be able to stop this.

KB: Why would you want to stop young people or anyone from exploring their gender anyway? Why would you want to stop young people from trying to come to an understanding about themselves?

JC: Yes, it's very hurtful to the many cis and trans and gender-expansive practitioners that this idea is being touted by some therapists and of course non-therapists too. What do you suggest we need or need to do as trans-affirming practitioners to challenge this, not only for our trans clients but also for our own support?

KB: Those of us who are privileged enough to be out LGBTQIA+ professionals need to speak up. There are far too many ordinary activists suffering from burn out because we are silent, because we do not put our heads above the parapet in training or even in forums where other therapists are mistakenly confusing the issues and defining our issues for us. Speaking up may seem the most obvious place to start but there is often too much silence about the ways that prejudice shows up, too much mythology that could be challenged but isn't. If we allow any of our siblings under the LGBTQIA+ umbrella to be bullied, pathologized or marginalized then we all suffer. Our silence will not protect us, to quote Audre Lorde (2017).

If our profession(s) were more accepting, less LGBTQIA+ phobic and more informed in a truly inclusive manner, perhaps it would mean that we would not be so afraid to challenge the cis heteronormativity. If our society was less discriminatory, perhaps that would filter down from the macro to the institutions. There is a lot of fear and ignorance, I think, arising from distorted narratives passed on by religious values which are pushed onto trans people and parroted by some within LGB communities – perhaps in the hope that they escape the violence of scapegoating. So, our trans-inclusive way of being, thinking, loving and living has somehow been twisted against us, despite being queer or non-cis-heteronormative people, and we are seen as the threat to lesbian, gay and bisexual people!

JC: Can you explain who is saying this and the impact it can have on us as practitioners and also on your trans and gender-expansive clients?

KB: The Christian right, the far right, the trans-excluding organizations that want to believe these ideologies, certain kinds of feminists, celebrities on social media, the mainstream media – they all seem to have joined the anti-trans 'debate'. Perhaps people with a lot of unprocessed unconscious bias are seeking to jump on the bandwagon of 'othering' trans and gender non-conforming people. They're attacking trans-ness and, by extension, queerness and non-conformity, using our own words and our own inclusive ideologies against us. I feel we need to resist this at all costs. It's as though their methodology for shaking up the world is to attack Stonewall and queer and trans individuals!

JC: What do you suppose might be driving this onslaught?

KB: While there is a swing away from the old establishment ways of thinking, and an embracing of the need for a new paradigm, a less harm-focused capitalist modality is being embraced across the global north by young people who have woken up to climate change, racial injustice, indigenous land rights and the ideology that there are enough resources on the planet but we are not using them wisely or fairly. As a result, there is a perceived threat to the capitalist neoliberal, socio-economic and hetero-patriarchal empire, and the 'old guard' are feeling threatened. There has been an exponential rise in others clinging to the certainty of 'traditional' values and ideals and the global pandemic has shaken up the idea that we as human beings are in control. So there is also something very unsavoury that has risen out of the collective unconscious of the global north – and the weakest and least established of the marginalized minority groups in society are being made scapegoats.

We all know that hating anyone for the colour of their skin, their sexuality or their gender is archaic nonsense and, as people who have worked within anti-hate groups say – me since I was 16, maybe 14 even, if you include being part of radical movements – 'No, you don't bring hate to our doors.' Hating trans people feels like a concerted effort to twist queerness into hate, and that is something that shocks me to the bone. This anti-trans ideology is trying to chop off the head as it were, so we no longer exist.

IM: Yes, that's right.

KB: Trying every angle to attack.

IM: I think, though, it's part of a strategy to remove social justice, worldwide. I do think there's a desire amongst many people witnessing the 'end' of a period of history since post-war Britain who want to restore something imperialistic about Britain. And part of that is making sure that the young people coming through are aware that they are male or female and that white power is actually how they need to understand the world. It's colonialist horror really.

I was reading something from Disabled People Against Cuts (DPAC) today; you know, disability rights, and how they attack all these very vulnerable groups and all of us are worn out. I'm fighting for disability rights, trans rights and queer rights, and I'm trying to teach a load of stuff about what's happening in terms of colonialism and imperialism and I'm aware that the support is not always there in teaching or in the universities because they are part of the same structure. Thankfully, I have been given space to teach around non-binary and trans and it's really wonderful. Thankfully, we're not yet at a point in the UK where the teaching manuals and the books that you can use are isolated like they are in the US. So at least at the moment, while I teach a course on non-binary, I can decide what the students will read, what I think they need to address and what ideas they can generate, and we can use all of that. However, I'm aware that it's a tough ask and this is where our profession falls down – it's not done the work.

JC: What work does our profession need to do, do you think, so that young trans and gender-expansive clients can be supported by therapists?

IM: Training and curriculum development and also social support for placements to understand how to be more expansive. Training of therapists, GPs, psychologists, psychiatrists, social workers, nurses and health professionals across the board needs to be expansive and intersectional. For 20 years, those of us from marginalized groups have recognized the need for a social justice agenda and have been saying, 'You need to be looking at intersectionality.' Some of our colleagues are out there doing research that only applies to the groups they are doing the research with. For example, plenty of students do research dissertations but usually spend no time at all thinking about demographics – as though it's just a nuisance factor. In reality, their research should *only* look at demographics or plainly say that the research can only apply to white, cisgender, able-bodied, middle-aged women, for example. The curriculum needs to reflect the social world – that's why there is such a reaction from 'the entitled' or those who think they should have a reflection of themselves alone.

JC: What do you think therapists should be learning?

IM: The learning should actually be in school but if it's not in school, when you get to a degree or a certificate, all of this should be included in the curriculum. Our profession (Moon, 2011) is riddled with structural inequalities such as racism, sexism, ableism and classism. How on earth we think we understand 'subjectivity' and 'self' when it is completely dislocated from 'the other', I will never know. Some students at doctoral level will say, 'I've never thought about being white, I've never thought about what it might mean to be a woman, a cisgender woman,' and I think, 'How can that form of subjectivity be completely off the map?'

Going beyond the traditional pedagogy around psychotherapy and counselling

KB: Because the traditional pedagogy around psychotherapy, counselling and psychology is white, middle-class, cisgender, heterosexual and heteronormative. That's the basis for it all, despite being aware of critical race and gender theories, and inclusivity. But inclusivity remains a marginalized ideology because it is considered to be 'too difficult' by many therapy training institutions to be inclusive.

IM: Yeah, I agree.

KB: So, somehow there's a danger of alienating white, middle-class professionals-to-be who are monied and have economic status and power. When I teach as a marginalized minority, I go into the organizations that will have me there, who want to learn about this stuff – I'm not part of the structures that teach. I'm brought in from the outside to teach something that feels fundamentally dangerous to the status quo because somehow you can't teach whiteness, you can only be white. You can be heterosexual but you can't teach people about marginalized sexual minorities because if you say you do that in the curriculum from the outset, you might not get students wanting to be therapists and counsellors. So this comes from the top of our profession and the very structures and institutions that say, 'But you can't teach that because that's going to shake things up.' And I say, 'Let's shake it up because it's about time!'

IM: I would agree.

KB: And that's us as queer and trans elders saying that. We need to be listened to.

IM: I think young people get used in this. They are a vehicle for absolute fear and anxiety, almost detestability of the direction, the orientation, a young person may choose in relation to sex, sexuality or gender. And then members of our profession add to their injury by saying these young people are confused, need more time to decide who they are or need to have time to explore their trauma that made them gay or trans, when in reality this simply is not the case. Young people who are questioning, or know they do not identify with the dominant gender norms in their society, have as much right as any cisgender, straight kid to not have that decision questioned by anyone, least of all a therapist.

We use younger bodies and we impose meanings onto those bodies

IM: So, they dominate discourse and when they sense their dominance is flowing away from them, they start making all sorts of demands of us and how we trans people need this and that according to them and their cis structures of thinking. The writer Casteneda (2002) talks about the way that we use bodies, younger bodies, bodies of what we might refer to as children, and we impose meanings onto those bodies. Casteneda (2002) refers to Darwin as referring to bodies of the savage as though that was one way to describe those who haven't yet met the European ideal of how to be in the world. What I mean is … I was listening to my mum recently; she was working in a mill at 13 years old. It was 1942, and at that time it was fully expected that the industrial heart and the money of this country would come from the working class. It came from a lot of the people in the north – my dad was on the railways at 14, at the same time mum was in the mill – and there was no discussion of them being children, you were not a child. In fact, we were looking in an old newspaper and there was a picture of a little boy in a mill and mum said straight away, 'I know exactly which part of the mill he's working in. He's eight years old and he's working in the part where the air is so bad it would likely give him tuberculosis.'

There were no rights for children then, and what I'm sort of saying is that we need to do here what they've tried to do in Scotland, which is to bring into domestic law the rights of the child, as ratified by the 90-odd nations at the United Nations Convention for the Rights of the Child, so that young people can be safe in exploring who they wish to be. I think that England and the whole of the UK and the world need to do the same. Then we can begin to unpack what it is that we are trying to do to these bodies that we refer to as children but that we insist are brought up, are manufactured, are delivered to society in a certain way. And we can go back to that conversation of those two young people earlier – you can't stop conversations; I mean you can do what you like – censorship; not letting them see things; refusing to allow them to wear certain clothes – but eventually 'change' and the future will push through. I really believe that, but we healthcare professionals and all of us involved in teaching and training do need to do a lot more than we're doing. We need to understand that we do not understand!

Biological essentialism is a construction

IM: For example, we need sex education – we need to realize that biological essentialism is a construction and that models of sex are the product of knowledge, debate and discussion, rather than certain people owning knowledge about the way sex is produced. The one-sex model followed by the two-sex model and now we have a pluralistic model – there are *not* just two sexes or two sexualities or two genders. We are not living in a therapeutic Noah's Ark where it's all two by two. Move on, get real, learn from other disciplines like sociology, anthropology, philosophy, English literature, African studies, queer studies, etc. or shut up.

We also need to review the way therapeutic organizations and institutes formalize their committees. For example, if those who are on the board of trustees, or the chairs of committees, use their power to negate change and spend time discussing why change takes time and how they need to think of their members, it tells me that either their committee is homophobic, transphobic, sexist, racist, etc. – as usually the way to stall change is to stall social justice – or their members are very badly trained. So that while they may spend hours talking about the 'self' and subjectivity, they fail to see that subjectivity is socially formed. As a non-binary person, my sense of self and who I am in the world is *not* the same as a cis person. Basically, we need a major paradigm shift to happen.

JC: Can you explain what that is?

IM: Quite often, transgender healthcare is underpinned by certain standards issued via organizations such as the World Professional Association for Transgender Healthcare. These are made up of professionals from a wide range of disciplines involved with trans healthcare, such as surgery, endocrinology, psychiatry, psychology, medicine, etc. It is interesting how some of these recommendations make their way into clinics and others do not. For example, in Argentina self-identification as trans is allowed whereas by comparison here in the UK trans people are assessed by predominantly cisgender people who have received no input about gender in their training, using an assessment tool they have basically put together themselves. It's not just incompetent, it's abhorrent. And dangerous. You know, at one level I just can't engage with this binary discourse. It's so maddeningly useless and I feel like we're in a Brexit conversation: stay or leave. Dreadful binaries. I think that young people will build a better future and they need our support.

JC: I agree – I think young people will build a better future. I read Juno Roche's *Gender Explorers* recently. It was great to read about the young people who are doing gender on their own terms that the rest of the adult world will have to come round to. They were at a Mermaids charity event for trans and gender-expansive young people and their descriptions of how they made gender work for them were wonderful. Can you say more about what issues your young trans clients bring to you?

KB: Most of my clients are QTBPOC so: racism, hormones, disability, trauma, homelessness, terror of being attacked on the street, in their education establishments, coming out, staying in, religion. The whole gamut of being trans in a world that is not trans-friendly, in a world that is not intersectionally aware.

IM: Survival, terror. 'Shall I kill myself?' And another one – and this to me is another very big worry. Sometimes the first port of call for a certain population of parents with a child who comes out as non-binary or trans and/or trans non-binary or trans binary is a private psychologist who is simply not equipped to deal with gender identity issues, and consequently falls back on their expertise, thus diagnosing ADHD or autism spectrum disorder. Inadvertently, this course of action and diagnosis allows the parents to effectively render the young person unable to decide about their gender, and gives them the complete right to say, 'you're not really trans, you're not really non-binary, you've got autism spectrum disorder and you're ADHD.'

I think we need to be a little bit mindful that we're living in a right-wing era when diagnoses are becoming quite prominent in executing people's lived experience of gender and neuropsychology – which I think flows through the rhetoric of the right wing; so, it's suddenly all neuro this and neuro that. I wasn't trained in the understanding of the brain; I was trained to talk about feelings and how people experience the world. But if we're going to start talking about brains and autism, these psychologists need to have incorporated in their training not only an intensive training about neuropsychology but also the widest spectrum of gender and race and ethnicity. You can't do an assessment if you haven't understood the world you're in. In effect, we are heading back to labelling theory of the 1970s in our profession, where some clinicians are willing to label clients without reflecting on the impact.

KB: Exactly, and it's interesting what you say. I see it as a class divide issue because most of my clients aren't going to psychologists: their families can't afford them. What's sitting on their parents' shoulders might be huge worry about their child. They are not taking their child to be diagnosed because they don't have those types of resources. They might be ostracizing their kids because of their fears or their worries or they might be doing it because of prejudice. So there's a binary economically and there may be a binary of, 'Let's see what we can do to sort this out for the child and then find that resource.' If it's a psychology resource, it's about diagnosis, it's about treatment and 'how can we fix this?'

Young people trying to articulate a different gender or sexuality might have to stay on the downlow for a long time

KB: The other end of the spectrum for the parent(s) might be, 'I'm not having any of that and I don't know what to do with that.' The young people might not be able to articulate that because they know full well that articulating gender or sexuality in a family that has not got the means to help them means they might stay on the downlow for a long time. They might find themselves more able to articulate their gender or sexuality when they are older or when they are taken to a priest to be told they need to pray that away. They might be articulating that and find themselves being taken to a counsellor who says, 'I don't know what this is.' Or they might be talking about self-harm and suicide because they feel so desperately isolated and lonely, and they might be taken to a CAMHS where they are further pathologized. Or they might be lucky and be part of the minority who have supportive parents. Or the GP might say, 'Go to the Tavistock.' There are so many ways the young person might be responded to by GPs, parents and school counsellors. If you're lucky, it's positive, and if you're not, then it's pathology or, 'Do you know what? You're an adolescent and I'm not having this in my home. Get out and find your way.' So, there are lots of different ways that young people are articulating gender and getting a response. What our profession does with it often, it would appear, is to try and pathologize it. But as you say, Igi, unless someone has themselves understood what an appropriate empathic response to this is, they're about as good as a chocolate teapot.

IM: I have to say, I find myself really shocked and I don't know why, having been in the profession for as long as I have. For example, we have been told clearly by certain organizations who do not agree that transgender is an acceptable identity that they will try to make the government weaponize young people in order to stop the conversion therapy ban protecting young people accessing treatment for gender and being able to receive puberty blockers. So, the idea that you've looked at the world and you've decided that a little group of young people who are vulnerable and without a voice are going to be targeted, with all your might and power, and that some of our fellow practitioners agree with these obtuse statements from these organizations and people who respond with, 'Well, we must protect the children' and 'The children must have time to explore.' In the meantime, knowing that there are plenty of therapists who do work with young people and do know what they are doing means that those therapists who are actively blocking the development of young people are responsible for the death of something. Whether it's an idea a young person wants to share or quite literally young people who can no longer face life – and it is something that our profession needs to wake up to.

KB: Absolutely.

Therapists have an ethical duty to look at our thinking and how we frame our ideas

IM: We have an ethical duty to look at our thinking and the way that we frame our ideas and the way that we decide in our profession who it is that we're going to help. The rhetoric that has been coming our way from some people within our profession is unethical and immoral and really is about them not wanting to explore within themselves. They colonise trans lives and they are willing to let trans people die in order that they can survive and their ideas that are damaging our society can continue.

We are complicit if we deny that trans people actually exist

KB: We are complicit if we deny that trans people actually exist. We can also be in denial, arising out of ignorance, about the reality of transphobia that transphobia often manifests as actual violence and harassment overtly – verbal, physical, street, interpersonal, familial, religious, and institutional violence. One only has to look at Twitter or the mainstream press to see manifestations of violence in the form of death threats, threats of violence that are sickening to behold. As therapists we need to really get our heads around how transphobia is perpetrated covertly, as micro- and macro-aggressions towards trans people, and encounter our own prejudices as part of the work with vulnerable youth. Saying to a young person, "I will not use your pronouns or recognise your gender identity" in the therapy room is a manifestation of violence from the therapist. This is also felt by the client as denial of their identity and self and this also must stop. Unconscious bias needs to be explored within supervision. Failing to honour the client's trans identity by constantly misgendering them in the privacy of supervision is a manifestation of the therapist's denial that transness exists and therefore that the client's identity exists. Supervisors need to get their heads around challenging this form of obliteration of the client's reality.

IM: Yeah, I agree.

KB: State and profession-sanctioned forms of violence.

IM: That is exactly it, Kris. I've come across some in our field suggest that the trans young people's charity Mermaids are 'shrieking about suicide' as though it's to be laughed at. It's barbaric.

KB: It is barbaric.

IM: And that's what I meant about the Brexit mentality and the rise of the right wing, but there's no opposition in place and that's what's more debilitating. I haven't heard anything from the opposition party about Stonewall. They don't dare stand up and say anything.

KB: No, because they agree! It's not even unconscious; there is a conscious complicity with what is happening around the proposed eradication of gender non-conformity of our youth. And therapists must start to recognize their complicity and do something about it.

JC: What else do you want to say to therapists working with trans kids?

KB: As my grandmother would say, 'Fix up!'

IM: And unless you know what you're doing, don't work with them because if a practitioner believes trans is embedded in trauma and is saying to a trans or gender-expansive child, 'You need to explore your trauma,' they need to go and explore their own bloody trauma!

KB: And their violence.

IM: Practitioners who don't believe that young people can be transgender say it's all down to trauma, that trans doesn't exist and it's only cisgender – and cisgender in the way that's understood in the UK, not as in the rest of the world where local knowledges may shape cisgenderism in different ways. For example, we know that gender in the UK has been shaped according to need, so that post-war need was for women to stay at home and men to be the 'breadwinners'. This wasn't about what men and women wanted so much as what the country needed and, therefore, there was emphasis on social role and gender role, as we can see in magazines produced throughout the 1960s and 1970s. But it was only aimed at the UK, obviously. I think what needs to happen – and we say this quite openly – some of these training courses need to incorporate not just social justice but …

KB: … an intersectional lens and to really understand that it's not about trying to create a hierarchy among different groups that are marginalized and oppressed or set us against each other. Rather, it's about what power, privilege and difference is about. I know that those of us who continue to say this continue to be ostracized by people in our profession.

JC: How has that impacted you, Kris?

KB: I don't think we have the space here to go into the ways that intersectional discrimination has manifested itself in my professional life, but I can say they need to get their act together. This is not about tokenism; it's not about having token trans people in training organizations. It's about really looking at the profession as a whole and what on earth we have been doing for the past 20 years to interrogate what we are teaching therapists about the whole gamut of discrimination and difference, power and privilege. And what are we teaching therapy students to understand about their role in relationships as human beings, our role as therapists in relation to other human beings, whether it's in private or state practice or the groups or charities we're running and setting up? We need to interrogate what we're taught in the first place because whole swathes of psychoanalysis, psychotherapy and psychology have not begun to embrace difference regarding class, race and gender. We haven't touched the tip of the iceberg in understanding ourselves as human beings; we don't understand minoritized people. The whole thing needs shaking up from the bottom to the top. There isn't a book big enough to teach people about how to respect people because there is so much shut down and repressed when we start to talk about it. We're in the twenty-first century, not the Victorian era; not every human being has the same experience – that would be a start.

If there are anxieties and fears about gender, sex or sexuality, explore what they mean for you

IM: If there are anxieties and fears about gender, sex or sexuality, then explore what they mean for you. If a client says they are non-binary or trans, sit with that instead of reacting negatively. We have entered a phase which is reactive and so sitting with things and really seeing what is going on is needed. So, for example, the thinking about reproductive rights has been enshrined in a binary configuration, but when you look at it in a different way, through a trans lens, you realize it can be far greater. Our understanding of a person's body and what it might mean for legislation and parenting, or even understanding one's own body, is expanded. And my sense is that, for some who are thinking or behaving in a way that is anti-trans, their fear is about this idea of 'transing' the world.

Transing the world

JC: What do you think is meant by that – transing the world?

IM: Transing means expanding our world view to include, incorporate, co-operate, negotiate and celebrate how people want to live with others and otherness in the world. It moves beyond boundaries and pushes gender rules and roles by asking us to reconsider what we have taken for granted when we think about 'the body', what we mean by 'male' or 'female' and 'masculine' or 'feminine'. Historically, I do think that some things are coming to an end and the world is changing, and with it are different ideas about bodies, psyches and feelings and the way we interact. It's going to be tough to get through, but at the other side of it, there will be a better world waiting. In between times, a lot of people are caught up in it.

KB: And young people specifically.

IM: Young people are the creative future subjectivity of the world and see the world in a very different way: they don't want the killing and murdering of people. You see that with certain people who want to talk of the impact of Islamophobia. There are concepts that make you rethink the world you live in, and they shift your thinking about a people, about a people that might be Palestinian, or Afghan; they shift your thinking and that's what those who feel they own this world and have the right to stop gender, sex and sexuality from changing seem to want to prevent. But shifting ideas is part of history-making.

Thinking is a lot of fun

IM: Many of those in the therapeutic professions and beyond who want to prevent change are terrified, I think. And our profession unfortunately also doesn't want to think about future change, whereas I think thinking is a lot of fun. Let's change the world! I think people are very frightened of that because I think with all due respect a lot of the people in our profession are getting older, they don't want things to change and are sort of thinking, 'if you don't mind, keep quiet about being non-binary because I don't want to have to change my ideas and I don't want to feel out of place.' Can you imagine all these young people coming in with all their ideas about intersectionality nailing that bunch and going, 'Go away! Your ideas are out of date!'?

KB: Yes, they are and it's not necessarily younger people that are making the change. There are people in the psychotherapy and counselling profession in their thirties and they are coming in from university education and saying, 'We already know this stuff. Why don't you? Why are you not fixing up? Why are you sitting there with these ideologies suggesting you don't have to look at this?' The institutions are coming up against new younger therapists saying, 'You're not fit for purpose! You cannot train us because you haven't even thought of this stuff.' Sometimes the trainee is the person punished for having these ideas and seen as being the danger, instead of the institution, and some institutions are saying, 'We want to change but we want to stay the same at the same time.' And they ask us to give this intersectionality stuff for free!

IM: I would agree with you there. What we need is people who want to change the way that things are being done and some of these young people are offering a completely different way of how to do it. But along the way there will be a slaughter of young people and older people and that's what necropolitics is about.

Necropolitics

JC: Can you explain necropolitics?

IM: It comes from Achille Mbembe (2019), who says the people that are fodder, we can be rid of them: the disabled, the people of colour, trans and non-binary people, it doesn't matter; they are part of the payoff for those who legitimize their power using the different forms of capital such as economic and social, but also what I refer to as 'psy capital.' The psy professions decide the worthiness of people depending upon what they can manage emotionally and how their mental health is managed within certain contexts. 'Psy capital' is a powerful and emerging force that we need to recognize as having the same power as other forms of capital. I am writing about this at present based on research findings. But eventually I do believe people, like those 13- and 14-year-old young people, talking about going off to explore gender is where we're headed. Because non-binary is about bringing something together that has relied very much on a binary in terms of language and feeling, and I think a lot of therapists find it quite frightening. They are people in the world who are frightened and need therapy to focus on their anxiety and fear of the changes coming about.

KB: And I think that all therapists need to admit we are people and not just professionals, that we are also subject to all of the conditioning that has fallen on everyone's shoulders. None of us are above it. I think there is a lot of work to be done by individuals in the institutions before you can work with trans young people. You have to have explored your own corners to do that without judgement. I don't have an agenda when I work with young people; they bring to me what their agenda is.

IM: Yeah.

KB: That's what we are supposed to be doing as therapists. We are supposed not to be deciding for the human beings in front of us. We are supposed to be following the basics of unconditional positive regard. Until we can stick to that for trans young people, we're stuffed. It's no good coming with a 'fix-it' denial or a 'debate' as a way of defending against looking at their own fears about gender and projecting that on to young clients.

IM: The question is, are they therapists? To my mind, that is not therapy.

KB: Not validating the human being that is in front of you as a starting point is already bringing in prejudices. For some young trans clients, they may be the first trans person that the therapist has met. Some of us might know what that feels like from our own youth, being the only BPOC queer person that a therapist has met, and if you're unlucky, you have to deal with the weight of that prejudice. I think it's a good question you ask, Igi. Are you doing therapy then? Are you getting the right kind of supervision and doing the right kind of personal work?

CHAPTER 12

Film summary: *A Normal Girl*

Valentino Vecchietti

Intersex experience is frequently excluded or absent from even those therapist trainings and books which do cover LGBTQ+ matters. Therefore, it was vital to include it in this collection, foregrounding the voices of intersex people themselves. We do this in two forms here.

First, writer and intersex equality campaigner Valentino Vecchietti writes an overview of the short documentary film *A Normal Girl*. Through a close analysis of gesture and expression, Valentino emphasizes that, in addition to research, therapists and psychologists must engage with intersex culture in order to gain key insights into the intersex experience.

Then we present a piece of research from the editor which includes intersex participants reflecting on their experiences of therapy, and what they would like therapists to know and do in terms of good practice. These pieces, amended and updated for inclusion in this book, both first appeared in a special issue of the British Psychological Society's *Psychologies of Sexualities Review* about intersex subjectivities (2021) and we would refer readers to this for more detail.

Intersex is an umbrella term to describe the naturally occurring physical variations in sex characteristics (VSC) that we can be born with. We comprise 1.7 per cent of the population – in the UK, that is over 1.1 million, and over 130 million worldwide. Although we gain knowledge through research and data, we connect through cultural representation. The following review aim is to convey the importance of engaging with intersex culture to extend knowledge of intersex lives for psychologists and therapists.

A Normal Girl (Bernier-Clarke *et al.*, 2019) is an American short documentary film by Aubree Bernier-Clarke. The film's focus is the life and activism of 34-year-old Pidgeon Pagonis (they/them). It highlights the issue of consent, by showing the consequences of asking parents to make decisions about the cosmetic appearance of their child's genitals, as well as other medical interventions, to which the intersex infant or child is too young to consent. For this short review, I will focus on the elements in the film that depict the parent/child relationship in the context of consent and medical practice.

In the opening scene, Pidgeon holds up a colourful artistic sign which says, 'Intersex is Beautiful.' The message is a joyful one. We see clips from their YouTube videos where they tell us that they were born with an intersex variation called androgen insensitivity syndrome (AIS), and that their body is non-binary. Later, the film switches to interview. In the intimacy of their home setting, we hear Pidgeon relaying their experiences of medical interventions as listed in their medical records:

> ... starting at six months of my life there was the removal of my testes; there was the reduction and removal of my clitoris because it was 'too big'; and there was female hormones pumped into me starting around aged ten; there was the vaginoplasty when I was eleven so that I could have 'normal sex with my husband'.

This film captures many contrasting moments; as in this case, when the act of speaking about othering, pathologizing, medical acts is in itself othering and pathologizing. This clear dislocation of emotion is somehow reset by Bernier-Clarke showing Pidgeon speak from the intimacy of home.

We cut to intersex activist Lynnell Stephani Long (she/they), who asks us, 'How can anything be normal after you cut off their clitoris?' The feeling when watching this film is visceral. Lynnell Stephani Long, who identifies as female, describes the simplistic thinking behind surgeons' decisions when they surgically assigned gender identities to both Long and Pidgeon:

> When I was born, they said, 'You have a micropenis, and we can work with that.' When Pidgeon was born, they were born with a vaginal canal, so they said, 'We can work with that.' So, for both of

us they tried to make one into a boy and one into a girl.

These cosmetic genital surgeries continue to be performed today on intersex infants and children in the UK, as well as globally. In all cases, when intersex surgery is performed below the age of consent, parental or guardian consent must be obtained.

The following scene makes explicit the importance of gaining knowledge through seeing gesture, expression and body language. It also highlights the relevance for therapists seeking to work with intersex clients and their families, of creating understanding, compassion and connection through engagement with cultural materials. It is one of the reasons I recommend that therapists and psychologists watch this film. Pidgeon remembers a specific surgery:

> Around the age of 11, I had a surgery, and they said it was going to be about my bladder and urethra; to fix those two things … I knew by feeling myself, by touching myself after the surgery that they had done a lot more than they told me they were going to do.

We meet Pidgeon's mother, Laurie Garcia (she/her), as she opens the door of her home and welcomes Pidgeon inside. Pidgeon and their mum are in the kitchen. Pidgeon is at the stove, cooking utensil in hand, stirring the contents of a tall cooking pot. Their mother is standing close by. This could be a typical family scene of intimacy and comfort. We are in close quarters; the light is broken by shadow.

Throughout the scene, Pidgeon's face is downcast, staring into the pot, eyes never leaving the contents, which we never see. We just hear the heat making it hiss and the sound of the utensil as Pidgeon stirs. We see the expression on Pidgeon's mum's face throughout their conversation as moments of pain register across her features. Pidgeon is asking their mum about what they remember of the surgery they recounted earlier.

Mum: 'I just remember crying – I was crying. I never wanted you to see me cry because I didn't want you to be more afraid.' The mother looks away, 'But I'll never forget they held you up. They were walking with you. You were crying.' Mum continues, 'It was so hard for me.' As she says this, her hand goes to her upper chest, double patting her skin in an emphatic gesture. Pidgeon, still looking down at the contents of the pot, utensil in hand, making small, repetitive, stabbing gestures at the ingredients.

Mum: '... and I wanted to hold you, and talk to you, and they said, "No, we'll hold her, and walk her up to the ... "' As she says this, her hand goes to her mouth, and she pauses – "'... up to the operating room.'"

The scene between Pidgeon and their mother creates space to consider the long-term impact of 'parental consent'. It makes explicit the vulnerability of both the parent and the child in the context of medical settings. This type of cultural evidence gives voice to the wider experience, and the impact of current medical practice beyond childhood. It is very rare to see or hear this kind of private and intimate conversation, and it is hugely relevant.

We cut to a room where Pidgeon's mum is being interviewed. Mum talking to camera:

> The doctors explained they were going to do a 'cosmetic' – because she [Pidgeon] would grow up with a complex, or whatever, because it would look funny down there. And I remember my husband at the time asking one last time, 'It's not going to interfere or do anything with the nerves?' And you know, [they] said, 'No, no.'

As she says this, we are shown a photo of Pidgeon's dad holding them as a much younger child, both smiling into the camera. Throughout this scene, we can hear the vulnerability and pain in Pidgeon's mum's voice and see it in her facial expressions.

Cut to a clip from Pidgeon's YouTube channel where Pidgeon says, 'It's hard to trust your parents, and even though I love them, and even though I see how they were caught up in the systematic erasure of intersex people, it's hard to trust them. And when you can't trust your parents, it's really hard to trust anybody else.' Cut to Pidgeon's mum: 'It's hard now knowing that I made this choice for my daughter, and it was the worst choice possible ... and now Pidgeon has to live with the choice I made. You can't change it.'

Our stories need to be shared with therapists, so that when we come to seek therapeutic support it is with a therapist who has done the research and understands us as cultural beings in society. We need widespread understanding that the current emergency which we face is not the birth of an intersex child; the emergency is the urgent need to provide doctors, surgeons and clinicians with mandatory and extensive training in diversity, equality and human rights in relation to bodily autonomy and intersex children.

In one of the final scenes of the film, we meet Orie and their mum. Orie is smiling into the camera and gesturing energetically with both hands to emphasize each word, 'Intersex is awesome!' Text on screen reads, 'Orie Turner, intersex activist, they/them'. As Orie speaks, their face is smiling, relaxed and confident, 'My name is Orie. I am ten years old, and my pronouns are they/them.' They sit side-by-side on a sofa with their mum, who looks on smiling as Orie continues, 'I met Pidgeon for the first time at Gender Odyssey two years ago. I thought Pidge was [whispers to emphasize] super cool.'

Orie's mum, Christina Turner (she/her), says, 'Pidgeon was the first time that Orie met another intersex person at a Gender Odyssey conference.' She turns to Orie and says, 'And that was actually when you learned about the surgeries and stuff.' Orie looks down, 'Uh-huh.' Orie turns to look at their mum as she continues talking:

We had a doctor that was really inappropriate. They tried to pressure my husband and I and said that our child could hate us for not doing surgery. I came in with a stack of research, and I basically was like, 'We want to get hormone levels checked, we want to know all this stuff, and what's going on, but there is no way we are going to do any surgery that is cosmetic or aesthetic.'

Orie is watching their mother, and smiles as she says this last bit. Orie's expression is relaxed; they appear safe and comfortable. Mum continues:

And they definitely recommended the typical: clitoridectomy, and 'gonads could lead to cancer', and of course I retorted back with the statistics that I had found. I was really lucky that we are millennial parents because I was able to go in there with my own research, and a lot of knowledge so that I knew what I was dealing with, and they couldn't manipulate me that way.

As their mother finishes talking, Orie, who has been watching their mother throughout, calmly turns to the camera; they look happy and relaxed.

It's sad to hear this parent talking about 'luck' in the context of being able to identify the need for bodily autonomy for their child. We can't expect every parent or guardian to be able to do the research necessary to make the kind of informed choices that Orie's mum was able to make. I would have liked to see a parent talking about the brilliant psychosocial support they were able to access. Therapists and psychologists could have a significant role to play in supporting intersex children and adults, their parents/guardians and families, but there simply is not enough psychosocial support available. And we need to change this. In the film's final shot, we see Pidgeon, via YouTube, smiling at us, with this simple parting imperative, 'Remember: intersex stories; not surgeries.'

CHAPTER 13

The truth that's denied: psychotherapy with LGBTIQ+ clients who identify as intersex

Jane Chance Czyzselska

This study is a qualitative investigation into the therapeutic experiences of clients who identify as both LGBTQ+ and intersex. I explain the terminology, introduce how intersex has been understood and how individuals in this group have been treated in the past, before considering how it has been dealt with – and often ignored – by the psychotherapeutic profession. I then reflect on reflexivity in relation to this study, and move on to the participants' experiences and views of therapy and what they think therapists need to know when working with this client group. There is scant psychotherapeutic literature about, and limited awareness of, the lived experiences of intersex people among the UK's psychotherapy and counselling institutions and practitioners. Clients with intersex variations are frequently conflated with transgender, LGB or gender non-conforming clients and not referred to specifically otherwise. Literature in this field parallels the medical protocols themselves which erase and obfuscate intersex variations, indicating a strong need for research on the experiences of clients with intersex variations.

Terminology

'Intersex' is an umbrella term that relates to naturally occuring variations in sex characteristics (VSC). It is used to refer to genitals, hormones, gonads and/or chromosome patterns that don't fit typical binary definitions of male or female. It is distinct from a person's sexual orientation or gender identity. A person who has an intersex variation may be straight, gay, lesbian, bisexual, asexual or any other sexuality, and may identify as female, male, both, intersex or neither. Roen (2015) notes that, since many individuals who are born with non-normative yet naturally occuring sex traits will not consider themselves as intersex, some prefer to use a diagnostic term to refer to their particular variation and some do not have any terminology to describe their sex development. It is also important to note that some members of this client group choose to use the term 'intersex', and some have various thoughts and feelings about how they relate to being included in the literature. Lev (2006) and others use the terms 'dsd' and 'diverse sex development', using lower case letters to signal a critical distance from the upper-case acronym DSD as used by some clinicians in reference to the pathologizing term 'disorder of sex development'.

Costello (2009) states, 'I am not defective. I am not disordered. I am an intersexed person. And if both doctors and people who speak in my name recoil in horror when I say that I don't identify as a man or as a woman, too bad for them.'

To identify as a diagnostic term could be considered collusion with the still current medical model reliant on the treatment practices as advocated by 1950s psychologist Dr John Money (Karkazis, 2008). Moreover, all these classifications are considered deeply problematic because of how they stigmatize and pathologize those with the variations (Roen, 2015). Roen (2015) explains that the focus on atypical genitalia makes it hard to talk about the diversities of sex development which are not related to genital appearance. Additionally, many activists challenge the term 'intersex' while also using it to 'disrupt the assumptions that diagnoses are real and that sex, gender and sexuality are natural, binary and correlated aspects of the body' (Davis, 2015, p. 521).

History of medical management and its consequences

Historically, the policing of gender and sexuality and the importance of distinct 'male' and 'female' categories have served to support the 'social sex order' (Dreger, 1998). Racist, colonial sexual dimorphism is also present – for example, in the work of Kraft-Ebbing (1886), who wrote, 'the higher the development of the race, the stronger the contrasts between man and woman'. Dreger (1998, p. 26) notes the 'disgust' and 'confusion' caused by 'human hermaphrodites' and by the 'homosexuals' who were categorized as 'behavioural hermaphrodites' by psychoanalysts such as Freud and Fairbairn in the first half of the twentieth century. This disavowal of those whose bodies and desires differ from cultural norms links to the erasure of intersex bodily variations described by Holmes (2009). Such erasure is central to the current medical treatment protocols used in hospitals in Britain today.

These protocols were established by psychologist John Money in the 1950s, who, with colleagues, 'proposed that the sexual reassignment of atypically sexed children would be possible if carried out before a critical age, and if the child was raised unambiguously within the gender role consistent with their new sex' (Roen, 2004, p. 127). Referring to 'female hermaphrodites', Money also insisted on life-long post-surgical secrecy. 'Then the girl can grow up oblivious of ever having had a problem. Her need for special sex education is then correspondingly minimised' (Money, 1968, p. 43). Griffiths (2018) notes that, while Money's protocols from the 1950s were ultimately globally impactful, their influence on healthcare in the UK in the 1950s was not immediate or complete. Indeed, Griffiths shows that, at this time in the UK, a normative and binary psychoanalytic understanding of sex and gender was more prevalent than it was in the US. Downing et al. (2015, p. 58) suggest that, although Money himself was bisexual, he believed the primacy of reproductive heterosexuality conferred on medical clinicians an ethical duty to 'impose "normality" on the sexual subject'. This protocol, which relies additionally on a policy of concealment, produces shame among both intersex individuals and their families. Paediatric urologist Justine Schober states, 'Surgery makes parents and doctors more comfortable, but counselling makes people comfortable too, and [it] is not irreversible' (Dreger, 1998, p. 30). Referencing the Hippocratic Oath, Schober questions whether surgery 'serves the best interests of our patients' (Dreger, 1998, p. 30).

Clinicians who have adhered to standard protocols have argued that advocating for patient bodily autonomy is a step backwards and creates 'psychological cripples' (Aaronson, 1999, p. 119). This utilization of psychosocial justifications for normalizing surgery has also been contested as a circular argument which posits that parent–child bonding and avoidance of discrimination is possible only through harmful and unnecessary non-consensual infant surgeries (Senate Community Affairs Committee Secretariat, 2013). Kessler (1998) has contributed a feminist social psychological critique of the heteronormative framework of understanding. Critical of the treatment protocols for those born with atypical genitals, Kessler claims the real problem is that doctors are given permission to make a decision on a baby's gender and make assumptions based on what they term 'natural' or 'true sex' when paradoxically they are trying to construct a sex through surgery. Although there are life-threatening risks to some children born with variations in sex characteristics, these can be diagnosed and treated early. There is no record of any life-threatening consequences of atypical genitalia. Yet invasive, heteronormative so-called 'corrective' surgical intervention is the norm. Roen (2015, p. 187) cites Brinkmann *et al.* (2007), who found that adult intersex participants had 'substantially negative experiences of treatment and found non-disclosure and secrecy particularly burdensome'.

Since 2013, infant genital surgery has been described as a human rights violation by the UN's Special Rapporteur on Torture, who called for a global end to 'genital normalizing' surgeries on intersex individuals because it causes profound mental suffering (Mendez, 2013). Psychologists Liao (2007) and Roen (2008) specifically challenged the heteronormative assumptions underpinning a number of intersex-related medical interventions – that is, the assumptions that a person needs either a penis or a penetrable vagina. Roen encourages academics to conduct work to support those in the psychological field working with this client group. Liao and Simmonds (2013) suggest those working with intersex clients and patients offer a 'values-driven and evidence-based approach to providing care in this highly medicalised context' (Roen, 2015, p. 192).

Psychotherapeutic considerations

The client-centred approach put forward by psychologists Roen, Liao and others contrasts with the earlier psychoanalytic emphasis on the maintenance of a 'stable gender identity' (see Hird, 2003). Hird (2003) observes that both a patient's medically assigned gender and the achievement of a heterosexual orientation have been valued above other non-normative taxonomies regarding gender and sexual preference.

Williams (2002) adds that a psychoanalytic preoccupation with the patient's 'true sex' limits what the client might want and need to explore, such as trauma from repeated invasive surgeries, doctors' examinations, the aftercare procedures from surgical alterations and difficulties with parental and familial relationships. Parents are told to withhold all information from their children about having intersex variations and are expected to mourn the loss of the fantasized perfect daughter or son. Guth *et al.* (2006, p. 71) advise psychotherapists working with intersex clients to learn about the 'social stigmatisation that prevents people with intersex conditions from sharing their experience with others' so that they can help clients acknowledge their isolation and any confusion they may feel about being intersex and work towards feeling more accepted. Roen (2015, pp. 184–185) suggests that some intersex people also 'avoid intimate relationships and health services in an attempt to avoid difficult conversations about their sex development and to avoid earlier trauma experienced in the name of healthcare'.

As we can see, the experiences of being surgically altered without consent and the repeated physical examinations and photographs – again without consent – result in significant distress. In the documentary film *Intersexion* (Mitchell *et al.*, 2012), a discussion about the impact of violated bodily boundaries through repeated non-consensual touching by the medical profession suggests an inability to distinguish or defend against intrusion from other adults:

> It's one of the awful consequences of growing up in a culture of silence that intersex children often fall victim to sexual predators. Our genitals have been touched right from when we're little, we've been taught never to talk about our different bodies, and so sexual predators are very good at picking out children who would make good victims. (Mitchell *et al.*, 2012)

Another key issue is shame. Since the 1990s, when Kessler (1998) critiqued the enforcement of sexual dimorphism through surgery for those who don't meet this cis-normative biological requirement, the existence and impact of the shame projected onto intersex bodies has not been acknowledged or addressed (and is more often than not worsened) by subjecting intersex people to Money's protocols. This insight suggests that a psychotherapy that supports intersex embodiment and autonomy could be a powerful resource in place of surgery. Psychotherapy can support clients' self-acceptance as intersex and create space for informed and consensual decisions about anything they do or don't want to do.

Basic therapeutic competencies

Guth *et al.* (2006, p. 71) and Harper *et al.* (2013) list a series of basic competencies for non-intersex psychotherapists working with intersex clients, emphasizing the need to educate themselves about intersex variations and the typical lived experiences they may have in order to best serve intersex clients. They suggest these therapists reflect upon how their attitudes and knowledge of intersex might affect their work with these clients. Examples of some of the basic competencies listed (Harper *et al.*, 2013, p. 28) include (1) understanding how the gender binary can be harmful to this group and how they might experience oppression, and (2) working as allies for people who are intersex. For example, by understanding the difference between the concealment- versus the client-centred model and the affirmation of the client's identity and lived experience where clients are treated respectfully and given all relevant medical information relating to their condition. Lev (2006, p. 34) cites Meyer-Bahlburg (1994, p. 22), who outlines some of the prospective issues for those born with intersex variations, including: 'body image problems associated with ambiguous genitalia, or with the development at puberty of gender-contrary secondary sex characteristics; prospective questions regarding sexual orientation; [and] gender insecurity or doubts about correct gender assignment'.

Lev notes that:

> there are three areas where psychosocial support has been absent or in some cases misdirected. These include (1) parents of newborn babies with dsd; (2) children and adolescents with intersex conditions; and (3) adults who are beginning to recognise that they were born with intersex conditions and were surgically altered as children. (2006, p. 35)

Commenting on the limitations of a psychoanalysis devoid of feminism and queer theory (Harris, 2005), Hird notes, 'counselling needs to be seen not in relation to how well the intersex client eases into their assigned or existing gender' but rather 'how successfully they are able to negotiate feelings of self-worth, trust and relationships with others' (2008, p. 61).

Referring to therapists working with clients with intersex variation(s), Liao (2003) believes psychoeducation can empower clients to control decisions relating to treatment and disclosure, and therapy can both offer opportunities to further explore meanings of different aspects of variations in sex characteristics and challenge notions of normalcy. 'Far from being an obscure area in medicine, management of conditions associated with atypical genitalia starkly exposes pervasive notions of "normal" sexuality that underpin research and practice in many areas of health and illness, and as such should concern health professionals in general' (Liao, 2003, p. 234).

Psychotherapeutic regulatory bodies and institutions

My research in the counselling field continues to reveal blocks to knowledge sharing. From the professions' regulatory bodies, to training institutions, and individuals, there is a striking lack of awareness about clients with VSC. The British Association of Counsellors and Psychotherapists (BACP) is the only regulatory body of the UK's 22 such organizations that specifically mentions intersex clients. Barker (2019) outlines some of the issues related to the structural stigmatization that might typically bring a client with intersex variations into therapy on their website. But these outlines are positioned as a resource rather than an explicit statement about what is expected of counsellors to meet this standard. There are currently no official guidelines for working with intersex clients in the UK. This suggests it could be difficult for an intersex client to lodge a complaint about a therapist who failed to follow guidelines.

The study

This study involved interviewing four participants aged 45 to 60 who all identified as intersex and as LGBTIQ+. Three participants identified as non-binary. One also identified as queer and trans masc; another also identified as genderqueer. All were involved in intersex activism. Three participants were white. All participants in this research preferred to use 'intersex' in place of a diagnostic term as an identity in and of itself, and to establish intersex embodiment. No participant fully identified with the sex category they were assigned at birth.

For example, Del, who was assigned female and who let their facial hair grow, now takes testosterone and defines as 'genderqueer, non-binary and intersex'. Seven, also assigned female, underwent a gonadectomy and now identifies as intersex, trans masc, non-binary and queer and has been on testosterone since 2018 after their body rejected the oestrogen they were put on from age 12. Jo, also categorized as female, uses she/her pronouns. After years spent trying to hide her facial hair, she no longer shaves and identifies 'in line with my intersex body, as an intersex person'.

Two participants – one AFAB and named Sarah, who changed their name to Seven Graham in 2018 when they 'transitioned to be whole' and uses he/they pronouns interchangeably, and Del (who uses the pronoun 'they') – decided against using pseudonyms to reclaim the subjectivity they felt had been taken from them by doctors. Seven had previously appeared 'anonymously' in a book about intersex child patients by paediatric and adolescent gynaecologist Sir John Dewhurst as a result of the surgery that Dewhurst conducted upon Seven. Regarding this, Seven explained:

> I understand the academic convention of anonymizing – it's the same dehumanizing, objectifying thinking that 'protects' the child in my gynaecologist's book – with a black stripe through the eyes. Therapy is supposed to see the individual and their humanity.

Wishing to use their name in this study, Seven said:

> My not being anonymous is a way to reclaim my power and body from 'science'.

Reflexivity

Due to the subjective nature of qualitative research, reflexivity is an important balancing influence on researcher bias. I was aware that the fate of my mother's twin – who had been 'left to die' 24 hours after birth in the early 1940s because of their atypical genitals and the prevailing medical protocols in rural England at the time – would make the research emotionally challenging and would touch upon unmetabolized intergenerational trauma, so I took this to personal therapy. Indeed, during the interviews and the process of data analysis, while I immersed myself in the transcripts and read the literature, I found that I initially felt overwhelmed by the trauma described by my participants. Additionally, I recognized my bias against the medical profession's approach to those with intersex variations. Yet the heteronormative-critical literature of key clinicians such as Liao, academics such as Roen and Karkazis, sociologists such as Hird and therapists such as Lev has also influenced my approach to this study.

A benefit of this queer feminist bias is that it runs as a validating counterinfluence to the pathologizing and harmful current UK practice, which privileges heteronormative values, beliefs, clinical practices and legal status regarding human bodies over and above those with atypical presentations regarding biology, hormones and chromosomes. Reflecting on my positionality in relation to this topic, and particularly the decision whether to reveal my family history, I knew my choice could potentially both open up and close down aspects of my conversations with participants. A family connection to the issues could be helpful in building trust with participants but I may nevertheless be seen as more of an outsider than an insider. My status as queer therapist could also be helpful in rapport-building, but also could distance me from those with prior negative therapy experiences.

Results

The focus of my analysis is on how a small cohort of LGBTIQ+ people with intersex variations experience therapy, the blocks to successful therapy and what therapists could do differently to ensure that they can work competently and ethically with this client group.

Client experiences of therapy

Identity and embodiment are primary themes for those with intersex variations. All four participants talked about the impossibility of being permitted to exist as intersex people in their own right. In this context, suspicion of the therapeutic process and of therapists themselves is common. All four participants said they were wary of their therapists either before or during the process. While one out of the four participants saw just one therapist, three saw different practitioners over many years. Two participants voiced fears about whether they would regard them and the issues they brought as 'legitimate' (Jo) or that they would feel 'less than' (Seven) their cisgendered therapist.

Starting therapy

Following their first experiences of therapy, three out of the four interviewees subsequently sought therapy at different points in their lives to help them process significant events and experiences such as bereavements, relationship and substance misuse issues. As well as discussing intersex-specific issues, all participants used the therapeutic space to modulate their disregulated arousal (Ogden, 2009) before reaching a point where it felt possible to expand their 'window of tolerance' (Siegel, 1999, p. 253) by working with painful and traumatic memories and feeling states, and mentalizing their experiences (Wallin, 2007).

For example, Seven, who had issues around substance and alcohol dependency, found that the 12-step model of therapy they came across in rehab helped them to 'break through denial and get in touch again with that spiritual part of myself'. They said it was with their therapist at this stage that:

> I came to realize that the only way this process was going to work was if I put the fact that I was intersex in my life story and start telling the truth of who I am, breaking through all the lies and dishonesty that fed toxic shame and my addictions. (Seven)

Exploring identity

Three of the four participants reflected on the way their identities were explored in therapy. Seven found that, whereas early in recovery they couldn't wait for their weekly therapy sessions because 'so much was coming up for me', over time their need for therapy gradually became less urgent. This then changed when they had a healing crisis aged 49 and their body rejected oestrogen. Therapy helped them to overcome their fear of doctors, so they were able to try testosterone shots and come to terms with a transition process that made them more visibly intersex, 'and face the risks to my personal safety that comes from having 38DD breasts and stubble'.

It is important to note that three out of the four participants had experiences with therapists who were able to engage on some level without the participants feeling they were being pathologized. This contrasts with the experiences they'd had with medical practitioners who – in two cases – quite literally erased their intersex bodies through unnecessary surgical intervention. Seven used therapy to address ongoing issues of self-acceptance and recalls the 'shame around my body'. However, the first time they mentioned they were intersex to a therapist:

> I had a tangible sense of connection with God – who I now called Goddex, a non-binary deity – in the room … and a sense of acceptance … the beginning of awareness that … that I was born this way for a reason and I'm perfect to Goddex as I am. (Seven)

Although therapy is still useful, Seven says their activism, creativity, writing and performing their solo play *Angels Are Intersex* and becoming the world's first intersex stand-up comic have helped them feel better about being intersex. Six years after they started therapy, they felt able to write about their story: 'I faced a lot of fears doing that and it was published, and I got a good response.'

Exploring shame

Being a visible intersex person has helped Seven with some of their feelings of shame. All participants talked about feeling shame at some point in their life as a result of the way they were treated because they are intersex:

> I realized that I did have [shame] but that I was very, very good at hiding it from myself. (Del)

Three out of four participants said they were not ashamed of their intersex biologies:

I felt ashamed that I was growing a beard, I felt I liked it, privately I liked it, privately I liked my genitals, privately my body, on the small, tiny world of me, I thought, 'Oh, this is OK, I like this,' but I was really aware that nobody else thought it was OK. (Jo)

Prior to being diagnosed as intersex and CAH (congenital adrenal hyperplasia), Jo thought she might be transgender. So, she went to a gender clinic from where she was sent to an endocrinologist who discovered she was intersex. Reeling from the revelation, Jo was told by a psychotherapist at the clinic that this diagnosis would help strengthen her case with doctors who require certain criteria to be met before the reassignment process is green-lit.

They didn't say, 'Yes, you were born with intersex characteristics, do you want to talk to someone about it?' That could have been a point of help. (Jo)

Being intersex 'wasn't considered to be something to do with a potential identity in itself, it's just something to fix'. Jo added that she didn't feel she could talk about being intersex at the gender clinic because, 'I didn't feel it was something I was allowed to talk about because of societal norms and pressures there.' Following this experience, she found another therapist:

She was very supportive, and she didn't try to re-contain something or to pathologize it, which is kind of frequently done where somebody is … categorizing (intersex) as a physical thing. (Jo)

For the first time in her life, Jo felt she had a therapist who was:

Just open to talking about it, to considering things or to seeing how I might feel, not in a way in which she was trying to learn anything from me or anything like that but just in a really healthy way. (Jo)

Therapeutic outcomes

The analysis showed that despite some unhelpful exchanges and enactments with some therapists, which I will outline below, all four participants found their overall experiences of therapy to be positive.

Seven felt lucky to work with a diverse range of therapeutic practitioners, from trauma specialists and therapy in rehab to couples' therapy, all of whom have played a part in an ongoing journey of holistic well-being:

I've been through some very dark spaces and I'm still here. I haven't attempted suicide in the past 20 years of being sober – I attempted suicide twice aged 14. I do look after myself, you know, I do eat well, I do exercise, I'm very satisfied in my professional, creative and my personal life. (Seven)

Del reported that, although they had not gone 'as deep as I would like' in therapy, they thought they were 'in a better place than I would have been' had they not sought it.

The blocks to therapy

As seen above, therapy produced positive outcomes with all clients; however, participants reported work at depth was not possible due to lack of therapist knowledge. The paucity of literature suggests that therapists are likely to be ignorant of this client group and, therefore, risk contravening the ethical standards required by the professional regulatory bodies. For example, the BACP's ethical framework asks members to agree to abide by professional standards by 'working within our competence' and 'keeping our skills and knowledge up to date' (BACP, 2016, p. 6). Therefore, those working with intersex clients must educate themselves on non-normative gender identities and bodies, or risk alienating and even doing harm to their clients, as was the case for Del.

Normative paradigms

Del said that in therapy they had discussed their thoughts and feelings about removing the breast implant that, at age 17, had been 'put into me without me wanting to, without fully informed consent', to balance their asymmetrical chest. Del's therapist asked about their relationship with their mother and father and what they felt about the therapist's own breasts. Del responded, 'I don't think about your breasts ...' and later, 'I don't want to cut my ... you don't understand, I'm not trying to cut my breast off because I hate being a woman.' In fact, Del simply wanted to remove the collapsed and unwanted implant, primarily for health reasons but also to 'stay true to my hermaphroditic roots'. What appears to underlie Del's bad experience is their therapist's difficulty in bracketing (Smith *et al.*, 2009) or holding her own experience and normative views about bodies while listening to and exploring the client's experience of and relationship with their own body.

All participants spoke of feeling anxious about being misunderstood by therapists who are not, themselves, intersex. This anxiety again suggests that the shame projected into intersex bodies and the 'conspiracy of silence' (Toal, 2014) is so often reproduced between clinicians, parents and their intersex children. This silence can be replicated in the therapy room when intersex awareness is not made explicit either verbally by the therapist or in their promotional material. It was this pervasive shame and silence about intersex lives that I believe underpinned Seven's comment:

> *Certainly, while my therapists were cisgendered, I kind of saw them as better than me in some way because I was this flawed intersex person, this less-than human, but I've been healed by being on the right hormones and transitioning. I felt 'less than' because I was trying to perform/act female and failing. I never was female but I had tried very hard to stay in the box. They cut bits out of my body to fit me in.* (Seven)

Knowledge gaps

As we have just learned, Del felt their lesbian psychotherapist was operating within a 'binary' understanding of gender, despite not being heterosexual. This made empathic exploration of their body impossible, causing repeated damaging enactments – that is, 'uncontrolled unconscious impulses that are mutually stimulated between analyst and patient' (Maroda, 1999, p. 125). Maroda believes such incidences are inevitable in the therapeutic process and advises practitioners to be cautious as to what is therapeutic, suggesting that enactment incidents are 'ripe for narcissistic gratification' (1999, p. 128).

What therapists could do differently

As we have seen, if intersubjectivity is an embodied process (Reis, 2009), then it is beholden upon practitioners to think about how this will affect their own sense of embodiment, in addition to researching the social construction of sex, gender and biology. All participants spoke of the need for therapists to educate themselves more about this client group. Seven found teaching their therapist as a client problematic, adding that this contributed to a feeling of 'disconnect' between them. Now, the multi-hyphenate writer, performer, comic, therapist and former UK government advisor on mental health is working with the Los Angeles LGBT Center as a consultant: 'to open a world-leading intersex clinic with both a medical and psychological wrap-around holistic approach as a professional with other professionals. Drawing on my experience as a therapist and person who has spent their life experiencing, often, what is counter-therapeutic in medicine for we intersex people, in a healthcare setting, is a whole different thing.' Two of the other participants didn't mind teaching their therapists about some aspects of intersex issues but wished they had known more.

Access to therapy

The issue of access was raised by three participants who referred to the difficulty some intersex individuals might have in knowing how to find intersex-aware counsellors, so signposting an intersex-aware practice or practitioners is suggested. The same participants also raised therapist fees as a block to access, with two suggesting that counselling should be provided for this client group for free or on a low-cost basis. Seven felt angry about paying for counselling, explaining:

> ... my body had forced me to have these unhealthy traumatic relationships with doctors for so many years and now my emotional pain and my mind was putting me in a similar situation where I was having to see another kind of professional ... and I really kind of resented it, and I think for me, the money part of the exchange was really problematic. (Seven)

Vicarious therapist trauma

During my research, I read harrowing testimonials from individuals with variations in sex characteristics who had been forced to undergo unnecessary surgical procedures in infancy or childhood (Mendez, 2013). The descriptions of the physical and psychological harm inflicted on their bodies penetrated my own body. Further, while reading Money (1968), I came across several black and white photographs of child and adult bodies displayed with legs splayed and/or fixed in place by hands that protruded from white clinical sleeves to expose the genitals. The bodies were 'anonymized' with a black strip over the eyes. I felt a visceral horror at the dehumanizing images. Although these individuals weren't my clients, the feeling reminded me how dissociated memories are often stored somatically not only as sensations that can be relived in the present, but also as non-verbal communications between client and therapist. I felt overwhelming sorrow about the deep trauma described by those who had been operated on without consent and by the way that the intersex individuals in Money's book had been treated and presented. This insight into the possibility of counter-transferential secondary trauma experienced by the therapist may be part of why some of the clients – and indeed therapists – were unable to explore some identity issues (among others) relating to their embodied intersex experiences.

Further to learning about intersex lived experiences, I suggest therapists working with this client group may need to incorporate a trauma-informed approach. This became clearer when Seven spoke of the potential barriers for therapists working at depth. They advised:

> No matter how great a therapist you are, you probably are going to be rejected, you probably are going to experience anger, you probably are going to experience a lot of negative emotional states and you really need to be grounded and you really need not to personalize that stuff. (Seven)

Discussion

To summarize, the research explored the therapy experiences of four LGBTIQ+ and intersex-identified individuals. The main research findings point to a reported lack of knowledge about VSC by therapists, which in some cases resulted in client mistrust of therapists and blocked in-depth therapeutic work around gender, bodies and sexuality. Participants emphasized the importance of therapist reflection on their own relationship with sexuality and gender and bodily integrity. There is also a possibility of vicarious therapist trauma.

Therapeutic practice

In addition to the lack of available literature for therapists, the reported lack of awareness about intersex lived experience in therapeutic environments can foreclose exploration of bodies, gender and sexuality in the therapeutic dyad. Caruth (1995) notes the power for both client and analyst if the analyst permits herself to be a witness who can attest to the truth of an event and the fact of its incomprehensibleness. Since all participants said they felt wary of therapists and feared not being seen as valid because they were intersex, such experiences of empathic witnessing could help to deepen the therapeutic bond as it disrupts client expectations of being pathologized.

Therapist education

Therapists working with intersex clients – regardless of how they identify – need to learn about variations in sex characteristics. Key texts that could be included in therapy training institution curricula include: *Contesting Intersex* (Davis, 2015), *Critical Intersex* (Holmes, 2009) and *Born Both: An Intersex Life* (Valoria, 2017). Documentary films by intersex activists such as *A Normal Girl* (Bernier-Clarke *et al.*, 2019) and *The Intersex Diaries* (Soni *et al.*, 2018), also add to the knowledge. Guth *et al.* (2006) note the social stigma and isolation of those with variations in sex characteristics. Finding community through activism helped all participants. Knowledge of resources such as Intersex Equality Rights UK, Organisation Intersex International, Intersex UK and InterACT may be helpful for both clients and therapist.

Access to therapy

Since intersex medical treatment protocols have rendered intersexuality invisible (Roen, 2004), it is suggested that therapists clearly signpost that they are intersex-affirming. Three of the four participants talked about financial access issues. If the damage done by medical institutions to this client group is truly recognized, reparative, free psychotherapy could be offered in these institutions.

Vicarious therapist trauma

Despite a spectrum of distress levels among those with intersex presentations, my experience of secondary traumatic stress (Sanderson, 2010), the distress described by three of the four participants and Schuetzmann *et al.*'s findings (2009) on the psychological distress of those who have undergone invasive surgeries, it is suggested that trauma-informed therapeutic support is considered with this client group. Further, Bollas (1989) as cited in Aron (1996, p. 104) says, 'insofar as patients use projective identification, they place into their analysts dissociated aspects of themselves'. Analysts become 'mediums for the psychosomatic processing of the patient's psyche-soma'.

Therapist reflexivity

Two of the four participants reported feeling uncomfortable about their biologies and gender expression. Therapists should interrogate any biases they may hold around sex, sexuality and gender. Additionally, reflection on relative bodily integrity privilege – again likely to be on a spectrum for practitioners – and what it might mean to live in a society that mitigates against intersex embodiment is encouraged. Suchet (2011, p. 183) notes that 'embodiment is not a given, but a complex process of acquiring a sense of ownership of one's material flesh, an investment in the bodily self' and understands that while it is 'influenced by physiological, cultural and unconscious process' it is also 'highly sensitive to traumatic disruption', as evidenced in the stories of all participants.

Limitations and future research

Since only one of the four participants was a person of colour, there was a lack of racial diversity in the study. This reflects the further marginalization that exists within already marginalized groups. The study focused on LGBTIQ+ adults who use either or both 'herm' or intersex as a marker of an aspect of their identity. The field urgently needs research on other adults with intersex variations as well as intersex children and young people's experiences of therapy. Although the research was qualitative and gave rich detail, therapists and others working in this field would benefit from a far greater number of studies on this client group with more participants.

Research into how clients feel therapists have helped them to explore their sense of intersex embodiment at depth is needed. A disturbing finding was the connection between surgeries and repeated medical examinations, and intersex people having a sense of having a 'violated body' and being subsequently 'vulnerable to' sexual abuse. This urgently deserves further research and may apply beyond intersex people to others with childhood experiences of genital surgeries or medical touch which was poorly explained and/or kept secret. Additionally, research into intersex client experiences of what it is like to see an intersex vs a non-intersex (aware) therapist would be beneficial. Further in-depth research about many diverse aspects of the lives of those with variations in sex characteristics – drawing out the implications for therapy – is required.

CHAPTER 14

Toward an intersectional therapy training

Sabah Choudrey

Most of the psychotherapy training we undertake comes from the colonized – hierarchical, white, cis, heterosexual, patriarchal – mindset. Key Black and Brown psychotherapy texts are still not included on many trainings. Nor too the many texts written by lesbian and gay practitioners. So how do queer psychotherapy trainees navigate these spaces? Sabah Choudrey reflects on their experience.

Clients from marginalized groups can find it hard to know where to start with therapy

JANE CHANCE CZYZSELSKA: Misery is a monthly club night for QTIPOC, right?

SABAH CHOUDREY: Yes, it's a collective, and during the Covid-19 pandemic it's been online, which is a great success as well.

JC: Fantastic.

SC: They had sober club nights last year and this monthly event is more focused on different themes. We've had therapeutic spaces focused around sexual health for LGBTIQ people of colour, spirituality and religion, grief, pleasure and trans-feminine health and well-being. It's a sharing and support space for 90 minutes. When they had the physical club nights, I was offering 20 minutes one-to-one support for anyone who wanted it. It was really awesome how they integrated mental health and well-being as part of the club night. So it's not just a club night or a space to be yourself but we also have someone who is listening to you and for a lot of people in our community it's not easy to just go and find a therapist. So many steps have to happen before that first conversation.

JC: What kinds of steps are you thinking of?

SC: Understanding what therapy actually is! And whether it is right for you as opposed to other kinds of therapy, such as bodywork, coaching or something more specialized or holistic. Another big thing is finding a legitimate therapist who is accountable to a governing body, who is safe and vetted, as anyone can call themselves a counsellor. Not many people know that. It can be hard to know what to look for and where to start. I put together this DIY Find A Therapist Kit to help others, as I would get similar questions on where to start with finding a therapist. Friends, young people and people I didn't know felt like they could ask me because I am quite open about training as a therapist.

Therapy training needs to be democratized and decolonized

JC: Tell me about your training journey so far.

SC: I did my undergrad in psychology and then a Level 1 and 2 in counselling skills in Brighton and it was really great. Because of the level the training was at, there were so many different people from different backgrounds, ages, identities and experiences who were part of it and that was really, really nice. Of course, when you get to Masters level it eliminates people of a certain socio-economic status and the people on the course are probably representative of the therapy profession today: white, middle-class, middle-aged women. I have been the only person of colour almost every year.

JC: Really? Wow!

SC: So I skipped the first year because of my previous training experience and started at Diploma Level 2. I had already taken the year out because I was looking after my dad, who's now passed, and it had been really up and down, but as well as being the only person of colour on the course, I was also the youngest. I am 30 now and started when I was 27, three or four years ago, and I was also the only LGBT person, so I felt a lot of differences.

JC: Yes, lots of intersections there.

SC: I don't think it was anything deliberate: there weren't any micro-aggressions, but I just really felt the difference. I did make friends and actively go to other people of colour or other people who I suspected were LGBT but there weren't really spaces to talk about those kinds of nuances. I don't know how we find out about other therapists in training who are queer or POC or similar.

JC: Pink Therapy's Facebook page is a good starting place for networking with other queer therapists. They welcome all trainees and qualified queer and GSRD therapists.

SC: Yes, I discovered that later into my training. BAATN – the Black, African and Asian Therapist Network – also has specific student groups. I had always planned to go but, for many reasons, I never made it to one. I think I was looking for something within the institution. My college attends London Pride every year, but they didn't seem to be doing much else, so I joined the college Pride committee. We had one or two meetings, but I think there was confusion about who it was for. Some thought it was for allies as well, and I had expected it to be just for LGBTIQ people and having that dialogue itself was a bit weird. I would have really benefited from an LGBTIQ-only space to talk about the cis- and hetero-normativity of the course and training, but having self-declared allies in that space felt weird. I kind of left it up to the group, so we started a thread on Moodle, but I don't know what happened. I think dad got ill again and I didn't do any more meetings and, when

I didn't do it, it didn't happen.

JC: Oh right, so it was left up to you, the only queer person in your year, not the college? Do you think the college should have done something else for LGBTIQ trainees re Pride, or something different maybe?

SC: Well, something good that happened before I started the Pride LGBT group was that I had joined a diversity and accessibility working group and they were reviewing the policy around taking leave if you're pregnant and I suggested they change the wording so it was gender-neutral. It was pretty understood, there wasn't any push-back, but I wonder what else could have been made more gender-inclusive. The toilets weren't gendered but that seemed to be more of a necessity due to the limited space in the building. Around the same time, I started the BME/people of colour working group and I asked the college to send an email out. I think I got replies from three or four people – bearing in mind there are hundreds of students there – who wanted to do something or have a working group for BME or POC trainees. But then dad got really unwell again and I didn't want to do it by myself, but nothing came of it because I couldn't do it. So, it was a lot of work to just even try and get a conversation started and this really mattered. There was only one black tutor I knew, but I didn't want to go to her and ask her for all the information about anything to do with race and culture within therapy. She was really supportive, and we had a few conversations about race and being POC in this profession but it was just this one space with the tutor.

Training institutions need to centre and support their LGBTIQ and POC students

JC: That's a problem, isn't it – the institutional structure is colonial and having one tutor that is a POC is not good enough in a training organization. How much power does that one person have to be able to fundamentally change things? The structure isn't there yet for that to be possible and it also puts a lot of pressure on that one person or you to talk about POC issues and difference and whiteness. Until, perhaps literally, George Floyd's death in May 2020, most white people weren't going to talk about whiteness.

SC: Yeah. I wonder what kind of conversations are happening in supervision and in these majority-white counselling schools. From the work in QTIPOC spaces and from doing reading, black folks need space to be held and heard, to grieve and receive empathy. White and non-black therapists need to understand why this is important through understanding the ways in which our own anti-blackness/whiteness shows up. It is crucial. In my first year, I had a really great tutor, Sheila Haugh, who is white and has written about whiteness and white privilege; we did a unit on power with her, and I really enjoyed being taught by her. I think it was a really good model for the white colleagues in the room to examine themselves but still it didn't feel like enough.

JC: Why was that?

SC: I think that was because it was just one module and it was on the broadness of power but considering how in-depth we go when we talk about insecurities, anxieties and traumas, there wasn't very much on whiteness or straightness. I did a presentation with a white colleague about race and power, but she expected me to tell her everything about race and what she needs to know as a white therapist. I did share with her, but I told her this is extra work for me.

JC: Right, it creates extra work, and it reproduces racialized power dynamics between trainees. Farhad Dalal (e.g. 2021) talks about race and group psychotherapy work, explaining how racism constructed race, which in turn creates power relations that are rigged against POC. Within the psychotherapy world, this challenges the foundational belief that things begin in the internal world.

SC: Exactly. When we did the presentation, my colleague told the group she had reflected on this with her supervisor, who was a person of colour, and it sounded like it was handled well. I was pushing for more to be done though. I'm not sure how it came about, but I did a short version of the privilege walk. Are you familiar with that?

JC: Yeah, when you step forwards or backwards from a starting line according to different social privilege markers or lack of them.

SC: And there's a version I have which goes beyond gender, sexuality and race that includes class, disability, language and immigration status. So, we did it using beads – not walking – and everyone had a certain number of beads.

JC: Oh, OK, cool.

SC: So, you'd take one or put one back and make a bracelet or necklace with the beads and it would represent your privileges. It was creative and it went down well; my colleagues said it really made them think. But if I hadn't done that, how would that kind of conversation and that awareness have happened? Yeah, that's always in the back of my mind. If I hadn't done that, then maybe it wouldn't have happened?

Non-LGBTIQ+ and white trainees need to take responsibility for their intersectional learning

JC: Some diversity courses are taught by white, cis, hetero male therapists.

SC: Yeah.

JC: Queer students often have to decide whether or not to bring most of the queer content into the training and it can come as an optional module in the latter part of the training. I think having out queer tutors is helpful in making queer students who are generally in the minority in trainings feel more included. Otherwise, hetero, white and cis assumptions are constantly centred. In one of my trainings, in group therapy class, I critiqued cis het culture and a fellow trainee said I sounded really anti-men. I was angry about how I was positioned for talking about the difficulty of being a lesbian under patriarchy. I felt unsupported by some of the other students. I emailed the tutor, who responded supportively, but there was overall little understanding of structural inequality and disempowerment. To be fair, I'm not sure I even understood it back then as I do now and I'm always learning more. It's problematic that queer people and POC have to bring so much of this education to tutors and colleagues and it's not woven into the fabric of our trainings.

SC: Yeah. I can relate to that. My training group so far has been all women apart from me and one cis man. So, the gender dynamics have been really strange. I've said things that colleagues told me sounded 'really anti-man'. I challenged some alpha male behaviour with a trainee who was talking positively about taking up space in a pub with his man friends. I said that is one of the reasons why I avoid pubs, and it came across as anti-man because there was only one cis man in the room. It was really weird because sexism still exists, even with one man in the room, and I don't know how to address that and speak about it in our profession. We need to encourage men to talk about masculinity and the constraints it has on our emotional development, as students, clients, therapists. But how do we do that in a feminist and inclusive way when some people are asking, 'Oh, what about the men?'

JC: You mean the hetero trainees are reproducing cis-heteronormativity in the classroom?

SC: Yeah.

JC: I think it's difficult to talk about this stuff within a normative context and therapy training is generally very normative. On Pink Therapy post-grad trainings, the awareness and sensitivity seems pretty different and recognizes how power structures can impact on LGBTIQ+ people. It's not that queer and QTIPOC therapists aren't affected by normative ideas; obviously we are: we internalize them and reproduce them unwittingly and we need to reflect on how we do that. But the whole vibe is different than in a majority straight, white, cis therapy training. I'm interested in what drew you to your college and the person-centred training. Did you think that they had a particularly good approach to queer and POC trainees?

SC: Yeah, definitely. When I studied Level 1 and 2, my tutor suggested the training and, when I looked into it, it was close to where I live. At the open day, it seemed really nice and really different to other counselling courses in that there's a lot of space for group process and time with your group, and that feels really important. Those moments have made it much easier for me to be authentic about being trans and other stuff that comes up around race or faith as well.

JC: Person-centred training does centre group work, doesn't it?

SC: Yeah, so I chose person-centred because I read about the approach, and I looked up feminism within person-centred theory and it made loads of sense. Like, of course my practice is going to be directed by the person in front of me and it felt like a practice that could hold the individual as well as the constructs that exist outside and the impact of that on that person, which was really important. I remember reading the author Gillian Procter, one of the key feminist writers in person-centred theory, and she simply wrote at the start of the book *Politicizing the Person-Centred Approach*, 'Is the person-centred approach political?' (Procter *et al.*, 2006, p. 1). That book cemented so much for me. This is what the person-centred approach is for me.

JC: So, you liked that she named the asymmetry of power?

Trainees need to think about how they hold power in and outside the therapy room

SC: I like that it's an approach that tries to … not balance the power because I don't think you can do that in the therapy room, but it tries to be honest about the power dynamics and hierarchies. It tries to keep it small, like I'm not just coming in and telling someone what they are doing or making any analysis for them. When I started working with clients, I thought the power dynamic was equal and now I realize it's not, but I'm trying to be aware of the power of the therapist in the room. This power is also really impacted by how I come across, like if somebody reads me as a cis or trans man, or if somebody reads me as young or as straight or gay or whatever, that also has an impact. This is why I think it's necessary for therapists to understand the facets of their own identity because it all has an impact on the work.

JC: Sure.

SC: Especially since so many of my colleagues' clients are majority POC and they were saying things like, pointing out whiteness means pointing out non-whiteness with clients. I brought questions like 'Is empathy colour-blind?' And when they talked about their clients, race was unspoken, and I wondered about the unconscious biases, especially around family or faith issues. As trainee volunteer therapists on low-cost therapy service placement, your clients are likely to be POC with different educational backgrounds and understandings or they may be migrants. English may not be their first language, so it's really important to understand those power dynamics and the power we hold.

JC: If someone was consulting you about setting up the therapy school of your dreams, what would you say was imperative?

SC: I would say definitely a diverse reading list and curriculum – like Dr Isha Mckenzie-Mavinga's *Black Issues in the Therapeutic Process* (2009). There are going to be key things to cover but teachers can add and recommend stuff and share little snippets from therapists from marginalized backgrounds. Even blogs such as BAATN articles and general discourse about therapy; it doesn't need to be from an academic source.

JC: Yeah. For example, your TEDx Brixton talk on being a proud, queer, trans Muslim would be a brilliant training tool.

SC: Thank you! I suppose, I forget that we can learn so much from personal lived experience. It doesn't have to be academic, a journal article, have references or be a case study. We're working with people, we're centring them in our practice, so it has to be in a way that we can really hear them and understand them. And usually, it is as simple as hearing someone speak.

JC: I agree, and for clinicians who work with clients from marginalized communities, if you don't mix with people who aren't like you, what you're suggesting is especially important.

The curriculum should be decolonized and include non-therapeutic texts

SC: Maybe even sharing what clients say about therapists and their experiences of therapy, too. I know my experience of therapy influences how I am as a therapist. I also think having tutors who are not afraid to be vulnerable and share themselves, as a person. For example, it meant so much when my teacher talked about her whiteness and being quite clear about it, and in that moment, I thought, 'Oh, I'm going to have to call something out or in,' but in fact, I could just sit back. That doesn't happen often, having race issues dealt with by white people in the room.

JC: What was it she was clear about?

SC: I can't remember. I think it felt like we were going to go down the rabbit hole of 'seeing race is a bad thing; if I see my client as a Black man, isn't that racist in itself? And putting that label on him, he's just a person.' I think it was just having her holding that bit of discomfort around my colleagues' whiteness in the room.

JC: It sounds like it was really important feeling you could relax because a white tutor was taking responsibility for talking about race and white privilege, and how white people are implicated in maintaining white supremacist structures, so you didn't have to. I'm going from my own experience as a queer person: the anxiety and frustration of tutors not naming heterocentrism and feeling like the whole picture isn't here. I feel like I don't exist here. And if I put my hand up to confront this, I'm going to be labelled the difficult queer who bangs on about queerness.

SC: Yeah, yeah, yeah. I feel like maybe I've gone the extra mile, but I feel I've had to do a lot of sharing around, 'Hey, this is Pink Therapy, they have this course if you want to know more about different relationships, or this is BAATN and they have a free podcast, it would be really good to listen to it.' Even those kinds of things added on to reading lists and the curriculum would be good. It's annoying because there are some types of colleagues who are more academic, who want to soak up all the knowledge and theory and intellectual stuff, but race and sexuality don't always fit into that.

JC: They do, sexuality and race have been theorized in our field – there's Judith Glassgold (Glassgold and Iasenza, 2004), Joanna Ryan (O'Connor and Ryan, 2003), Igi Moon (2008), MJ Barker (2019), Resmaa Menakem (2017), Lara Sheehi (2020), Lynne Layton (Layton and Leavy-Sperounis, 2020). I was lucky in mine having some tutors who did, but often white, straight tutors don't know, and as a rule they don't bring it into trainings.

SC: It's harder to bring yourself into it as well if you're constantly theorizing about these things. Some of the best discussions around these kinds of issues are not academic texts; they are books and info and podcasts and stuff. I think having other things that work is important, like having group process time with colleagues and a tutor who is interested in having discussion.

JC: Yeah, we live life in practice not in theory. And feeling safe and seen in your difference and not being othered for it is crucial in trainings.

SC: I think it's hard, at least within my experience of the person-centred classroom, because everyone is hands off. Because it's a non-directive approach compared to other approaches, I think that can mean we're quite passive as therapists. I've definitely been like, 'What do I do?' like, 'If I say something now, is it too directive?' I see that happen with my classmates too but I'm trying to think about how we can counter the person-centred approach when it comes to learning about ourselves and power. Power is directive but it's the opposite of a non-directive approach, but it's so important to be able to engage with it in the therapy room.

JC: It is, and there are ways of engaging with the power, I think. But also, many of the theories come from white, cis, het men and women who have used their dominant ideologies, their privilege if you like, to defend against what they call 'politics' but we could call 'othered lives' in the therapy room. I really like what Foluke Taylor and Robert Downes (2020) suggest in their fantasy intersectional decolonised relational therapy school. They imagine they are studying at therapy schools where you can choose what and how you study. The organizing principle is kind of, unless you are in a training context that feels holding and expansive, how can you become what or who you need to be as a therapist? Taylor and Downes position themselves – like Moten and Harney (2004) – as 'fugitive knowers' or a community of outcast thinkers who reject and resist normative values and structures. Which sounds really liberating to me. What else have you found hasn't worked for you?

SC: I think the training has often felt quite two-dimensional for me. Really digging into parts of ourselves and what shapes us as people and therapists, and it still feels like there's not enough joining the dots. I am a product of the experiences I've had growing up when it comes to attachment and relationships and any traumas, but I've also learnt things from the media and the role models in my life. Also, there's so much pressure to find a placement, any placement, and there's so much demand and they pressure you on your hours, seeing clients and recording with clients. I feel the work with clients is a low priority; it's all about hours.

JC: Yes, that's really true about the pressure. I think in a way our trainings are too short. Robert Downes (personal communication) says we need more time to cook. For many queer trainees I've spoken with, what doesn't work is that differences such as neurodivergence or differences in ability, sexuality, gender, race, class and whether you're cis or trans aren't thoroughly examined. That's really problematic for clients ultimately because we don't get to explore and question those aspects of ourselves in the way that those from marginalized groups have to way before starting therapy training.

SC: Yeah.

JC: As white trainee therapists, we are rarely asked to think about our white privilege. Obviously, race is a construct, but white people often aren't considered as racialized, only people of colour are. And even that isn't addressed. How can you become the hated white object if you aren't examining your issues regarding your white privilege? For example. Or heterosexual therapists who haven't explored their sexuality because it's only an optional model in the third year. This lack of exploration can lead to unethical behaviour by straight therapists with their LGB clients.

SC: Gosh.

JC: So I think all that needs addressing in our trainings.

Think about where the medical model comes from and how it differs from psychotherapy

SC: It reminds me that we've covered mental health and diagnosis and pathologization and when we did that I was thinking of the origins of the DSM. And lots of these things are culturally insensitive, the diagnosing people of different cultures and faiths and stuff, and there was so much missing around that. I mean, let's think about who's in the mental health system and what percentage of them are from POC backgrounds and why that might be. It wasn't very intersectional; it was very two-dimensional and there's so much more that we need to think about.

JC: There was no critique of the DSM?

SC: Only that diagnosis/disorders is incongruent with person-centred theory. When it came to the origins of the DSM, I brought it up.

JC: Apart from you?

SC: No, I don't think so. I think with mental health the really popular stats are that women suffer more with depression and anxiety and men have higher suicide rates than women (Mental Health Organization,

2021), and that's about it. There's no nuance around why that is, what is it about masculinity and the workplace or the nuances of being from a LGBT or POC background, for example. There's no reflection on the DSM being racist. The first edition, DSM-1, was published in 1952. What was it like for people of colour in the 1950s? Segregation was prevalent, racism was normal, so it was literally written into societal norms. And institutional racism in psychiatry is not hidden; even today, POC are often misdiagnosed with psychiatric disorders, becoming medically institutionalized and hospitalized, impacting their lives permanently. Actually, when we studied the medical model, my awesome white tutor always challenged the use of the word 'disorder' and said no one is disordered; rather there are personalities, but not personality disorders. It was so simple and so effective; it changes how you see things.

JC: I agree. Using terms like 'syndrome' and 'disorder' when, for example, talking about people with variations in sex characteristics, is problematic and pathologizing.

SC: Language makes such an impact, so you need to be careful what you say when you're in a position of power. The language you use can replicate harmful power dynamics.

JC: Yeah, definitely. So, what needs to change? From my perspective, your Misery work has been part of the change: making it accessible outside of conventional therapeutic space. I guess you may need to be paid at some point. Lots of therapists do offer concessions or have a free slot in their private practice, but I wonder how possible it may be to continue to provide it to everyone for free?

Learning about marginalized people and experiences is a priority

SC: The work with Misery is great. It's run by the community for the community and by people who have different experiences of therapy. It's a really good starting point. It's not a solution, but one of the organisers who runs it is also trained in counselling skills. They had this idea and we talked about what the service would look like. We thought, let's try 20- or 25-minute slots and think about whether people can sign up in advance or come on the day. It was a really thought-through model and we are still learning as we go along. It's going to be different almost every time, depending on what is happening and who is there. I think that's positive. I've learnt already; I was expecting attendees to answer questions about really vulnerable things about sexual and mental health, forgetting that not everyone knows what therapy is like, not everyone knows or likes how therapists talk. I've just spent years in these academic white spaces and of course my default way of therapizing will reflect that. I can feel that it's not my voice when I am with POC clients or a POC space because I feel uncomfortable in myself, and the words don't feel authentic! Next time, I'll think about the language I'm using and maybe even talk about my own relationship to sexual and mental health, start off gently, not straight in with, 'How are you feeling about this?' but, 'What do you think about sexual and mental health?' Really simple things. Not everyone knows how they feel about these things when they haven't had a chance to think about them.

JC: It's interesting to think about what you might talk about because I imagine it's important to not open things up too much. Maybe they'd need to have some kind of aftercare, and thinking about how 20 minutes can be a holding environment in a club context.

SC: At Misery, I'm always upfront about what to expect and what 20 minutes is and can be with the person in front of me and with myself – including that it might not be the right thing for them. There are so many reasons why clients won't talk to the person in front of them; it's not always going to be about race and gender or sexuality, but we acknowledge that these things could also be in the mix. I've definitely made assumptions about clients, thinking probably this is going on for them with their gender but actually I need to listen to what they are saying first, keeping in mind that's a possibility, but it might be happening in an unconscious way. And I need to be aware of my own unconscious judgements to clients based on perceptions. In the therapy room with clients, I don't open up or disclose information, personal experiences or identities about myself, which I think is the appropriate practice. But there's so much already written on my skin, in my name, in my gender presentation that it feels like there's often stuff that is already in the room, whether I like it or not.

JC: I suppose doing things differently to how they are now in most trainings would mean, as Dominic Davies says (Chapter 15), having a diverse training cohort that's led by tutors robust enough to be able to work with all the stuff that might come up and who could make the space feel safe enough so people could explore their biases. That was missing in my training. I didn't feel I was taken to a place where I could explore my biases around class, race, gender or cis-ness. It's so important to examine one's own lived experience and what kinds of values and assumptions we have and what we have blind spots about and prejudicial thoughts and ideas that we can soak up from the culture. All that stuff needs to be rinsed through.

Talking about internalized biases and micro-aggressions is important

SC: I also think talking about micro-aggressions would be good. That has come up in one of our groups: I introduced it, and no one had heard of the term. It's a really good way to understand how systems of oppression can look and how they work at everyday levels and how we can reproduce them too.

JC: Can you give an example of what you told them?

SC: I explained about how the little jokes, stereotypes, off-the-cuff remarks that we make about people all add up. If you hear the same small thing over and over again about your race, gender or sexuality, it's going to feel massive. It's not just 'a bit annoying' that I get asked, 'Where are you really from?' It's racist and absolutely exhausting because it happens so often. That was new for them to hear, but when I spoke about sexist micro-aggressions, I think most of them understood it. It's hard to educate my colleagues like this because it makes me so exposed and visible. I'm telling them about my personal experiences as well. I also would add that a lot of my colleagues would say, 'I've got this trans or Muslim client; how should I approach this?' And while I'm happy to share information and resources, I'm thinking, 'Why isn't training giving you the confidence to know what to do?'

JC: Yeah, right – it really isn't.

SC: I don't think I'd go to a Black friend and say, 'Oh, I have a Black client; how should I approach them?' I think I would try and give myself the tools I need to understand the differences.

JC: There should be more of a lead from the colleges and tutors, and they need to look at who they have in their teaching cohort. I've heard tutors say, 'We don't want to spoon feed you' when they're confronted by LGBTIQ trainees who want more of a critique of normative ways of being a human. I think that response is so telling; it's a cis-het fragility. Can I end on a final question? I'm interested in what you think is the most important thing you've learned in your training, either about yourself or the training for work with clients.

SC: I think it's about what a counselling relationship with a client can look like. I've had a lot of thoughts about what good counselling or good therapy looks like. It's not always seeing a change in ten to twelve sessions; it's not even getting to talk about that reason the person came to therapy. It can just be that relationship and, even if we don't talk for the whole session or if the first five sessions were really awkward or uncomfortable, I've realized it's about so much more than my experience of it and what I think I should be saying or focusing on or what I've missed. After an ending with a client, they emailed me and said, 'Thank you so much. I know I didn't say anything in the last session; it was a really awkward goodbye.' I realized there are always things going on that I'm not aware of and I don't need to be aware of. I think trusting in the client is the most important thing I've learnt. Just trust the client who's in front of me and get out of my own head a bit too.

CHAPTER 15

Navigating dual relationships

Dominic Davies

As the community of LGBTIQA+ therapists continues to grow, it is likely that we will encounter each other outside of as well as in the therapy room, either as therapists and clients, as supervisors and supervisees, at events, or on social media. So, how do we ethically and skilfully move between these increasingly interconnected spheres? Pink Therapy co-founder Dominic Davies advises on dual-role boundary issues for queer therapists.

JANE CHANCE CZYZSELSKA: Many of us were involved in our communities through work or activism as well as pleasure and leisure activities before we trained. Now, as practising therapists, it's likely we will find ourselves working with clients who are connected to colleagues or friends or whose partners are in the same friendship groups as our other clients. Our clients may also be therapists, so we might see them in our networks or at events. If we or they are in poly and/or kink relationships, our polycules or kink networks may overlap with those of other clients, colleagues or friends. And for therapists living in remote areas, these issues can be even more pressing. How do you suggest we manage these potential overlaps?

You have a right to a private life as a queer therapist

DOMINIC DAVIES: It's my view that you have a right to a private life as a queer therapist, which means participating as fully as you want to online and in real life. So, you have the freedom to cruise, use sex apps, visit saunas and play parties if you so choose. Of course, some may say they have no desire to do that, but for those who do want to, you absolutely should do so because research tells us that participation in community activities is a protective factor against minority stress. This is something that as queers we are wrestling with in the same way that many of our clients are. If I hear a supervisee is isolating themselves from community events and activities because they think they might run into clients, I sometimes start to worry. My concern is that they sometimes might run the risk of living their queer identities primarily in their therapy rooms with their queer clients, and with diminished social support they might be looking to their clients to meet their emotional queer relational needs. This could be a slippery slope for weakening the boundaries and the frame that makes it a safe container. I think therapists who are most at risk of this are those living in more isolated areas, with little access to queer friends and who may not be in satisfying intimate relationships.

JC: I agree about the value of community events; that's always been important for me.

You don't have to marry or assimilate into heteronormativity to be valid and whole

DD: I think a great many therapists feel shame about cruising and having casual sex or even being single. You know, here we are, supposedly 'relationship experts' helping people to navigate the world and maybe we are having trouble finding a significant other or emotional connection in our own lives and that can feel like a source of shame. Perhaps there is work to be done here, maybe asking yourself if there's something about you that's keeping you single. Sometimes I think therapists develop very high standards and expect their potential partner to be incredibly psychologically well-evolved, but that's not always possible unless you find another therapist as a partner. So maybe it's about looking at yourself and what is important to you, what your values are. Of course, it's perfectly fine to be single.

JC: Absolutely, and how 'out' do you think therapists can be on dating apps?

DD: You might want to consider whether you want to use a face pic and be open about your sexual preferences and interests or decide to show your face pic once you've seen the other person's, and so hopefully know who you're talking to. I did some research a few years ago with gay and bi men therapists, who were using sex apps like SCRUFF, Recon, Grindr and the like. I asked if they used face pics and about half of them did, half of them didn't. So, if your sexual interests are fairly conventional and normative – that is, you're looking for people around the same age as you and you're not into kink-oriented play – a face pic is OK. You will probably find it easier to meet people because generally you get more responses with a face pic. But if you're into kink or kink-oriented practices, then maybe that's a lot of private info that you're putting out there that your clients might come across. So, while it may be helpful for your clients to know that you're queer, and maybe if you're kinky, the specific detail of what you're into is probably best left out of the public domain. That said, apps like OkCupid insist on a face pic as a condition of membership and then they have an extensive set of moral and ethical values-based questions for you to opt into for improved matching. By answering all these different questions, they can match you up with other people who share similar ideas and interests, and this could be a more effective way to meet partners. But many therapists might feel as though they're revealing too much of their personal and political identities and sexual practices in these ways.

JC: Yes, true. Moving away from the apps towards social media usage: how do you ascertain when a client comes for the initial consultation whether they know people in your social circle?

DD: Personally, I tend to do a quick check on Facebook and just see if their name pings up among my close mutual friends. If I find I'm about to see someone for an initial session who is a really close friend of a really close friend of mine or we share many mutual friends, I'm probably going to think this might not be the best person for me to work with. So I go into that appointment thinking let's redirect them to someone else. You may have five free slots in your diary, but you do need to think about the potential boundary problems of too many of these dual relationships and the impact it could have on your social life. So far, I have found it's really cut down on how often I run into clients in small social gatherings. It isn't foolproof but it helps. For therapists living in fairly small geographical communities where there may be small gay/kinky communities, I'd say, keep in mind that you don't need to be *the* one to see all the kinky queer people in your area. You could refer people in your immediate closest circle to someone online. Thanks to online queer therapy networks like Pink Therapy, no one has to be the only queer in the village anymore.

Live as openly as you can

DD: I do think it's important to live as openly as you can, though. In terms of your identities, this means working on your own internalized shame about them and includes choosing a modality which values your openness and authenticity. I think that some therapeutic modalities are encouraging of that and consider that a cornerstone; in particular, some of the more humanistic ones. In some of the more analytic modalities, that's not always the case and so it might be a challenge for queer people to be able to live their most authentic selves. While you may choose not to wear your sexuality or your gender identity on your sleeve, not all of us get that choice; for example, some trans women perhaps or some non-binary folk, or gay men who are naturally quite effeminate.

JC: Or masculine-of-centre lesbians and queer women.

DD: Yes, they may be outed as soon as they walk in the room or open their mouths. So, I think we probably do need to be open to answering questions about our identities where relevant and in the context of the therapeutic work. If a therapist wants to work psychodynamically or psychoanalytically and chooses not to say in their profiles or web pages that they are queer, that is their choice and that's fine. I think if a client asks if you're queer then you need to answer that question honestly and not bat it away. It's OK to explore it, asking 'And what would it mean if I was and what would it mean if I'm not?' But to refuse to answer, I think, is unethical and anti-therapeutic. Even some progressive psychoanalytic schools would agree the classical

Freudian notion of the blank screen simply doesn't exist. We can't be blank screens.

JC: Yeah, my understanding is that the blank screen was the 'neutral' default created by white, able-bodied, cis-heteronormative therapists. Psychoanalyst Susan Vaughan (2000) wrote about her counter-transferential expectation of rejection by a heterosexual female client. I don't think we can escape internalized prejudice but it's important to be reflexive about our relationship to it and how that might impact our client work. Interestingly, when Vaughan eventually revealed her sexuality to her straight client, her client's acceptance further repaired Vaughan's own earlier developmental wounding around keeping her lesbian desire secret.

DD: Yes, if you have to sit on your hands, that can be problematic. We know from the research that it is the relationship that heals; the modality isn't that important. It's about the relationship, so you need to be able to bring your whole self into the therapy room and not sit on those hands and be afraid of gesticulating in case it might give you away. As a consequence of hypervigilance and minority stress, many queer clients may have already checked out their therapists before they've arrived by asking friends or Googling and found out about whether you are lesbian or gay or kinky. I see this as an indication of looking for psychological safety, as in: 'Are you safe for me to be open with?' That's not to say you need to have the same gender or sexual identity to be safe for that person, but you do have to feel comfortable to be able to answer that question honestly and not think, 'Well, if I tell them I'm straight, they won't want to work with me.' That's unlikely to be the case; don't rob them of that experience.

Create a personal and professional boundaries statement

DD: Creating a personal and professional boundaries statement will help you and your client navigate the potential for dual relationships. You can put it on your website or in your first email to potential new clients, so they can see what your fees and terms are but also your professional boundaries statement. This can facilitate a conversation about how you both manage the complexity of living and working within the community. Clients may not understand the rather arcane rules of therapy and the things that govern our ethical behaviour. They may not know what's allowed and what isn't and what questions they can ask us, and they can get very tied up in that. The rules about our ethical behaviour originate in rules developed in the earliest days of medical and psychotherapeutic practice to protect cis women from cis men; in other words, to stop powerful cis men from seducing their vulnerable cis female patients. Even with those rules, they don't keep women clients that safe because there are still breaches in ethical practice, more so among cis males/females within the heterosexual community than in the queer community, but there are breaches in the queer community as well, so the rules don't necessarily stop it happening. Pope (2001) reports that 4.4 per cent of therapists (7 per cent of male therapists; 1.5 per cent of female therapists) are perpetrators when data from US national studies are pooled on this issue. So, the majority of this, it would appear from the stats, is male therapists abusing female clients.

JC: Female therapists are not immune to this either. It makes me very concerned about the limited opportunities for reflection on sexuality and desire in therapy training courses. It speaks in a different way to what you were saying about therapists who don't live their sexual lives openly – they might end up using their clients in a harmful way.

DD: Yes, I think I can understand why some of these boundaries get broken. It is partly that relational therapies are about making love, it's about intimacy, it's about loving someone unconditionally and being there and showing deep interest in them and their well-being. All the kinds of things that good lovers do, except good lovers probably extend that to a physical plane and have sex with the person. The client–therapist relationship is non-sexual. Nevertheless, it is natural for two people to develop strong feelings of intimacy and then perhaps if we're talking about sex and sexuality and our desires, it can create a highly charged atmosphere. If as a therapist you don't have good support and other outlets for your emotional and sexual life, you may come to rely on having those kinds of conversations with clients and this can trip over into boundary violations. So, by paying attention to one's own sexual, relational and mental health, we take care of our own needs.

JC: Right, yeah, that's a really good point.

As queer therapists, we need to create our own cultural guidelines

DD: As queer therapists, I think we also have to be creating our own cultural guidelines which are sensitive to the norms operating within our smaller, overlapping and often highly sexualized communities. I can't imagine the BACP putting out a policy that is culturally sensitive about how therapists should use Tinder and Grindr. They're just not going to go there. They are frightened of looking at it because it's a nightmare. But my colleagues and students are having conversations about how we manage these things because we recognize the importance of being part of these communities and we are not robots; we need to have ways to manage our needs appropriately. It's never acceptable to have sex with a client. I want to make that very clear. I don't think that's ever acceptable and, in most cases, probably not an ex-client. If people think they can make a case for it, where they've fallen for an ex-client, they should probably consider waiting at least two years after the work has ended and then take it to supervision and therapy and be sure. If this relationship came to light, can they represent themselves as behaving ethically and being morally OK? The power dynamic could still be there for life with some therapeutic relationships.

There may be situations where, for example, you only saw someone for six sessions, perhaps about them moving to the area or their new career; it wasn't that deep or intimate, so there wasn't a huge level of intimacy that entered into the relationship and maybe then, meeting someone two years later is a different thing. Sex with clients is not acceptable but we are likely to run into our clients and often in sexualized arenas. Many years ago, I ran into a client at a sauna but because I had a protocol in place, I knew how to operate and my client knew how to as well. I left the space, we discussed it at the next session, it was done in a way that wasn't shaming of the client being there, we acknowledged that we both had needs and it was handled in an appropriate way.

JC: What would you say about bumping into clients in non-sexualized spaces, like at the swimming pool or clubs and queer events? In my own practice, I generally talk about that pretty much at the start. If I'm going to be going somewhere like a queer arts festival, Pride and other political protests, I may bring it up again: 'In case we bump into each other, what I suggest we do is acknowledge each other and move on. If you don't want to be acknowledged that's absolutely fine too.' In the main, people say, 'Yes, let's nod and a smile and move on.'

DD: I think you're absolutely right; raise the possibility of going somewhere if you think they might be going there too and explore how it might be if you were to see each other there. Most of these non-intimate spaces are really OK. Some clients might feel uncomfortable seeing their therapist out in public but it's mostly not a big deal. I think it's more of a big deal if you know a client has a crush on you and you end up meeting each other at an event. Then there can be a tension there until you have managed to work through that. Those erotic transferences or counter-transferences can be recurring and need supporting and managing in the therapy room. Good supervision is essential here. Having a supervisor you can bring your whole self to.

Learn how to manage erotic transference and counter-transference

JC: Can you say a little about how you might do that?

DD: It helps to make them aware that this is often a natural occurrence originating in the relationship that you two have created. John Shlien's paper 'A counter-theory of transference' is important here. I always remember the opening quote: '"Transference" is a fiction, invented and maintained by the therapist to protect himself from the consequences of his own behavior.' The paper deconstructs Joseph Breuer and Anna O's relationship and Breuer's conversations with Freud when they co-create this theory of transference. Shlien was initially trained as a psychoanalyst and retrained and worked with Carl Rogers. He was a Harvard psychology professor. It's a great paper. It's pretty long and freely available online. It's a really useful way of learning about how we got to the point of thinking about transference as being the only explanation for what's happening in the therapy room. He coins the term 'originalance'. It's not a great word but it's about the origination of something that's occurred between the two of you. So he's saying look there first and understand why and how that might happen because in that intimate, warm, accepting relationship, loving feelings are going to develop and we have loving feelings for them. Therefore, it's understandable how clients – and therapists – might fall in love with each other.

JC: Yeah, it's true about the love. There are so many types of love which aren't sexual, which don't involve eros, anyway: I'm thinking of the ancient Greek term for universal love, 'agape'. And some therapists might also think, 'If this wasn't a therapeutic relationship, I can imagine being your friend.' So, processing the sorrow of that is important, I think – in supervision, though, not with the client. Even if the client stopped therapy, I don't think it would be appropriate to befriend them.

DD: I wouldn't necessarily write that off if it's later down the road. I think having some time and distance to think is important but if the therapy has finished and you run into each other – yes, you may still be their therapist in their mind, but I don't think its necessarily an issue that you can't share a social space or a meal together in that context. You might end up working on the same political project together and some of those dynamics work themselves out a bit and you get to see each other in different contexts as well.

Learn how to run your social media and navigate it with your clients

JC: How about social media? Nowadays I advise clients not to follow me on social media.

DD: I am aware of what I put on social media, so I don't share really personal stuff. In bygone years, I had a separate Facebook page with a fake name with my close friends and the Pink Therapy one that I used for work. Then they closed the ones with fake names, and you needed to provide evidence, so I had to bring my closest friends into my work Facebook page. I didn't want the people I meet through clubbing to know about my work, so I made a filter group so I can send messages just to my closest friends that are separate from my therapy colleagues. I can't control who follows me on Twitter and LinkedIn, but on Facebook I might rant in the Pink Therapy group a bit but I'm careful that I'm only bitching to other queer therapists.

JC: What about peer or group supervision? Could they become a problem for queer therapists because of our extended networks and increased likelihood of multiple relationships?

DD: But everyone in the group is bound by confidentiality by their professional association. I would still be mindful about not revealing too much about identifying features though. When you're working in a small geographical area as the only queer kinky therapist, you know everything that's going on between partners and lovers, but as a therapist you have to keep things confidential. Sometimes it's a nightmare because you have to hold all these secrets.

JC: It's a lot to hold. I didn't realize that when I was a trainee. There's a lot I didn't know and couldn't have known when I was a trainee.

DD: It's true, and trainees probably don't realize they're going to spend five years and £20,000 to £30,000 on training!

JC: Yes, the expense of training is problematic in terms of access for many people in our communities and these are really useful practical considerations. Talking of training, if you were to study at the queer therapy training school of your dreams, what would be on the curriculum? What would the organizational principles and values of the school be?

DD: Training from scratch, do you mean? Rather than what I'm doing, which is postgraduate training?

JC: Yes, from ground-level entry. Think back to your own training or what you know of current preliminary trainings. For me, an easy one would be normalizing pronoun use so trans and non-binary people feel properly acknowledged.

DD: I'd want to see 'out' queer faculty where queer psychological issues are incorporated throughout the curriculum and where intersectionality is front and centre. I'd want to see bursaries for people coming from disadvantaged and under-represented communities, which is one of the things we are doing for trans and non-binary counsellors – only one in each cohort but of a cohort of nine that could be significant. And because trans and non-binary people are generally disadvantaged compared to regular queers, for instance, you might spend five to ten years trying to figure out your gender stuff and that pulls you out of the normal career trajectory that your cisgender peers go through. Then you might have to spend a lot of money on your transition. QTIPOC people are really under-represented because of systemic racism, so they may have less money and fewer opportunities for work, so bursaries would be a good thing. It also brings a more diverse group and that creates an incredibly rich learning experience. Then you need staff who can manage the differences. It might play into white fragility, or some cis people might get freaked out or they can't respect 'they' pronouns. They would be my first thoughts on what courses need to be including. We recently created an endorsement programme which will give generic training courses a Pink Therapy endorsement stamp. The stamp will be a sign that they are including queer issues all the way through their courses, that they don't assume gender or other hierarchies and that they challenge them. This will make it easier for queer students to find safe places to learn and train and it might encourage other courses to up their game too.

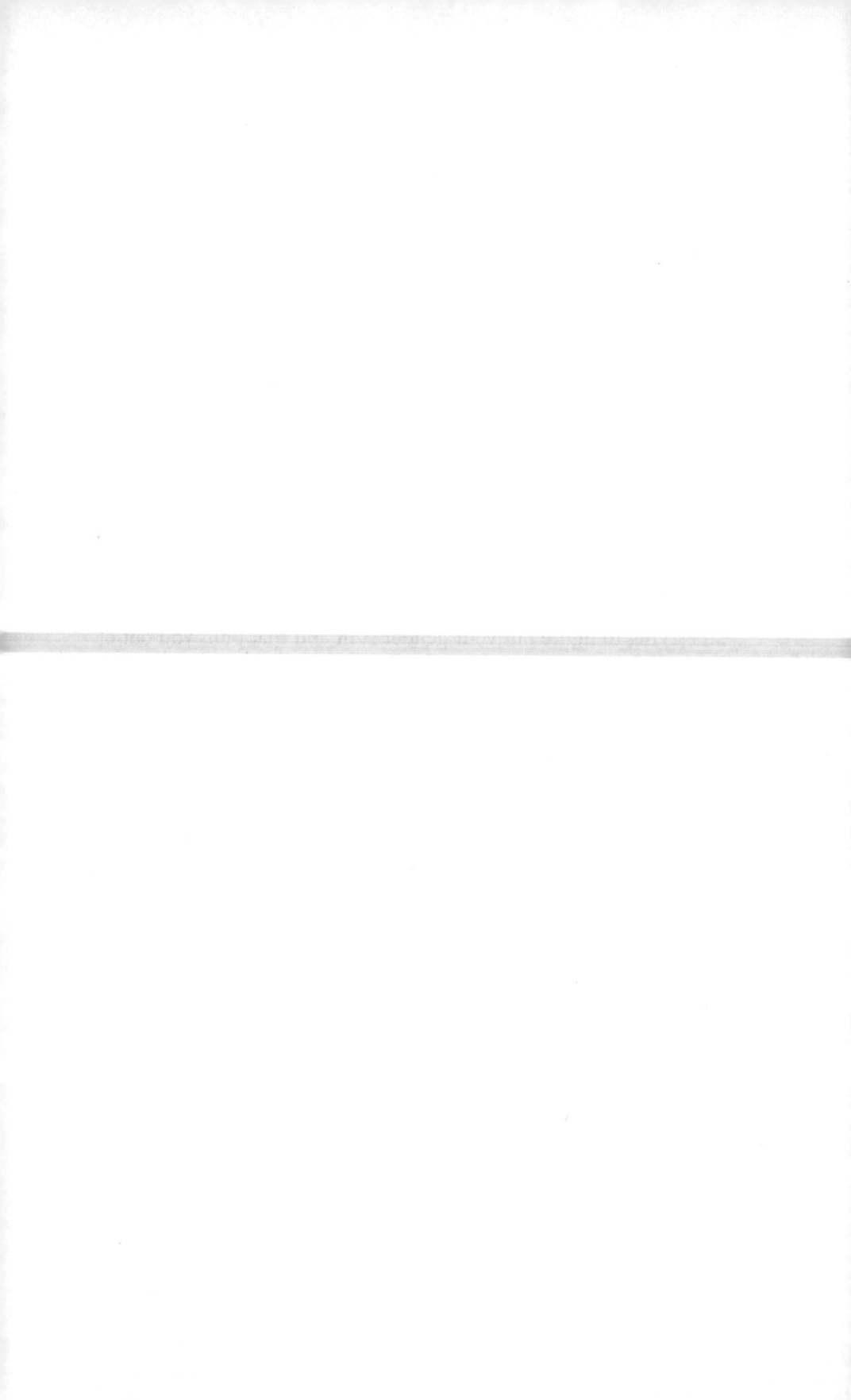

CHAPTER 16

Emotional diaspora

Bay De Veen

Bay De Veen reflects on her search for a deeper, more nuanced kind of supervision, a practice that she re-names supra-vision to support and nurture her therapeutic work.

Displacement

I'm looking out to sea right now as I write this. I'm high up at the top window of an old Victorian building and, as I look out towards Beachy Head, I notice a small boat in the distance. I wonder if it carries more displaced people in search of something. The possibility of a new home or place of safety. At this point, more than 65 million people globally are seeking refuge somewhere. There is no global plan of action to address this human disaster, even though under international law anyone in need of protection has a right to claim asylum.

I find myself reflecting further on the strangeness and the brutality of the times; so many people uprooted from their homes with little or no humane options for living in dignity or safety. Home for many can become uninhabitable, unintelligible. I remember the line from a book by Ocean Vuong (2019, p. 12): 'What is a country but a life sentence?' Being within or beyond national boundaries can determine your value or worthlessness as a human being. This is also relevant to whole ecosystems. Traumas enacted over time through colonization, exploitation and extraction, and the emotions these practices inevitably ignite in response; antagonism, xenophobia, war, genocide and ecocide all stem from the traumatic repetition of inequality and injustice and the disassociation that accompanies such trauma.

Supra-vision

This is what fills our global matrix of existence, and I am in need of a supra-visioner to support my unpacking of this emotional diaspora. Most of us are displaced in various ways. This can be a chosen or an enforced predicament, or somewhere in between. It is my life's work to see this in individual stories as well as feeling into the magnitude of the bigger picture, but I also need to be held in this seeing by my wise and trusted people.

Supervision means literally overseeing, or seeing more, or seeing more broadly, yet in my experience – and in research too (Ladany *et al.*, 2013) – a lot of supervision is actually rather narrow and limited, and even damaging. It is in the context of this supervision that can't see itself and its limitations that I imagine a supra-vision. *Supra* comes from the Latin meaning 'above and beyond'. So supra-vision is a supervision that goes above and beyond what exists, particularly in keeping an eye on the well-being of practitioners and, by extension, the profession as a whole, because supervision is meant to be the way in which we monitor our work in this field.

My search for a deeper, more nuanced supra-vision to support and nurture my own work began two years previously, when a very wise person once said that it is essential, when seeking any form of help for ourselves, that we choose the right practitioner. One who can see us and hold what we bring. Only then can we really heal from injury and be adequately supported.

Something about this recognition that we need to seek someone 'who can see us' landed for me in a profound way, both on the day I heard it and over time at different moments. It brought to mind the many instances in which this had absolutely not happened. Accumulations of conscious and unconscious acts of harm or omissions, like small eruptions, laid themselves out: neglect, thoughtlessness and violence laced into mundane or normalized acts within the mainstream health/care professions and institutions. I include psychotherapy and supervision within this health architecture. Much of it is a lack of care or concern. Not really seeing who we are. An inability to be present in a fully human way. No attention to detail. It led me to a mindful practice of choosing my people.

The second supra-vision session

What follows is a blend of real events, fiction or fabulation and 'theratopian' longing in the form of a 90-minute monthly meeting, and this is our second meeting. It's late summer and we decide to meet for a walk between Lewes and Glyndebourne, East Sussex. The weather is warm and calm, held in by the deep, blue Sussex sea.

Oriel Wycker is a 60-year-old supervisor and energy therapist who agreed to be one of my supra-visioners. She soon became one of my people. We had an initial discussion in person and decided to continue meeting every six weeks.

ORIEL WYCKER: I have been looking forward to our meeting today and I prepared by thinking about us individually and also what surrounds us, what is present in the matrix? I wanted to bring things from our different environments to anchor us somehow; so, I have a stone from Fairlight Glen for you – there you go – and a shell from Malta, my special place. It has a comforting feel in my hand and helps me focus. I thought you might like something elemental.

BAY DE VEEN: Thank you, wow! I love that gesture. It's also amazing to be out of the confines of rooms and screens. Being in nature is my centred place.

OW: Yes, a different energy, and sometimes I think it's helpful to know we can change what and how we do these meetings. That seems important to both of us as we navigate this supra-vision process. I'm curious where you want to begin today.

BDV: I have been thinking a lot about migrations, movement over time but in different contexts. In the global frame, displacement is massive and ongoing. The world is in so much chaos and flux right now, yet as a therapist in the twenty-first century I feel like there is a stuckness, a rigidity and lack of dynamism in the institutional culture of therapy. It doesn't seem responsive enough to these colossal changes we face. Something about old structures and new challenges being out of sync. What has always attracted me to this work is its dynamic possibilities, but the more static and over-regulated it seeks to become, the less I want to be in it.

OW: I see, big stuff there. Let's think about how we can get into the detail of that. Can you say more about this rigidity, stuckness?

BDV: Well, like almost everything else, therapy is a business now; it's commodified. Each cycle of anxious regulation creates a business opportunity based on ever more fears about how to avoid complaints from clients or being sued for malpractice. So, fear is now a central defining feature of this profession. The result is a loss of the centrality of the use of self, creatively and instinctively. That's why so much of standard supervision feels like going to confess all your bad moves and screw-ups. Training is increasingly singular, isolated themes or topics-based, and outdated by its desire to reside under the dying wing of nineteenth-century medicine. We look at symptomatic things like depression and anxiety instead of the whole person within a context. Oscar Wilde (2016, p. 26) once said that, 'We teach people how to remember, we never teach them how to grow.' And you can't grow and develop if you are stunted by fear and a need to know everything and get everything right all the time.

OW: Yes, I see this too, but how has it impacted you?

BDV: I gave up on the marketplace that is workshops and mainstream CPD ages ago. There are a few exceptions but the creative rigor mortis I consistently felt at these events, not to mention the expense in money and time, left me feeling quite determined to find my own way through. I knew I needed to expand, recalibrate on what I needed in order to become the kind of practitioner I wanted to be. I needed to look beyond the usual places and offerings to find mentors, coaches, writers, poets, teachers and supra-visioners. I have always had a strong internal sense of direction. I trust my instincts, so I suppose my response was to go my own way.

OW: Indeed. It takes quite a while to connect with the people you need to have around you to do the incredibly precious work that I know you do with clients. We are our best tool. Insightful, gifted practitioners are like delicate instruments and they, you, need to be cared for.

BDV: Thank you, Oriel. I realize I don't hear that kind of feedback from other professionals. But in my practice, I always had a bag of tricks. You know? Queer Tarot decks, crystals, clay, interesting articles and websites that I share with clients, but I realized more and more how meaningful therapeutic work happens when we really connect to and curiously engage with the uniqueness of a person's experience. So being able to respond to that uniqueness requires significant adaptability, flexibility. We must do this by any means necessary and, for me, creativity is the key to connecting with people, and that connecting is the cornerstone of therapy. Fear will always disrupt that. Sounds obvious, right? But I started to notice that being open and really present is actually really difficult for so many people, in life and in therapy. So, when we encounter it, it can be mind-blowing and being seen for the first time, possibly ever, becomes transformative. Theoretical moorings can both support and obstruct being present. Relating can get lost when we become a bit too techniquey. There is an increasing 'how to work with …' culture in psychotherapy and perhaps a concomitant anxiety in many therapists that needs the reassurance of a 'how to' approach. Or maybe this approach stoked the anxieties?

OW: So true, the simple things can get overlooked. Though it sounds like you used your own inner guide to nourish yourself, your practice?

BDV: I think that's it. I love being in a state of ongoing learning, so initially I shifted from reading hundreds of textbooks on psychotherapy and ideas to broader related interests, from quantum physics to neuroscience to psychobiotics. I got hooked on the beauty and mystery of biology and plant communication and eventually everything I read about or researched just began to connect up and became exciting. I had an increasing feeling of having enough, and being enough, and was able to really feel enlivened in sessions in a new way. I found that a broad and open curiosity about everything opened up increasingly new ways to view things, the world, people and life. It feels limitless. It feels like the opposite of fear.

OW: How joyous that sounds, like finding a hidden portal.

BDV: Adrienne Rich (2003, p. xvi) describes poetry in a way that reminds me of therapy at its most vital best: 'The disorderly welter of subjectivity and imagination.' I think poetry and therapy are similar; they are both mostly short form and intense. We attempt to squeeze everything into that 50-minute window and sometimes it's a perfect distillation. A wonderful welter.

Tea and space

BDV: I have some tea with me. Would you like some?

[From my special travel flask, I pour a very hot, black tea called Herringbone, a smoky concoction mixed in the Samovar Tea House, a tea shop in Ely that closed in the pandemic only to rise again as an online trader. A wafting aroma of peat-like smokiness reminds me of Lagavulin whiskey and campfires.]

OW: Oh, yes please, it smells amazing. Oh, I like that. Thank you.

[We talk tea for a while and take in the view silently for some time.]

BDV: Oriel, I'm really liking the pace of today.

OW: Me too. What a gift to be surrounded by all this green and sparkly sea.

BDV: It's gorgeous. Not many days pass without a feeling of gratitude for it all.

The knowing body

OW: So, you mentioned earlier a few things we could go back to that I'm curious about: migrations and outmoded medical models that influence the therapeutic organizations' direction of travel.

BDV: Migrations links nicely there with 'direction of travel'. I feel like I have always been migrating in one way or another. This is being formulated as I speak so I hope it doesn't drift off.

OW: I can help you out with that if you like?

BDV: OK. So, pretty much every culture has a history of helping people with problems in life through priests, witch doctors, elders, wise ancestors, herbalism, rituals. The same aim but different approaches. All of these things make up the common pathway of the eventual emergence of therapy but because today power seems to be settling around medicine and science – in an attempt to create legitimacy and measurability – it is creating a conservative vortex of sameness and rigidity. But – as is always the case – there are dissenters, heretics. So, in some ways, you're right when you say I have resisted and found my own way. But I know things felt better to me when our diverse communities of therapists had more freedom. I also know that when people have any kind of issue in life that needs help and support, usually it requires different types of input because we are complex; I mean our bodies, environment and history, etc. I also know that I don't have all the answers. I feel as if I am navigating away from this rigidity and my own experience is guiding me.

OW: I'm wondering if your health and body have informed your learning? We did talk about it briefly last time we met.

BDV: I sometimes describe my body as the pain-body. Pain has been a strong reoccurring theme for me for a lot of my life, but particularly since menopause. I could write a book on the menopausal experience! Reading Molly McCully Brown's *Places I've Taken My Body*, our experiences are hugely different, but I feel deeply what she means when she says, 'My life is built to flex unconsciously around new pain' (2020, p. 3). This can be physical or emotional pain. It creates a different sort of being in the world. It's weighted somehow. I feel strongly that we must find a way to help each other with our pain and trauma in a kind and gentle way because I know how it feels to be on the receiving end of bad practice in medicine and therapy. Our bodies can teach us so much if we pay attention. Even Bessel Van der

Kolk (2014) had to challenge the rigid status quo to better understand the biology of trauma. The lack of knowledge and awareness when he was starting out was astounding.

OW: We know as therapists that abuse, trauma and harm are in most of our clients' stories and this isn't the exception but the norm. The harm becomes normalized and minimized and there is nowhere for those feelings to go. It's culturally frowned upon to talk about our pain, though our language is full of violence: 'fighting' a virus or 'battling' cancer, even the use of 'trigger' as the start of a panic response. Even the pandemic is responded to as if we are at war, when what we need to understand is our interdependency with our environment.

I recently read *The Mind Fixers* by Anne Harrington (2019) and she really brings together the sheer lack of understanding and knowledge, not to mention brutal experimentation, that was psychiatry and medicine, and those ghosts are still present.

BDV: Yes, ordinary people have been traumatized by the so-called care institutions over hundreds of years and it leaves scars. This is, of course, partly why regulation or ethical frames exist. But practitioners will be better able to work ethically if they are well supported enough to think for themselves instead of passively following protocols.

Some of my experiences with therapy and supervision have come about because I have questioned quite a lot of things and some people have seen this as an unwelcome challenge rather than the beginning of a conversation. Supervision has sometimes felt like a closed system where the rules have to be intuited.

Harmful practice

BDV: I remember one supervisor who was great in some ways, but suddenly lost their moorings and started interrogating me about why I didn't believe in therapy because I had rarely had much of it myself. How did I think I could possibly offer anything unless I toil for years with my own therapist? I was being asked to justify myself for not needing lots of therapy. It was as if there could only be one way for a psychotherapist to get what they need. The thing is, they didn't seem aware that they were attacking me. Something switched in them, I could see it, and I wondered if it was because I came into the therapy profession in a different way to most people, who seem to come to it because they have had therapy themselves. I only heard one psychotherapist, Dr Betty Cannon (2015), who described coming to therapy in a similar way to me, which was through an interest in existential philosophy. Getting interested in that and phenomenology led me to psychotherapy. It felt like its practical manifestation, but that interest helped me deal with my own mental health issues earlier in life. I realized that curiosity can be the antidote to depression, and it works well in therapy if it is genuine.

We all come to ourselves in different ways

BDV: We all come to ourselves in different ways. It isn't OK to punish and exclude people for thinking differently. Diversity is good in and of itself because I believe it creates and maintains caring communities. And strong communities nurture the uniqueness of its individual members; this is a principle within anarchy. My ideal philosophy would be a blend I call anarcho-marxistentialism. When I have that, I don't need much therapy. I prefer supra-vision but, because it only partly existed, I found it necessary to invent it.

There are lots of examples of what I call big-picture bullying too, where some supervisors have really not understood the importance of clients seeing what happens to them as systemic, and this is part of queer experience in normative cultures. It can be useful in orienting our queer understanding of ourselves, our positionality and context. We can then challenge clients' beliefs about their not being good or valuable enough by exposing the limitations of the hetero-dominant hegemony that creates hierarchies of value that exclude queers, people with disabilities, those with neurodivergence, BIPOC, etc.

Some supervisors would argue with me endlessly about the personal being more important than the political and variations on these themes. It just matters sometimes for some people that they become aware of the system creating their situation. It also helps to know that there is a potential solidarity in being outside of things. You can feel at home outside as well as inside. I have in the past felt unsupported and misunderstood and it takes its toll. If I didn't have a belief in myself, I may have given up. I did eventually find my practitioners though. My eclectic terroir in which to grow.

OW: Terroir! Oh, I like that image.

[We laugh at this.]

BDV: Something needs to be said about systemic violence. The word violence creates challenge, but it isn't individual events as much as the steady accumulation over a long time of being seen as somehow 'wrong/odd/different' and how that weighs in on you. How these normalizing and continuous oppressions feed into what you could tenuously call a 'collective consciousness', which then traumatizes some, but also makes space for irrational outbursts of hate against certain groups. That's how violence quietly mounts in small ways over time so as to hide itself in plain sight. It is how white, cis hetero-dominant society perpetuates such violence by simply maintaining or reproducing itself and its norms. We become emotional acrobats trying to navigate this. Or we don't. Often clients will say they left therapy with someone who they felt judged by and who didn't understand queerness, race, class or even pain and illness. Not being seen is harmful and so much gets in the way of seeing clearly. Privilege of one kind or another stops us seeing what it's like for the other person. That's what supervision is for – self-examination.

OW: We also have to hold all that for clients, but in supra-vision this multiplies. Between us, it's a lot to contain. Shall we let the sand fall through the hourglass for a while? Perhaps to gently hold the enormity of displacement internally and externally, many of us have taken flight from ourselves in an attempt to escape from what feels overwhelming and unstoppable.

[Some reflective time passes, and we enjoy the warm sun.]

BDV: I think though, in relation to what you said about taking flight from ourselves, that it is probably an obvious trauma response in a violent world: this disassociation, disconnection and excessive busyness.

So many of us are lost to ourselves and to what really matters. On a collective level, that's how we got to this point, slowly over time terrible things start to feel normal so that the suffering of others can easily be forgotten. But we are also trying to navigate ourselves back to or maybe towards something different. This is part of the human condition.

OW: I know your experience of the menopause was a real challenge. The first time we met you were in a lot of pain I seem to remember.

Menopausal body

BDV: What I learned in different journeys with pain is a new body-specific language. It is a very different kind of communication, not always clear or obvious and so often overlooked or ignored. The intense and anarchic menopause I had forced me to understand this communication in more detail. All the interconnected complexity that is me and my physicality meeting my specific environment. It was so much to deal with, and I felt as if I had been given a different body overnight.

There is no one-size-fits-all answer to dealing with these hormonal changes, and that's partly why I had to become my own healer. Doctors were dismissive, not interested, patronizing and wouldn't even agree to simple diagnostics. So, I had to find answers elsewhere, take control of my own health in new ways. A deep kind of research became necessary because it's hard to find reliable and personalized information. I learned so much about how amazing our bodies are, the intelligence in their design and adaptation. The sheer volume of activity going on inside us made me question aloneness and will. The gut, it turns out, is more of a brain than the brain. It's definitely in the driving seat.

Now, I cannot feel alone with all the inner discussions, teeming microbes, nerve endings and signalling, as well as feeling ancestors nearby and strange coincidences, because when you really slow down and pay attention, universes expand and everything becomes so interesting, so much more complex. A real concatenation.

I had to re-learn most of what I thought I knew about health, and I managed to become pain-free in a year, but it was quite an intense and often challenging experience. The pain comes back; it's an ongoing journey and conversation with my body, my choices – and how much I can hold for others I work with and in my life. In many healthcare settings, being a middle-aged woman was a real eye-opener because we are so objectified and because medicine only treats individual symptoms, not the whole person. I have worked with so many women who are treated as if they are mad for coming with symptoms that medicine can't and will not understand. It's one example of the antiquated approach of medicine to the health of complex bodies.

All this over time made me realize that having different viewpoints is useful and we have to question things, live more consciously. I stopped feeling a lack, and just feel so much gratitude and wonder. The practice of therapy began to feel more of an art again, as I saw how many more possibilities there are. Pain is a difficulty and a revelation. I realized the freedom that can come from taking back the power to decide what works for me on my terms and that really influenced what kind of practitioner I was becoming.

OW: I so hear you.

Indigenous ideas

OW: You have reminded me, as I listen to you, of *Braiding Sweetgrass*, that life-changing book by Robin Wall Kimmerer (2020). Such a loving and nourishing read. Poetry and science in one place. She says in that book that seeing all the gifts from nature helps us feel a sense of abundance and that, 'Recognising abundance rather than scarcity undermines an economy that thrives by creating unmet desires. Gratitude cultivates an ethic of fullness, but the economy needs emptiness' (Kimmerer, 2020, p. 111). Nature helped me through and beyond menopause, I do relate.

BDV: I love that book too, and in fact, Indigenous wisdom and knowledge really helped me shift my thinking on almost everything. Our disconnection from nature, each other and ultimately ourselves creates a state of homelessness or non-belonging and nothing makes sense anymore. But it mostly can feel like hopelessness and powerlessness until we start paying more attention to detail.

Tyson Yunkaporta is an interesting guy, a wise academic and Indigenous thinker, but the thing I got from him was the idea about all of us being at one time or other taken away from our place of origin, possibly many times throughout our ancestral past, and we became 'a global diaspora of refugees severed not only from land, but from the sheer genius that comes from belonging in symbiotic relation to it' (Yunkaporta, 2019, p. 2).

OW: So most people are more distanced from who and what they really are? A kind of emotional/internal diaspora? I also get a sense here of layers of things, time, history, nature, the body, the geo-politics of the time, among other things, all gathering for you, and what does all that do in you, how is it held or expressed?

BDV: I like that idea: emotional diaspora. It kind of syncs up with the way we think about dysregulation in the body, that constant triggering of the vagus nerve, its wandering and stabilizing communication in the full length of the body. So much is going on within us that we are unaware of, so people often say they feel hijacked by their own bodies when 'triggered'. It always helps to know the biology of that dysregulation so we can learn how to navigate it and centre ourselves. Speak the language of our bodies.

In terms of what helps, or how I deal with it all – talking it out with someone who gets it, that's all I need. So, thank you for being one of those people. Talking things out like this is a bit like untangling, letting a breeze blow through all the density of everything gathering. I really appreciate you right now.

OW: I love working this way. It's satisfying, 'all-of-a-piece' somehow. And that's great that it works for you too. I will check in on that though. Have we spent much time on queerness in all of this? I'm mindful to make room for our different queernesses! But also to weave it into experiences. I know it's come up, but I imagine there's so much more.

BDV: Interestingly, this is another thing that has changed for me in the last three or four years. Being a lesbian is an important historical, political and cultural marker for me. I don't like the way some people are trying to narrow its range and potential. Transphobia depresses me so much. Lesbians understand that we are often hated and feared, so seeing that anti-trans hate rise in our numbers feels like amnesia to me. We need all the comrades we can get, particularly if erasure is such a problem. I had to smile though, when a trans woman I know recently told me she had decided to refer to herself as a 'transbian' so as not to piss anyone off. I like that inventiveness.

Asexual biophilia

BDV: But since menopause, I also occupy a space that I describe as asexual biophilia. The natural world is phenomenal, and it makes me happy, and I feel that I'm part of it, but in an ever-expanding pretty profound way. I found gradually that I wasn't interested in sex, and it was a careful process of working things out with my partner so we could recalibrate our relationship. It was tricky but brilliant and I didn't want to feel shame or be corrected just because some hormone levels had dropped. And libido decline is the only thing some medics want to treat. I think, looking back, I always had an asexual part of me waiting for a moment to shine. After menopause and what for me were the labours and pains of living with this specific female anatomy, I could have a new relationship to my body in a sensual world on my own terms. It is a freedom to be expansive and immersed in things other than sex. Though its hormonal, it's also natural and I don't feel a need to 'correct' anything.

It's interesting too because I talk to so many young people who have chosen to identify as asexual, partly because sex feels dangerous for lots of reasons. It can be difficult to connect and trust people; consent is misunderstood or just ignored in our violent culture. And of course, these days, it's a bit less taboo to say, 'No thanks, not interested' in these sex-positive times if you are on the asexual spectrum. Though so many people think they can't say no to anything. No is powerful, radical. It's seen by many as a character flaw if you're not ready and willing to be used. There are many variations of asexuality and it's a natural thing, whether it's always been there or whether it arrives at a certain point in life. Pleasure has infinite forms.

Queernesses

OW: So, a lesbian asexual biophilic? Wow.

[I nod in agreement.]

OW: And I'm seeing the evolving nature of these identities. I could share something about me if you would be OK with that?

BDV: Yes.

OW: I think I moved around with sexuality exploration in my early life and had some gender confusion for a while, which faded out, but since my late thirties it's stayed pretty fixed. People assume I'm straight but I'm bi and demi-sexual and it can be annoying when your queerness isn't seen. I do like the increasing visibility of the asexuality spectrum; it's so diverse. So much prejudice on the subject.

BDV: Thank you for sharing that, I didn't know you were demi-sexual. So much stays out of sight. Hetero-dominance can feel so oppressive and invalidating just by its unresponsive existence and if this is ever articulated, people who aren't queer get upset or offended. All the time gets spent mopping up their pain and you rarely get close to what needs to be talked about and repaired. So much therapy is about this cis hetero-patriarchy causing so much trauma and pain.

The queers in families often become the 'problem', the 'attention seeker', the 'selfish one', the 'weak one'. All the blame and shame gets stored in that role that the queer has to carry and be responsible for and nobody else can see or acknowledge it.

In the therapy system, there is a carelessness or a disregard for the diversity and complexity of queer people. They don't see or really get our diverse standpoints, but they want to benefit from our knowledge and experience by getting us to commodify and perform our 'queer particularity' as if it's a separate topic from life. In a learning context, like race, it's seen as a little topic to be examined. We are not seen as part of the complex matrix of life, we are treated as problematic, exceptions.

Yet, it is precisely this separation that gives queer people their viewpoint and potential for empathy. It's a long view, far from the feeling of home.

OW: An institutional blindness, then. All the learning is focused outward to the 'other' to be analyzed or made sense of within the limits of normativity. Or one could say that white, cis hetero-patriarchy cannot see itself and, therefore, doesn't understand its oppressive relationship to whatever it doesn't understand. I hear you. So many clients will say how their previous therapist was pretty good, but they just didn't get the queer stuff, right? Neither do many families for that matter.

BDV: I hear that a lot! And it's not about becoming an expert in queerness; it's about understanding yourself, your power and how a lack of empathic understanding gets oppressive and shaming when these useless binaries of 'normal' and 'abnormal' perpetuate and create and maintain hierarchies of value.

In Indigenous philosophy, there aren't really boundaries of existence, rather everything is interdependently in relationship, and everything has subjectivity and therefore value. But psychotherapy sits within the medical model that seeks to isolate everything from source and examine it out of its context. So, on many trainings we learn in chunks of isolation, depression, self-harm, bisexuality, etc. Connections and continuities are not made within that model of learning. It's not expansive or phenomenological.

OW: I think there are still places to learn in a more holistic way. As you said before, there is always dissent.

Coming home

BDV: When I think of Carl Rogers, I'm reminded of the difficulty in simply becoming who we are. How difficult a task. Yet so much in life now stops all of us getting in touch with who we really are because distraction is everywhere and stops us thinking very much at all so we can just buy stuff to fill the void.

We are so often out of our minds with stress. There is little time for quiet and rest and that gets in the way of everything important. We are constantly abandoning our needs and desires to the 'shoulds' and expectations or values of others. Those aspects of ourselves that we disavow, split off from or cast out become a diaspora of ourselves, forever in exile unless we can find a tender heart to help us come home.

But in the words 'become who we are' is an invitation to emerge into something we know has been lost somewhere along the way, but also to explore openly the not yet known. We are not fixed, imprisoned entities, but rather full of potential, possibility. Though they would be unlikely bedfellows, Rogers leads me to Munoz, a much-missed queer academic, who gives this idea both a queer slant and a more collective focus when he says:

> The here and now is a prison house. We must strive, in the face of the here and now's totalising rendering of reality, to think and feel a then and there. Some will say that all we have are the pleasures of this moment, but we must never settle for that minimal transport; we must dream and enact new and better pleasures, other ways of being in the world, and ultimately new worlds. (Munoz, 2009, p. 1)

OW: Yes, I can see the meeting point, the motion in these ideas.

BDV: Sometimes being in the moment is wonderful. Noticing flowers, a drink with friends or just being still and at peace, but there are so many other possibilities of being we haven't tapped into, and we must explore. I use these ideas and lots of other things to help clients feel this freedom, to know that life doesn't have to be only as they have lived it so far. The idea of emergence or becoming is important. It's about honouring process, an unfolding that allows time to review, deconstruct, reconstruct, change your mind and your direction. I am learning this too.

Lost queers

BDV: In 2021, we lost a queer elder and radical thinker in Lauren Berlant. *Cruel Optimism* (Berlant, 2011) was one of those important texts that, despite being difficult to understand in places, nonetheless challenged the capitalist lies about what constitutes happiness. Basically, what they were saying is that the things you think you must be or acquire to be happy are in fact the things that will stop you flourishing. This is why often people will say, 'Oh, I'm so privileged, so lucky, I have a great job, money, a partner, a dog, holidays, but I feel so depressed and anxious all the time.' Or maybe we think 'something's missing'. How colonized we are that we only ever feel a lack of something. Not surprising in a competitive, masculinist culture. The constant feeling that you don't have what is needed to be happy drives people crazy. If we always want more, when will it be enough? How will we know?

Audre Lorde (2007, p. 31) said that we are all more blind to what we have than to what we have not. We need to think differently to appreciate the reality of that.

OW: This is me doing my energy thing, but I just feel that you are, despite what you said earlier about psychotherapy, definitely at home in yourself. Perhaps this is why you are feeling and seeing so much. Maybe at last you have enough?

BDV: I'm at home in the welter of existence. The migrations of my many ancestors have brought me here to welcome and witness the many stories and journeys I must hold for those yet to make sense of them. What a privilege that is.

Glossary

Language is an ever-changing medium; definitions move and are different for each person who uses them, so some of the terms listed below may well be considered outdated in the next few years. This being the case, please treat this glossary as a snapshot from 2022.

Ableist Adjective used to refer to systemic, interpersonal and other forms of discrimination and social prejudice against Disabled people. For further information see the Social Model of Disability, developed by Disabled people, which describes people as being disabled by barriers to society, not by impairments or difference.

AFAB Acronym for assigned female at birth.

Ally Someone who speaks up for and challenges prejudice, structural or otherwise, towards people with whom they do not share an identity, such as a white person who is an anti-racist ally, or a heterosexual or cis person who is a gay, lesbian, bi and trans ally.

AMAB Acronym for assigned male at birth.

Anti-racist Adjective or noun for a person or organization actively working to disrupt systemic racism and white supremacist colonial structures, power dynamics, and interpersonal and intra-psychic ideologies.

Aromantic Adjective and noun for people who feel little or no romantic attraction towards others.

Asexual Adjective and noun for people who feel little or no sexual attraction towards others. Sometimes shortened to Ace. *See also* **demi-sexual,** below, and **aromantic**, above.

BAME Acronym for Black, Asian and minority ethnic. Used in the UK by some and considered problematic by others who say that it implies all ethnic minorities are a homogenous group and that it comes from a white construct of race. *See also* **POC, BIPOC** and **QTIPOC**, below.

BDSM Acronym for bondage and discipline, dominance and submission, and sadomasochism. An umbrella term for sexual and erotic practices, relationships and communities which involve playing with control, power, roles and/or sensation. Also called kink/kinky.

Binders A garment that is worn to flatten the appearance of the chest area. Chest binders are manufactured and sold commercially but are also often made at home from tight-fitting garments or tapes/bandages. Chest binding is most common among transgender, non-binary and androgynous people. However, it is not exclusive to these communities. Over time, and with persistent use, binding can cause a range of physical health issues, such as back pain and poor posture.

BIPOC Acronym for Black, Indigenous and people of colour. Used mainly in the United States to centre Black and Indigenous people's lives and also to demonstrate solidarity between all communities of colour.

Bisexual Adjective and noun used to describe people who are attracted sexually and/or relationship-wise to more than one gender (or to both same-sex gender and other gender partners).

Certified sexological bodyworker (CSB) A qualified, trained professional working within the field of sexological bodywork. This can include one-way touch and bodywork from practitioner to client.

Chemsex Originating from the gay men's health sector, the term refers to the use of a combination of drugs, including crystal methamphetamine, mephedrone and/or GHB/GBL (gamma hydroxybutyrate/gamma butyrolactone), before or during sex, enabling sex that can last for hours, or even days.

Cisgender A person whose gender identity corresponds with the sex they were assigned – based on their genitals – at birth, by medical clinicians.

Also used in the shorter form 'cis'. Cis is a dominant category that positions those who are trans as 'other'/marginal.

Cis hetero-patriarchy A feminist term referring to socio-political systems that primarily privilege cisgender heterosexual males over those with marginalized sexualities and gender identities.

Cis-normative lens A subconscious and/or conscious belief in cis experiences as the 'natural human norm', and anything else as an anomaly or a deviation from that norm; only being able to understand trans experiences as they relate to the 'standard' of cis experiences.

Cis normativity An expectation or assumption that all bodies and genders are binary: cis male or cis female. As with heterosexuality, there's nothing wrong with being cisgender. However, like heteronormativity, cis normativity is a problem – at an interpersonal or societal level – because it excludes anyone who does not fit the cis norm (e.g. trans people) and imposes rigid standards on those who are cisgender.

Consensual non-monogamy (CNM) Someone who practices CNM may or may not be partnered and is committed to negotiating multiple relationships with sexual and/or romantic partners. They may use words like polyamorous, open relationship, ethical non-monogamy or relationship-anarchy to describe their relationship styles.

Demi-sexual Someone who feels sexual attraction to others only when they have developed an emotional bond with them.

Disorder of sex development (DSD) This emerged from debate and the subsequent creation of a Consensus Statement after a convention in Chicago in 2005, where it was agreed that the term 'disorder of sex development' (DSD) would replace 'intersex' and 'hermaphrodite' in medical literature. The term is controversial because of the implication that what is naturally occurring should be considered a 'disorder'. Some people, using lower case 'dsd', redefine DSD as 'diversity of sex development' instead, for this reason. *See also* **endosex, intersex** and **VSC,** below

Endosex The term used for someone who doesn't have variations in sex characteristics. *See also* **DSD** above, **intersex** and **VSC** below.

Family constellation The people, structure, dynamics, themes and patterns within someone's family of origin.

Gay Adjective and noun used to describe male same-sex attraction, relationships and sex but is also used by women and non-binary people to describe non-heterosexual attraction, relationships, behaviours and sex.

Gender non-conforming/-expansive Someone who behaves or expresses their gender in such a way that doesn't conform to the normative social expectations for people of that gender. *See also* **non-binary** and **genderqueer**, below.

Genderqueer People who are both male and female, neither or beyond these categories. Sometimes used in a more political sense than **non-binary** (see below) in opposition to the normative cultural gender binary.

GSRD Acronym for gender, sexual and relationship diversity. Popularised by Pink Therapy to accommodate the various identities that exist beyond the colonising categories the term incorporates non-normative sex, sexuality and relationship styles and preferences and provides an alternative to the ever-growing LGBTIQA++ acronym which can also be limiting and exclusionary.

Heteronormative Assuming of heterosexual identities and relationship(s) dynamics, including marriage, children, so-called 'male' and 'female' roles, duties and expectations.

Intersectional Term developed by Kimberlé Crenshaw (1991) to acknowledge the multi-faceted nature of the lived experiences of Black women (originally in a legal context) and, as many Black feminists attest, that have still not been addressed. Used here to describe an approach and awareness that considers how different aspects of oppression and experience, such as race, gender, class, age, sexuality and ability, impact a person's experience of themselves and the world and how the world interacts with and relates to them.

Intersectionality A theory that various forms of discrimination centred on race, gender, class, disability, sexuality and other forms of identity do not work independently but interact to produce particularized forms of social oppression. As such, oppression is the result of intersecting forms of exclusionary practices. It is thus suggested that the study of identity-based discrimination needs to identify and take account of these intersectionalities.

Intersex This umbrella term relates to sex traits and the variations that can naturally occur in people who are born with sex characteristics – genitals, hormones, gonads and/ or chromosome patterns – that do not fit typical binary definitions of male or female. It is distinct from a person's sexual orientation or gender identity. Somebody who has an intersex variation can have a sexual orientation that is straight, gay, lesbian, bisexual or asexual, they can have a gender identity that is cis, trans, female, male, both or neither just like anyone else in society. Some prefer the term **variation in sex characteristics (VSC)**, below. The opposite of intersex is **endosex**, above.

Lesbian Adjective and noun used to describe female same-sex or same-gender attraction, relationships and sex. Used by women and non-binary people to describe non-heterosexual attraction, relationships, behaviours and sex.

LGBTIQA+, LGBTQIA+, LGBTIQ+, LGBTQQAI+ Acronym for lesbian, gay, bisexual, transgender, intersex, queer and questioning, and asexual. The acronyms are used variously to describe the marginalized sexual and gender identities. The plus is used to signify the other identities not referenced by a letter, such as kinky, polyamorous, agender, aromantic, etc. *See also* **GSRD**.

Non-binary People who are neither exclusively male nor female. As with other genders, there are as many ways to be non-binary as there are individuals. Non-binary people can have any biology and express their gender in any number of ways.

Packers A person who doesn't have a cisgender penis might use a packer to create the feeling and appearance of having one. Commercial packers are usually made from silicone or neoprene and generally resemble the bulge of cisgender penises in size and shape. Some people also opt to 'pack' with soft everyday items, such as rolled-up socks. It is also common that a person may use an STP (stand-to-pee) packer, which is a prosthetic that not only gives the appearance of a bulge but also allows the wearer to urinate through the device while standing up.

Pansexual Adjective and noun describing a person whose sexuality is oriented towards all people regardless of gender or sexuality, and assumes that gender exists beyond binaries. Describes someone who has the potential for emotional, romantic, or sexual attraction to people of any gender though not necessarily simultaneously, in the same way or to the same degree.

POC Acronym for people (or person) of colour – which includes Black, Brown and other people of colour. When there is no QTI in front of the POC, heterosexuality and cis-ness is assumed.

Polyamorous Having more than one relationship that is negotiated between all partners. One, both or more people in a partnership might also be in other multiple relationships.

Polyvagal theory Developed by US psychiatrist and neuroscientist Stephen Porges in 1994, polyvagal theory examines the role of the vagus nerve in emotional regulation.

Pro-domming The provision of BDSM services for money, where the sex worker takes the role of the top or dominant partner. May or may not include sexual contact.

Psy-complex A term used in reference to the various psy professions (psychology, psychotherapy, psychoanalysis, psychiatry, etc.) that focus on work with the human psyche, and the role that these professions play in regulating family life, sexuality, mind and rationality. Derived from the work of Foucault and others.

QTBPOC Acronym for queer, trans, Black and other people of colour.

QTIPOC Acronym for queer, trans and intersex people (or persons) of colour.

Queer Noun or adjective used to describe a range of sexual identities and orientations that are not mainstream. The term can also be used to describe people who are trans, non-binary and gender-expansive. Used until the 1980s against gay and lesbian and bi people, queer as a term emerged in the 1990s as a radical anti-capitalist and anti-mainstream gay term and has since then been re-appropriated by many in the LGBTIQ+ communities.

Quintimacy Beck Thom's UK-based somatic sex education and bodywork practice. The focus of Quintimacy is cultivating queer intimacy with ourselves and others through trauma-informed and embodied connection. www.quintimacy.com.

Section 28 Legislation introduced by Conservative Party Prime Minister Margaret Thatcher which prohibited the so-called 'promotion of homosexuality' in schools and local authorities from 1988 to 2000.

Sex critical Sex positive and also understanding that not all people want sex or have sexual feelings that need expression with another human. Critical of any norms around sex and sexuality, whether mainstream or non-normative.

Sex positive Affirming of ethical and consensual sexual desire and agency, especially in relation to women and other groups culturally considered sexually passive.

Soma Of the body.

Somatic sex educator (SSE) Supports people (individuals, couples and groups) to develop their erotic practices, connect with their bodies and address issues relating to sex and sexuality. This does not necessarily involve physical touch.

Systemic therapy A therapeutic approach that works from a relational perspective; by taking account of the relationships, meanings and contexts that clients inhabit. There is a focus on interaction, pattern and communication.

Transgender or trans This term comes from the Greek trans as in 'on that side' and is posited as being opposite to cis, which is 'on this side', used in reference to – and by – people whose gender does not correlate to the one they were assigned at birth. Transgender is not related to sexual orientation and trans people may describe their sexuality as straight, gay, lesbian, bisexual, asexual, etc. Some use trans* as an encompassing term where the asterisk could stand for -gender, -sexual, -vestite, -sitional, etc.

Tucking A way to hide the penis and testes. During tucking, the penis and testes can be moved between the buttocks and secured with tape and/or a tight-fitting garment. Alternatively, the testes can be eased into the inguinal canals before the penis is pulled back towards the buttocks and secured in place. This is usually done to create the appearance of no external genitals.

Variations in sex characteristics (VSC) This is an umbrella term for people born with naturally occuring variations in sex traits. *See also* **intersex**, above.

White supremacy Global and local socio-cultural, political and economic systems of social power, organization, associated ideologies and structures, legislation, etc. that exist worldwide and privilege whiteness and often Christianity to the detriment of other racialized and faith-defined ethnicities and minorities.

Bibliography

Introduction

Bachmann, C.L., & Gooch, B. (2018). LGBT in Britain, Health Report. Stonewall. https://www.stonewall.org.uk/system/files/lgbt_in_britain_health.pdf [Last accessed 15.06.22]

Ban Conversion Therapy Coalition (2022). Protecting Trans Victims of Gender Identity Conversion Practices. p.1. https://www.banconversiontherapy.com/s/BCT-briefing_22-April-2022.pdf [Last accessed 01.06.2022]

Crawford, M.J., Thana, L., Farquharson, L. and Palmer, L. (2018). Patient experience of negative effects of psychological treatment: Results of a national survey. *British Journal of Psychiatry*. https://doi.org/10.1192/bjp.bp.114.162628

Hartman, S. (2019). *Wayward Lives, Beautiful Experiments: Intimate Histories of Social Upheaval*. New York, NY: W.W. Norton & Company.

Lorde, A. (2017). Poetry is not a luxury. In: *Your Silence Will Not Protect You* (pp. 7–11). London, UK: Silver Press.

Munoz, J.E. (2009). *Cruising Utopia: The Then and There of Queer Futurity*. New York, NY: New York University Press.

Rimes, K.A., Ion, D., Wingrove, J. and Carter, B. (2019). Sexual orientation differences in psychological treatment outcomes for depression and anxiety: National cohort study. *Journal of Consulting and Clinical Psychology*, 87(7), 577–589. https://doi.org/10.1037/ccp0000416

Roche, J. (2019). *Trans Power: Own Your Gender*. London, UK: Jessica Kingsley Publishers.

Chapter 1

Agard-Jones, V. (2012). What the sands remember. *GLQ: A Journal of Lesbian and Gay Studies*, 18(2–3), 325–346.

Alexander, M.J. (2005). *Pedagogies of Crossing: Meditations on Feminism, Sexual Politics, Memory and the Sacred*. Durham, NC: Duke University Press.

Bion, W.R. (1959). Attacks on linking. *International Journal of Psychoanalysis*, 40, 308–315.

Bion, W.R. (1962). A theory of thinking. *The Psychoanalytic Study of Thinking. International Journal of Psychoanalysis*, 43, 306–310.

Bion, W.R. (1970). *Attention and Interpretation*. London, UK: Karnac.

Campt, T. (2014). *Black Feminist Futures and the Practice of Fugitivity*. Barnard Center for Research on Women. www.youtube.com/watch?v=2ozhqw840PU [last accessed 07.02.2022]

Campt, T. (2017). Quick soundings: The grammar of Black futurity and Coda. Black futurity and the echo of premature death. In: *Listening to Images* (pp. 13–46 and pp. 101–118). Durham, NC: Duke University Press.

Coel, M. (2020). *I May Destroy You*. Falkna Productions. London, UK: BBC One.

Halberstam, J. (2011). *The Queer Art of Failure*. Durham, NC: Duke University Press.

Hartman, S. (2021). *Wayward Lives, Beautiful Experiments: Intimate Histories of Riotous Black Girls, Troublesome Women and Queer Radicals*. London, UK: Profile Books Ltd.

Klein, M. (1980). Envy and gratitude and other works (1946–1963). *The Writings of Melanie Klein, Volume 3*. London, UK: Hogarth Press.

Lorde, A. (1984a). Poetry is not a luxury. In: *Sister Outsider* (pp. 36–39). New York, NY: The Crossing Press.

Lorde, A. (1984b). Uses of the erotic: The erotic as power. In: *Sister Outsider* (pp. 53–59). New York, NY: The Crossing Press.

Munoz, J.E. (2009). *Cruising Utopia: The Then and There of Queer Futurity*. New York, NY: New York University Press.

Spillers, H. (2003a). All the things you could be now if Sigmund Freud's wife was your mother: Psychoanalysis and race. In: *Black, White and in Color: Essays on American Literature and Culture* (pp. 376–427). Chicago, IL: Chicago University Press.

Spillers, H. (2003b). Mama's baby, papa's maybe: An American grammar book. In: *Black, White and in Color: Essays on American Literature and Culture* (pp. 203–229). Chicago, IL: Chicago University Press.

Winnicott. D.W. (1982). *Playing and Reality*. London, UK: Routledge.

Winnicott. D.W. (1990). *The Maturational Process and the Facilitating Environment*. London, UK: Routledge.

Chapter 2

Barker, M.J. and Iantaffi, A. (2017). *How to Understand Your Gender*. London, UK: Jessica Kingsley Publishers.

Hird, M.J. (2003). A typical gender identity conference? Some disturbing reports from the therapeutic front lines. *Feminism & Psychology*, 13(2), 181–199.

Iantaffi, A. (2020). *Gender Trauma: Healing Cultural, Social, and Historical Gendered Trauma*. London, UK: Jessica Kingsley Publishers.

Kraft-Ebbing, R.v. (1886). *Psychopathia Sexualis: Eine Klinisch-Forensische Studie (Sexual Psychopathy: A Clinical-Forensic Study)*. Stuttgart, Germany: Ferdinand Enke.

Linnaeus, C. (1758). *Systema naturae per regna tria naturae :secundum classes, ordines, genera, species, cum characteribus, differentiis, synonymis, locis* (in Latin). Stockholm, Sweden: Laurentius Salvius.

Lugones, M. (2016). *The Coloniality of Gender.* Durham, NC: Worlds & Knowledges Otherwise.

The Museum of Transology. Museum documenting trans, non-binary, and intersex lives. www.museumoftransology.com

Peters, T. (2021). *Detransition, Baby: A Novel.* London, UK: Serpents Tail.

The Trevor Project (2020). US charity for LGBTQ youth. www.thetrevorproject. org/research-briefs/pronouns-usage-among-lgbtq-youth/ [last accessed 22.06.22]

Turner, D. (2021). *Intersections of Privilege and Otherness.* London, UK: Routledge.

Watkins, M. and Shulman, H. (2008). *Toward Psychologies of Liberation.* London, UK: Palgrave Macmillan.

Chapter 3

Baldwin, J. (1990). *The Fire Next Time.* London, UK: Penguin Books.

Brown, B. and Burke, T. (Eds.). (2021). *You Are Your Best Thing: Vulnerability, Shame Resilience, and the Black Experience.* New York, NY: Penguin Random House.

Charura, D. and Lago, C. (Eds.). (2021). *Black Identities + White Therapies: Race, Respect + Diversity.* London, UK: PCCS.

De Young, P. (2015). *Understanding and Treating Chronic Shame: A Relational and Neurobiological Approach.* New York, NY: Routledge.

Eigen, M. (2015). Shame. In: *Image, Sense, Infinities, and Everyday Life* (pp. 61–86). London, UK: Routledge.

Fanon, F. (2008). *Black Skin, White Masks.* London, UK: Pluto Press.

hooks, b. (1992). Eating the other: Desire and resistance. In: *Black Looks: Race and Representation* (pp. 21–39). Boston, CT: South End Press.

hooks, b. and Harris-Perry, M. (2013). *Black Female Voices.* The New School. New York, NY. https://livestream.com/accounts/1369487/events/2477970/videos/34324981

Kalsched, D. (2013). *Trauma and the Soul.* London, UK: Routledge.

Kaufman, G. and Raphael, L. (1996). *Coming Out of Shame.* New York, NY: Main Street Books.

Layton, L. and Leavy-Sperounis, M. (Eds.). (2020). *Toward a Social Psychoanalysis Culture, Character, and Normative Unconscious Processes.* New York, NY: Routledge.

Mendez, J. (2013). *Report of the Special Rapporteur on Torture and Other Cruel, Inhuman or Degrading Treatment or Punishment.* UN HRC.

Rilke, R.M. (2005). I am prayer again. In: *Rilke's Book of Hours: Love Poems to God* (p. 137). New York, NY: Riverhead Books.

Stern, D.B. (2019). *The Infinity of the Unsaid – Unformulated Experience, Language, and the Nonverbal.* London, UK: Routledge.

Taylor, F. and Downes, R. (2020). Re-imagining the space and context for a therapeutic curriculum. In: D. Charura and C. Lago (Eds.). *Black Identities + White Therapies* (pp. 88–97). London, UK: PCCS.

Trevarthen, C. and Aitken, K.J. (2001). Infant intersubjectivity: Research, theory, and clinical applications. *Journal of Child Psychology and Psychiatry and Allied Disciplines,* 42(1), 3–48.

Young, W. (2020). *To Be a Gay Man.* London, UK: Virgin Books.

The title of this chapter is an amalgam of work by Coyote and MacDougall, and Rainer Maria Rilke and all permissions have been requested.

Chapter 4

Ahmed, S. (2010). *The Promise of Happiness.* Durham, NC: Duke University Press.

Bachmann, C.L. and Gooch, B. (2018). *LGBT In Britain Health Report.* www.stonewall.org.uk/system/files/lgbt_in_britain_health.pdf [last accessed 07.02.2022]

Barker, M.J. (2018). *Rewriting the Rules: An Anti-Self-Help Guide to Love, Sex and Relationships.* London, UK: Routledge.

Barker, M.J. and Iantaffi, A. (2019). *Life Isn't Binary.* London, UK: Jessica Kingsley Publishers.

Beauvoir, Simone de (1953). *The Second Sex.* New York, NY: Knopf.

Bridgeman, L.L. (2015). *The Butch Monologues.* www.thebutchmonologues.com [last accessed 07.02.2022]

Butler, J. (2006). *Precarious Life: The Powers of Mourning and Violence.* New York, NY: Verso.

Fisher, J. (2017). *Healing the Fragmented Selves of Trauma Survivors: Overcoming Internal Self-Alienation.* New York, NY: Routledge.

GALOP. The UK's LGBT+ Anti-Abuse Charity. https://galop.org.uk/ [last accessed 26.01.2022]

Halberstam, J. (2011). *The Queer Art of Failure.* Durham, NC: Duke University Press.

Herman, J.L. (2015). *Trauma and Recovery: The Aftermath of Violence – From Domestic Abuse to Political Terror.* New York, NY: Basic Books.

Iantaffi, A. (2020). *Gender Trauma: Healing Cultural, Social, and Historical Gendered Trauma.* London, UK: Jessica Kingsley Publishers.

McRuer, R. (2006). *Crip Theory: Cultural Signs of Queerness and Disability.* New York, NY: NYU Press.

Moon, L. (Ed.). (2008). *Feeling Queer or Queer Feelings? Radical Approaches to Counselling Sex, Sexualities and Genders.* Oxon, UK: Routledge.

Nuno Nodin, N., Peel, E., Tyler, A. and Rivers, I. (2015). *LGB&T Mental*

Health Risk and Resilience Report. www.queerfutures.co.uk/wp-content/ uploads/2015/04/RARE_Research_Report_PACE_2015.pdf [last accessed 26.01.2022]

Pratchett, T. (2009). *Unseen Academicals.* London, UK: Doubleday.

Roche, J. (2019). *Trans Power: Own Your Gender.* London, UK: Jessica Kingsley Publishers.

Walker, P. (2018). *Complex PTSD: From Surviving to Thriving.* Scotts Valley, CA: Createspace Independent Publishing Platform.

Chapter 5

Ahmed, S. (2006). *Queer Phenomenology.* Durham, NC: Duke University Press.

Angelides, S. (2001). *A History of Bisexuality.* Chicago, IL: Chicago University Press.

Benjamin, J. (1988). *The Bonds of Love: Psychoanalysis, Feminism and the Problems of Domination.* New York, NY: Pantheon Books.

Booth, R. (2022). More than one in 10 young women now identify as lesbian, gay, bisexual or other. *The Guardian.* https://www.theguardian.com/society/2022/ may/25/more-than-one-in-10-young-women-now-identify-lesbian-gay-bisexual-or-other [Last accessed 15.06.22]

Burch, B. (1997). Family romances and Sexual solutions. In: *Other Women* (Chapters 1 and 2). New York, NY: Columbia University Press.

De Lauretis, T. (1999). Letter to an unknown woman. In: R.C. Lesser and E. Schoenberg (Eds.). *That Obscure Subject of Desire: Freud's Female Homosexual Revisited* (pp. 37–53). New York, NY: Routledge.

D'Ercole, A. (1999). Designing the lesbian subject: Looking backwards, looking forwards. In: R.C. Lesser and E. Schoenberg (Eds.). *That Obscure Subject of Desire: Freud's Female Homosexual Revisited* (pp. 115–129). New York, NY: Routledge.

Elise, D. (2002). The primary maternal oedipal situation and female homoerotic desire. *Psychoanalytic Inquiry,* 22(2), 209–228.

Freud, S. (1920). The psychogenesis of a case of homosexuality in a woman. *The International Journal of Psychoanalysis,* I(2), 125–149.

Freud, S. (1932). Femininity. *New Introductory Lectures on Psychoanalysis,* SE22, 112–135.

Gilman, S. (1993). *The Case of Sigmund Freud: Medicine and Identity at the Fine de Siecle.* Baltimore, MD: The Johns Hopkins University Press.

Gilman, S. (1993). *Freud, Race, and Gender.* Princeton, NJ: Princeton University Press.

Gilman, S. (1995). *Freud, Race and Gender.* Oxford, UK: Princeton University Press.

Gleeson, J. (2021). Judith Butler: We need to rethink the category of woman. *The Guardian.* www.theguardian.com/lifeandstyle/2021/sep/07/judith-butler-interview-gender [last accessed 06.02.2022]

Government Equalities Office (2018). *National LGBT Survey*. https://assets. publishing.service.gov.uk/government/uploads/system/uploads/attachment_ data/file/721704/LGBT-survey-research-report.pdf [last accessed 06.02.2022]

Harris, A. (1999). Gender as contradiction. In: R.C. Lesser and E. Schoenberg (Eds.). *That Obscure Subject of Desire: Freud's Female Homosexual Revisited* (pp. 156–179). New York, NY: Routledge.

Human Dignity Trust (2021). *Map of Criminalisation*. www.humandignitytrust. org/lgbt-the-law/map-of-criminalisation/?type_filter=crim_sex_women [last accessed 06.02.2022]

Lesser, R.C. (1999). Introduction: In the shadow of Freud. In: R.C. Lesser and E. Schoenberg (Eds.). *That Obscure Subject of Desire: Freud's Female Homosexual Revisited* (pp. 1–9). New York, NY: Routledge.

Lesser, R.C. and Schoenberg, E. (Eds.). (1999). *That Obscure Subject of Desire: Freud's Female Homosexual Revisited*. New York, NY: Routledge.

O'Connor, N. and Ryan, J. (1993). *Wild Desires and Mistaken Identities: Lesbianism and Psychoanalysis*. New York, NY: Columbia University Press.

Office of National Statistics (2020). *Experimental Statistics on Sexual Orientation in the UK*. www.ons.gov.uk/peoplepopulationandcommunity/culturalidentity/ sexuality/bulletins/sexualidentityuk/2018#sexual-orientation-data [last accessed 06.02.2022]

Oyěwùmi, O. (1997). *The Invention of Women: Making an African Sense of Western Gender Discourses*. Minneapolis, MN: University of Minnesota Press.

Rich, A. (1980). Compulsory heterosexuality and lesbian existence. *Signs*, 5(4), 631–660, Women: Sex and Sexuality (Summer, 1980). Chicago, IL: University of Chicago Press.

Rieder, I. and Voigt, D. (2020). *The Story of Sidonie C.: Freud's Famous Lesbian Patient*. Reno, NV: Helena History Press.

Roth, D. (2004). Engorging the lesbian clitoris: Opposing the phallic cultural unconscious. In: J.M. Glassgold and S. Iasenza (Eds.). *Lesbians, Feminism, and Psychoanalysis: The Second Wave* (pp. 177–189). New York, NY: Harrington Park Press.

Yellin, J. (2007). Such stuff as dreams are made on: Sexuality as re/creation. In: K. White (Ed.). *Attachment and Sexuality in Clinical Practice* (pp. 11–37). London, UK: Karnac.

Some of the material in this chapter first appeared in a Stillpoint Spaces blog on Medium.com in October 2020. https://medium.com/stillpointspaces/ freuds-famous-case-of-female-homosexuality-a-book-review-on-the-story- of-sidonie-c-328e09111c4b [Accessed August 2022.]

Chapter 6

Ahmed, S. (2014). *The Cultural Politics of Emotion*. Edinburgh, UK: Edinburgh University Press.

Butler, J. (2006). *Gender Trouble, Feminism and the Subversion of Identity*. London, UK: Routledge Classics.

Caro Lancho, M. (2015). *Contributions to Bisexual Erasure*. Barcelona, Spain: University of Barcelona.

Davies, D. and Neal, C. (Eds.). (2000). *Pink Therapy Vol. 3: Issues in Therapy with Lesbian, Gay, and Bisexual and Transgender Clients*. Buckingham, UK: McGraw Hill International.

Ferenczi, S. (1949). Confusion of the tongues between the adults and the child – the language of tenderness and of passion. *International Journal of Psycho-Analysis*, 30(4).

Freud, S. (1905). Three essays on the theory of sexuality. *The Standard Edition of the Complete Psychological Works of Sigmund Freud, Volume VII (1901–1905): A Case of Hysteria, Three Essays on Sexuality and Other Works*, 123–246.

Freud, S. (1920). The psychogenesis of a case of homosexuality in a woman. *The International Journal of Psychoanalysis*, I(2), 125–149.

Freud, S. (1923e). The infantile genital organization. In: *An Interpolation into the Theory of Sexuality. The Standard Edition of the Complete Psychological Works of Sigmund Freud*, 19, 136–146.

Freud, S. (1932). Femininity. *New Introductory Lectures on Psychoanalysis*, SE22, 112–135.

Freud, S. (1951). Letter to an American mother. *American Journal of Psychiatry*, 107, 787.

Freud, S. (1981). Femininity. *New Introductory Lectures on Psychoanalysis*. New York, NY: W.W. Norton. First published in 1936.

Freud, S. (1999). The psychogenesis of a case of homosexuality in a woman (1920). In: R.C. Lesser and E. Schoenberg (Eds.). *That Obscure Subject of Desire: Freud's Female Homosexual Revisited* (pp. 13–33). New York, NY: Routledge.

Goldener, V. (1991). Toward a critical relational theory of gender. *Psychoanalytic Dialogues*, 1, 3, 249–272. Berkeley, CA: The Analytic Press.

Goldman, R. (2014). List of 58 gender options for Facebook users. *ABC News*. https://abcnews.go.com/blogs/headlines/2014/02/heres-a-list-of-58-gender-options-for-facebook-users

Gramsci, A., Hoare, Q. and Nowell-Smith, G. (2005). *Selections from the Prison Notebooks of Antonio Gramsci*. London, UK: Lawrence & Wishart Ltd; Reprint edition.

Janet, P. (1903). *Psychological Automism*. Paris, France: Germer Baillière et cie.

Janov, A. (1970). *The Primal Scream. Primal Therapy: The Cure for Neurosis*. New York, NY: Dell.

Keleman, S. (1989a). *Emotional Anatomy*. Berkeley, CA: Center Press.

Keleman, S. (1989b). *Your Body Speaks Its Mind*. Berkeley, CA: Center Press.

Kinsey, A., Wardell, B. and Martin, Clyde E. (1948). *Sexual Behavior in the Human Male*. Philadelphia, PA: W.B. Saunders.

Layton, L. (2000). The psychopolitics of bisexuality. *Studies in Gender and Sexuality*, 1(1), 41–60.

Lorde, A. (2007). Age, race, class, and sex: Women redefining difference. In: *Sister Outsider* (pp. 114–123). Berkeley, CA: Ten Speed Press.

Lowen, A. (1958). *The Language of the Body*. New York, NY: Simon and Schuster.

Lowen, A. (1975). *Bioenergetics*. London, UK: Penguin.

McDougall, J. (1989). *Theatres of the Body: A Psychoanalytic Approach to Psychosomatic Illness*. London, UK: Free Association Books.

Neal, C. (2013). A body of experience, Annual PCSR Conference keynote address. In: *Transformations. Journal of Psychotherapists & Counsellors for Social Responsibility*, August.

Neal, C. (2014). *The Marrying Kind? Lives of Gay and Bisexual Men Who Marry Women*. Scotts Valley, CA: CreateSpace.

Neal, C. and Davies, D. (Eds.). (2000). *Pink Therapy Vol. 2: Therapeutic Perspectives on Working with Lesbian, Gay and Bisexual Clients*. Buckingham, UK: McGraw Hill International.

Perls, F., Hefferline, R. and Goodman, P. (1951). *Gestalt Therapy: Excitement and Growth in the Human Personality*. New York, NY: Dell.

Rapoport, E. (2009). Bisexuality in psychoanalytic theory: Interpreting the resistance. *Journal of Bisexuality*, 9(3–4), 279–295.

Reich, W. (1925). *The Impulsive Character: A Psychoanalytic Study of the Pathology of the Self*. Vienna, Austria: Internationaler Psychoanalytischer Verlag.

Reich, W. (1933). *Character Analysis*. New York, NY: Farrar, Straus and Giroux.

Roche, J. (2019). *Trans Power: Own Your Gender*. London, UK: Jessica Kingsley Publishers.

Storr, M. (Ed.). (1999). *Bisexuality: A Critical Reader*. London, UK: Routledge.

Theil, M. (2021). Non-binary author Alok Vaid-Menon expertly deconstructs gender in powerful clip. *Pink News*. www.pinknews.co.uk/2021/08/02/alok-vaid-menon-non-binary/ [last accessed 15.02.2022]

Williams, K.D., Forgas, J.P. and Von Hippel, F. (2005). *Social Outcast: Ostracism, Social Exclusion, Rejection, and Bullying*. New York, NY: Psychology Press.

Chapter 7

Anderson, H. and Goolishian, H. (1992). The client is the expert: A not-knowing approach to therapy. In: S. McNamee and K.J. Gergen (Eds.). *Therapy as Social Construction* (pp. 25–39). Newberry Park, CA: Sage Publications.

Benjamin, J. (2017). *Beyond Doer and Done to: Recognition Theory, Intersubjectivity and the Third*. London, UK: Routledge.

Burnham, J. (2018). Developments in the social GRRRAAACCEEESSS: Visible-invisible and voiced-unvoiced 1. In: B. Krause (Ed.). *Culture and Reflexivity in Systemic Psychotherapy* (pp. 139–160). London, UK: Routledge.

Falicov, C. (1995). Training to think culturally: A multidimensional comparative framework. *Family Process*, 34, 4, 373–388. https://pubmed.ncbi.nlm.nih.gov/8674519/

Foucault, M. (1977). *Discipline and Punish: The Birth of the Prison*. New York, NY: Random House.

Menakem, R. (2017). *My Grandmother's Hands: Racialized Trauma and the Pathway to Mending Our Hearts and Bodies*. Las Vegas, NV: Central Recovery Press.

Nicholas, M. (2004). Lesbian sexuality/female sexuality: Rethinking 'lesbian bed death'. In: *Sexual and Relationship Therapy*, 19, 4, 363–371.

Wallin, D.J. (2007). *Attachment in Psychotherapy*. New York, NY: Guilford Press.

Chapter 8

Adventures in Time and Gender. A non-binary person's story into the history of gender. https://adventuresintimeandgender.org/

Bellwether, M. (2010). *Fucking Trans Women: A Zine About the Sex Lives of Trans Women*. Scotts Valley, CA: CreateSpace Independent Publishing Platform.

Bornstein, K. and Bergman, S.B. (Eds.). (2010). *Gender Outlaws: The Next Generation*. New York, NY: Avalon Publishing Group.

Carrellas, B. (2012). *Ecstasy Is Necessary: A Practical Guide to Sex, Relationships, and Oh So Much More*. New York, NY: Hay House.

Carrellas, B. (2017). *Urban Tantra: Sacred Sex for the Twenty-First Century*. Berkeley, CA: Ten Speed Press.

Erickson-Schroth, L. (2014). *Trans Bodies, Trans Selves – A Resource for the Transgender Community*. New York, NY: Oxford University Press.

Fielding, L. (2021). *Trans Sex: Clinical Approaches to Trans Sexualities and Erotic Embodiments*. New York, NY: Routledge.

Games, F. (2021). *Top To Bottom: A Memoir and Personal Guide Through Phalloplasty*. London, UK: Jessica Kingsley Publishers.

GIRES Gender Identity Research and Education Society. www.gires.org.uk [last accessed 24.01.2022]

Iantaffi, A. and Barker M.J. (2018). *How to Understand Your Gender*. London, UK: Jessica Kingsley Publishers.

Jesse, C. (2021). *Ethics for Outlaws*. Video. www.erospirit.ca/ethics/ [last accessed 23.01.2022]

Laffy, C. (2013). *Love Sex: An Integrative Model for Sexual Education*. London, UK: Karnac.

Martin, B. and Dalzen, R. (2021). *The Art of Receiving and Giving: The Wheel of Consent*. Eugene, OR: Luminare Press.

Price, D. (2018). *Gender Socialization Is Real (Complex): No One Is Simply 'Socialised Male' or 'Socialised Female'* . https://devonprice.medium.com/gender-socialization-is-real-complex-348f56146925 [last accessed 23.01.2022]

Quintimacy https://quintimacy.com [last accessed 08.06.2022]

Roche, J. (2018). *Queer Sex*. London, UK: Jessica Kingsley Publishers.

Roche, J. (2019). *Trans Power: Own Your Gender*. London, UK: Jessica Kingsley Publishers.

Tanenbaum, T.J. (2020). I was socialized trans. *An Injustice Mag*, 7 August. https://aninjusticemag.com/i-was-socialized-trans-b2fa870866a4 [last accessed 02.05.2022]

The Gender Dysphoria Bible. https://genderdysphoria.fyi/en [last accessed 23.01.2022]

Thom, B. (2022). *Boundary Statement*. https://quintimacy.com/ [last accessed 29.04.2022]

Treleaven, D.A. (2018). *Trauma-Sensitive Mindfulness: Practices for Safe and Transformative Healing*. New York, NY: W.W. Norton.

Van der Kolk, B. (2014). *The Body Keeps the Score: Brain, Mind, and Body in the Healing of Trauma*. New York, NY: Viking Press.

Wheeler, S. Sharon. Wheeler's ScarWork. https://scarwork.uk [Accessed August 2022.]

Chapter 9

Bennachie, C. (2010). *Comment on Farley's 'What Really Happened in New Zealand After Prostitution Was Decriminalized in 2003?'* www.academia.edu/1039197/Comment_on_Melissa_Farleys_claims_regarding_decriminalisation_of_sex_work_in_New_Zealand [last accessed 06.02.2022]

English Collective of Prostitutes (ECP). *Network Campaigning for Safety and Decriminalisation*. https://prostitutescollective.net

Farley, M. (2003). Prostitution and the invisibility of harm. *Women & Therapy*, 26(3–4), 247–280.

Hammond, N. and Kingston, S. (2014). Experiencing stigma as sex work researchers in professional and personal lives. *Sexualities*, 17(3), 329–347.

National Ugly Mugs. Ending Violence Against Sex Workers. https://www.nationaluglymugs.org

Office For National Statistics (2019). *Child Sexual Abuse in England and Wales: Year Ending March 2019*. www.ons.gov.uk/peoplepopulationandcommunity/crimeandjustice/articles/childsexualabuseinenglandandwales/yearendingmarch2019 [last accessed on 06.02.2022]

Pollock, K. (2019a). *Stop Shaming People for Faking Orgasms*. https://counsellinginnorthumberland.com/2019/08/04/why-we-need-to-stop-shaming-and-blaming-people-for-faking-orgasms/

Pollock, K. (2019b). *Sex Work and Minority Stress*. Academeu. www.academia.edu/53388953/Sex_work_and_Minority_Stress

SWARM Sex Worker Advocacy and Resistance Movement. Sex worker collective campaigning for the full decriminalisation of sex work https://www.swarmcollective.org

Tits and Sass. Service journalism by and for sex workers. https://titsandsass.com

Chapter 10

Ahmed, S. (2004). *The Cultural Politics of Emotions*. Edinburgh, UK: Edinburgh University Press.

Bastian, J. (11 October 2021). Interview by Young, N.

Bateman, A. and Fonagy, P. (2016). *Mentalizing-Based Treatment for Personality Disorders*. Oxford, UK: Oxford University Press.

Bion, W.R. (1962). *Learning from Experience*. London, UK: Heinemann.

Bower-Brown, S., Zadeh, S. and Jadva, V. (2021). Binary-trans, non-binary and gender-questioning adolescents' experiences in UK schools. *Journal of LGBT Youth*. www.tandfonline.com/doi/full/10.1080/19361653.2021.1873215 [last accessed 30.10.2021]

Butler, J. (2006). *Gender Trouble: Feminism and the Subversion of Identity*. Abingdon, UK: Routledge.

Clark, K.A., Dougherty L.R. and Pachankis, J.E. (2021). A study of parents of sexual and gender minority children: Linking parental reactions with child mental health. *Psychology of Sexual Orientation and Gender Diversity*. https://psycnet.apa.org/record/2021-46343-001 [last accessed 30.10.2021]

Craig, S.L., Eaton, A.D., McInroy, L.B., Leung, V.W.Y. and Krishnan, S. (2021). Can social media participation enhance LGBTQ+ youth well-being? Development of the Social Media Benefits Scale. *Social Media + Society*, January–March 2021, pp. 1–13.

Crenshaw, K. (1989). Demarginalizing the intersection of race and sex: A black feminist critique of antidiscrimination doctrine. *Feminist Theory and Antiracist Politics*. University of Chicago Legal Forum, 1, 8, 139–167.

Du Bois, W.E.B. (1994). *The Souls of Black Folk*. Mineola, NY: Dover Publications. Reprint of the A. C. McClurg and Co., Chicago, 1903 edition.

Espinoza, R. (2013). 'Coming out' or 'letting in'? Recasting the LGBT narrative. *Huffington Post*. www.huffpost.com/entry/coming-out-or-letting-in_b_4070273 [last accessed 17.10.2021]

Firmin, C. (2020). *Contextual Safeguarding and Child Protection: Rewriting the Rules*. Oxon, UK: Routledge.

Freire, P. (1970). *Pedagogy of the Oppressed*. New York, NY: Seabury.

Freud, S. (1923). *The Ego and the Id*. London, UK: Hogarth Press.

Furley, S. (4 October 2021). Interview by Young, N.

Harris, P. (2021). Welcome. In: *Poetry in Child Psychotherapy*. Unpublished work.

Holmes-Brown, C. (4 October 2021). Interview by Young, N.

Jones, O. (2021, 3 September). The shocking rise in anti-LGBTQ hate crime shows bigotry is still ruining lives. www.theguardian.com/commentisfree/2021/sep/03/anti-lgbtq-hate-crime-bigotry-britain [last accessed 30.10.2021]

Jones, O. (2021, 17 October). *The Establishment War on Stonewall and LGBTQ Rights*. https://www.theguardian.com/commentisfree/2021/sep/03/anti-lgbtq-hate-crime-bigotry-britain

LGBT Manifesto (2020). www.lgbtmanifesto.co.uk/the-manifesto [last accessed 30.10.2021]

Metro Charity (2014). *Youth Chances*. https://metrocharity.org.uk/sites/default/files/2017-04/National%20Youth%20Chances%20Intergrated%20Report%202016.pdf [last accessed 11.02.2022]

Mills-Koonce, W.R., Rehder, P.D. and McCurdy, A.L. (2018). The significance of parenting and parent–child relationships for sexual and gender minority adolescents. *Journal of Research on Adolescence*, 28(3), 637–649.

Moon, L. (Ed.). (2008). *Feeling Queer or Queer Feelings?: Radical Approaches to Counselling Sex, Sexualities and Genders*. Oxon, UK: Routledge.

Mordanti, D. (29 October and 1 November 2021). Interview by Young, N.

Ofcom (2021). *Children and Parents: Media Use and Attitudes Report*. https://www.ofcom.org.uk/__data/assets/pdf_file/0025/217825/children-and-parents-media-use-and-attitudes-report-2020-21.pdf [last accessed 11.02.2022]

Panksepp, J. (1998). *Affective Neuroscience: The Foundations of Human and Animal Emotions*. Oxford, UK: Oxford University Press.

Porges, S. (2017). *The Pocket Guide to the Polyvagal Theory: The Transformative Power of Feeling Safe (Norton Series on Interpersonal Neurobiology)*. New York, NY: W.W. Norton & Company.

Poushter, J. and Kent, N. (2020). The global divide on homosexuality persists. Pew Research Center. www.pewresearch.org/global/2020/06/25/global-divide-on-homosexuality-persists/ [last accessed 11.02.2022]

Simon, G. and Whitfield, G. (2000). Systemic and social constructionist therapy. In: D. Davies and C. Neal (Eds.). *Pink Therapy Vol. 2: Therapeutic Perspectives on Working with Lesbian, Gay and Bisexual Clients* (pp. 144–162). London, UK: Open University Press.

Stockton, K.B. (2009). *The Queer Child or Growing Sideways in the Twentieth Century*. Durham, NC: Duke University Press.

Stonewall (2017). *The School Report: The Experiences of Lesbian, Gay, Bi and Trans Young People in Britain's Schools in 2017*. www.stonewall.org.uk/school-report-2017 [last accessed 11.02.2022]

Tilsen, J. B. (2013). *Therapeutic Conversations with Queer Youth: Transcending Homonormativity and Constructing Preferred Identities*. Lanham, MD: Rowman & Littlefield.

Trevarthen, C. (2001). Intrinsic motives for companionship in understanding: Their origin, development and significance for infant mental health. *International Journal of Infant Mental Health*, 22(1-2), 95–131.

Vaid-Menon, A., interview with Baldoni, J., Heath, J. and Plank, L. (2021). ALOK: The urgent need for compassion. *The Man Enough Podcast*. https://www.youtube.com/watch?v=Tq3C9R8HNUQ [last accessed 30.11.2021]

Winnicott, D.W. (1949) Mind and its relation to the psyche-soma. *British Journal of Medical Psychology*, 1954, 27(4), 201–209. Also published in *Collected Papers: Through Paediatrics to Psycho-analysis* (pp. 243–254). London, UK: Tavistock, 1958.

Winnicott, D.W. (1988). *Human Nature*. London, UK: Free Association Books.

Young-Bruehl, E. (2012). *Childism: Confronting Prejudice Against Children*. New Haven, CT; London, UK: Yale University Press.

Chapter 11

Castaneda, C. (2002). *Figurations: Child, Bodies, Worlds*. Durham, NC: Duke University Press.

Lorde, A. (2017). *Your Silence Will Not Protect You*. London, UK: Silver Press.

Mbembe, A. (2019). *Necropolitics: Theory in Forms*. Durham, NC: Duke University Press.

McManus, J. (2021) Media watchdog Ofcom quits Stonewall diversity scheme. BBC. www.bbc.com/news/uk-58336116

Mermaids Charity for gender-diverse kids, young people, and their families. https://mermaidsuk.org.uk

Moon, L. (2011). The gentle violence of therapists: Misrecognition and dis-location of the other. *Psychotherapy and Politics International*, 9(3), 194–205.

Roche, J. (2020). *Gender Explorers*. London, UK: JKP.

Scheff, T.J. (1974). The labelling theory of mental illness. *American Sociological Review*, 39(3), pp. 444–452. American Sociological Association.

Stonewall Charity for LGBTQ+ rights and advocacy. www.stonewall.org.uk

Chapter 12

Bernier-Clarke, A., Pagonis, P. and Lipton, S. (2019). *A Normal Girl*. US, WMM. NY: New York.

Vecchietti, V. (2021). Film review: *A Normal Girl*. In: L. Wignall (Ed.). *British Psychological Society Psychologies of Sexualities Review* Special issue, 12(1), Summer 2021, pp. 67–69.

Chapter 13

Aaronson, I.A. (1999). When and how to screen? Editorial comment on 'The Child with Ambiguous Genitalia'. *Infectious Urology*, 12(4), 113–119.

Aron, L. (1996). *A Meeting of Minds: Mutuality in Psychoanalysis*. New York, NY: Analytic Press.

BACP (2016). *Ethical Framework for the Counselling Professions*. www.bacp.co.uk/media/2176/bacp-ethical-framework-for-the-counselling-professions.pdf

Barker, M.J. (2019). *Gender, Sexual, and Relationship Diversity (GSRD): Good Practice Across the Counselling Professions 001*. www.bacp.co.uk/media/5877/

bacp-gender-sexual-relationship-diversity-gpacp001-april19.pdf

Bernier-Clarke, A., Pagonis, P. and Lipton, S. (2019). *A Normal Girl*. US, WMM. NY: New York.

Bond, T. (2004). *Ethical Guidelines for Researching Counselling and Psychotherapy*. www.bacp.co.uk/media/1959/bacp-ethical-guidelines-researching-counselling-psychotherapy.pdf

Brinkmann, L., Schuetzmann, K. and Richter-Appelt, H. (2007). Gender assignment and medical history of individuals with different forms of intersexuality: Evaluation of medical records and the patients' perspective. *Journal of Sexual Medicine*, 4(4), 964–980. https://doi.org/10.1111/j.1743- 6109.2007.00524.x

Caruth, C. (1995). *Trauma: Explorations in Memory*. Baltimore, MD; London, UK: The Johns Hopkins University Press.

Costello, C.G. (2009). *Intersex Roadshow*. https://intersexroadshow. blogspot.com/search?q=I%27m+not+defective [last accessed 15.03.2021]

Czyzselska, J. (2021). The truth that's denied: Psychotherapy with LGBTIQ+ clients who identify as intersex. In: L. Wignall (Ed.). *British Psychological Society Psychologies of Sexualities Review* Special issue, 12(1), Summer 2021, pp. 20–33.

Davis, G. (2015). *Contesting Intersex: The Dubious Diagnosis*. New York, NY: New York University Press.

Downing, L., Moreland, I. and Sullivan, N. (2015). *Fuckology: Critical Essays on John Money's Diagnostic Concepts*. Chicago, IL: Chicago University Press.

Dreger, A.D. (1998). Ambiguous sex or ambivalent medicine? *The Hastings Center Report*, 28(3), 24–35.

Dreger, A.D. (1998). *Hermaphrodites and the Medical Invention of Sex*. Cambridge, MA: Harvard University Press.

Graham, S. (2020). *The Alchemy of Authenticity: Turning Your Shit into Gold*. https://freethework.com/article/seven-graham-authenticity [last accessed 09.03.2022]

Graham, S. (2021). Speaking to *Invisible No More: The Need For Intersex Stories*. Writers' Guild of America. https://www.youtube.com/watch?v=T6xn1sMJoNc [last accessed 09.03.2022]

Griffiths, D.A. (2018). Diagnosing sex: Intersex surgery and sex change in Britain 1930–1955. *Sexualities*, 21(3), 476–495. https://doi.org/10.1177%2F1363460717740339

Guth, J., Witchel, R., Witchel, S. and Lee, P. (2006). Relationships, sexuality, gender identity, gender roles, and self-concept of individuals who have congenital adrenal hyperplasia: A qualitative investigation. *The Journal of Lesbian & Gay Psychotherapy*, 10(2). https://doi.org/10.1300/J236v10n02_04

Harper, A., Finnerty, P., Martinez, M., Brace, A., Crethar, H., Loos, B., …Lambert, S. (2013). *Competencies for Counseling with Lesbian, Gay, Bisexual, Queer, Questioning, Intersex, and Ally Individuals*. www.counseling.org/docs/ethics/algbtic-2012-07

Harris, A. (2005). *Gender as Soft Assembly*. New York, NY: Analytic Press.

Hefferon, K. and Gil-Rodriguez, E. (2011). Methods: Interpretative phenomenological analysis. *The Psychologist*, 24. https://thepsychologist.bps.org. uk/volume-24/edition-10/methods-interpretative-phenomenological-analysis

Hird, M.J. (2003). A typical gender identity conference? Some disturbing reports from the therapeutic front lines. *Feminism & Psychology*, 13(2), 181–199. https://doi.org/10.117 7%2F0959353503013002004

Hird, M.J. (2008). Queer(y)ing intersex: Freud, polymorphous perversity and the construction of identity. In: L. Moon (Ed.). *Feeling Queer or Queer Feelings: Radical Approaches to Counselling Sex, Sexualities and Genders* (pp. 54–71). London, UK: Routledge.

Holmes, M.M. (Ed.). (2009). *Critical Intersex*. Farnham, UK: Ashgate Press.

InterACT: Advocates for Intersex Youth (2021). www.interactadvocates.org

Intersex Equality Rights UK (2021). www.consortium.lgbt/member-directory/intersex-equality-rights-uk/

Intersex Human Rights Australia (2021). www.Ihra.org.au

Intersex UK (2021). www.intersexuk.org

Karkazis, K. (2008). *Fixing Sex: Intersex, Medical Authority, and Lived Experience*. Durham, NC: Duke University Press.

Kessler, S.J. (1998). *Lessons from the Intersexed*. New Brunswick, NJ: Rutgers University.

Kraft-Ebbing, R.V. (1886). *Psychopathia Sexualis: eine Klinisch-Forensische Studies (Sexual Psychopathy: A Clinical-Forensic Study)*. Stuttgart, Germany: Ferdinand Enke.

Langdridge, D. (2007). *Phenomenological Psychology: Theory, Research and Method*. London, UK: Pearson Prentice Hall.

Lev, A. (2006). Intersexuality in the family: An unacknowledged trauma. *The Journal of Lesbian & Gay Psychotherapy*, 10(2). https://doi.org/10.1300/J236v10n02_03

Liao, L.M. (2003). Learning to assist women born with atypical genitalia: Journey through ignorance, taboo and dilemma. *Journal of Reproductive and Infant Psychology*, 21(3), 229–238. https:// doi.org/10.1080/0264683031000154971

Liao, L.M. (2007). Towards a clinical-psychological approach to address the heterosexual concerns of intersexed women. In: V. Clarke and E. Peel (Eds.). *Out in Psychology: Lesbian, Gay Bisexual, Trans and Queer Perspectives* (pp. 391–408). Hoboken, NJ: John Wiley & Sons.

Liao, L.M. and Simmonds, M. (2013). A values-driven and evidence-based health care psychology for diverse sex development. *Psychology & Sexuality*, 5(1), 83–101. https://doi.org/10.1080/1941989 9.2013.831217

Maroda, K.J. (1999). *Seduction, Surrender, and Transformation: Emotional Engagement in the Analytic Process*. New York, NY: Analytic Press.

Mendez, J. (2013). Report of the Special Rapporteur on torture and other cruel, inhuman or degrading treatment or punishment. Promotion and protection of all human rights, civil, political, economic, social and cultural rights, including the right to development. UN HRC. www.ohchr.org/en/special-procedures/sr-torture

Mitchell, M., Lahood, G. and Keir, J. (2012). *Intersexion*. New Zealand: Ponsonby Productions.

Money, J. (1968). *Sex Errors of the Body: Dilemmas, Education, Counselling*. Baltimore, MD: Johns Hopkins Press.

Ogden, P. (2009). Modulation, mindfulness and movement in the treatment of trauma-related depression. In: M. Kerman (Ed.). *Clinical Pearls of Wisdom: 21 Leading Therapists Share Their Key Insights* (pp. 1–13). New York, NY: W.W. Norton.

Organisation Intersex International (2021). http://oiiinternational.com/

Reis, B. (2009). Performative and enactive features of psychoanalytic witnessing: The transference as the scene of address. *International Journal of Psychoanalysis*, 90, 1359–1372. https://doi.org/10.1111/j.1745-8315.2009.00216.x

Roen, K. (2004). Intersex embodiment: When health care means maintaining binary sexes. *Sexual Health*, Vol. 1, Institute for Health Research, Lancaster University, Csiro Publishing and Minnis Communications. www.publish.csiro.au/journals/sh

Roen, K. (2008). 'But we have to do something': Surgical 'correction' of atypical genitalia. *Body Society*, 14(1), 47–66. https://doi.org/10.1177%2F1357034X07087530

Roen, K. (2015). Intersex/DSD. In: C. Richards and M.J. Barker (Eds.). *The Palgrave Handbook of the Psychology of Sexuality and Gender* (pp. 183–197). Basingstoke, UK: Palgrave MacMillan.

Sanderson, C. (2010). *Introduction to Counselling Survivors of Interpersonal Trauma*. London, UK: Jessica Kingsley Publishers.

Schuetzmann, K., Brinkmann, L., Schacht, M. and Richter-Appelt, H. (2009). Psychological distress, self-harming behavior, and suicidal tendencies in adults with disorders of sex development. *Archive of Sex Behaviour*, 38(1), 16–33. https:// doi.org/10.1007/s10508-007-9241-9

Senate Community Affairs Committee Secretariat (2013). *Involuntary or Coerced Sterilisation of Intersex People in Australia*. Canberra: Senate Printing Unit. www.aph.gov.au/Parliamentary_Business/ Committees/Senate/Community_Affairs/Involuntary_Sterilisation/First_Report

Siegel, D. (1999). *The Developing Mind*. New York, NY: Guildford Press.

Smith, J., Flowers, P. and Larkin, M. (2009). *IPA: Theory Method and Research*. London: Sage.

Soni, A., Dicks, E. and Ower, G. (2018). *The Intersex Diaries*. London, UK: BBC.

Suchet, M. (2011). Crossing over. Psychoanalytic dialogues. *The International Journal of Relational Perspectives*, 21(2), 172–191. https://doi.org/10.1080/10481885.2011.562842

Toal, P. (2014). *Is It a Boy or a Girl? The Lived Experience of Intersex Individuals in Ireland*. Dublin, Ireland: Dublin City University. Unpublished MSc Dissertation.

Valoria, H. (2017). *Born Both: An Intersex Life*. New York, NY: Hachette Books.

Wallin, D. (2007). *Attachment in Psychotherapy*. New York, NY: Guildford Press.

Williams, N. (2002). The imposition of gender: Psychoanalytic encounters with genital atypicality. *Psychoanalytic Psychology*, 19(3), 455–474. https://doi.org/10.1037/0736-9735.19.3.455

Chapter 14

Barker, M.J. (2019). *Gender, Sexual, and Relationship Diversity (GSRD): Good Practice Across the Counselling Professions 001*. www.bacp.co.uk/media/5877/bacp-gender-sexual-relationship-diversity-gpacp001-april19.pdf

Black, African and Asian Therapist Network (BAATN). www.baatn.org.uk/

Choudrey, S. (2015). Brown, trans, queer, Muslim and proud. TEDxBrixton. www.youtube.com/watch?v=w6hxrZW6I9I&t=6s [last accessed 09.02.2022]

Choudrey, S. (2019). *DIY Find a Therapist Kit*. http://sabahchoudrey.com/2019/12/17/diy-find-a-therapist-kit/ [last accessed 09.02.2022]

Choudrey, S. (2022). *Supporting Trans People of Colour: How to Make Your Practice Inclusive*. London, UK: Jessica Kingsley Publishers.

Czyzselska, J.C. (2016). *Group Analysis and Racialisation*. www.pesi.co.uk/blog/2016/july/group-analysis-and-racialisation [last accessed 08.08.20]

Dalal, F. (2021). Taking the group (really seriously: Race, racism and group analysis. *Group Analysis* https://doi.org/10.1177/05333164211041549

Glassgold, J.M. and Iasenza, S. (Eds.) (2004). *Lesbians, Feminism, and Psychoanalysis: The Second Wave*. New York, NY: Harrington Park Press.

Haugh, S. (2016). The white therapist: Privilege and power. In: D. Charura and C. Lago (Eds.). *The Person-Centred Counselling and Psychotherapy Handbook: Origins, Developments and Current Applications* (pp. 246–255). London, UK: Open University Press.

Layton, L. and Leavy-Sperounis, M. (Eds.). (2020). *Toward a Social Psychoanalysis Culture, Character, and Normative Unconscious Processes*. New York, NY: Routledge.

Menakem, R. (2017). *My Grandmother's Hands: Racialized Trauma and the Pathway to Mending Our Hearts and Bodies*. Las Vegas, NV: Central Recovery Press.

Mental Health Organisation. (2021). *Men and Mental Health*. www.mentalhealth.org.uk/a-to-z/m/men-and-mental-health

Mental Health Organisation. (2021). *Women and Mental Health*. www.mentalhealth.org.uk/a-to-z/w/women-and-mental-health

Mckenzie-Mavinga, I. (2009). *Black Issues in the Therapeutic Process*. London, UK: Bloomsbury Publishing.

Moon, L. (2008). (Ed). *Feeling Queer or Queer Feelings: Radical Approaches to Counselling Sex, Sexualities and Genders*. London, UK: Routledge.

Moten, F. and Harney, S. (2004). The university and the undercommons: Seven theses. In: *Social Text 79*, 22(2), 101–115. Durham, NC: Duke University Press.

O'Connor, N. and Ryan, J. (2003). *Wild Desires and Mistaken Identities: Lesbianism and Psychoanalysis*. London, UK: Routledge.

Procter, G., Cooper, M. and Sanders, P. (2006). *Politicizing the Person-Centred Approach: An Agenda for Personal Change*. London, UK: PCCS.

Sheehi, L. (2020). Talking back. Introduction to Special Edition: Black, Indigenous, Women of Color Talk Back: Decentering Normative Psychoanalysis. *Studies in Gender and Sexuality*, 21(2), 73–76. https://doi.org/10.1080/15240657.2020.1760012

Taylor, F. and Downes, R. (2020). Re-imagining the space and context for a therapeutic curriculum. In: D. Charura and C. Lago (Eds.). *Black Identities and White Therapies* (pp. 88–97). London, UK: PCCS.

Chapter 15

BFI Flare LGBTIQA+ film festival. www.bfi.org.uk/flare

DIVA magazine. For LGBTIQ+ women and non-binary people. www.divamag.co.uk

Gabriel, L. and Davies, D. (2000). The management of ethical dilemmas associated with dual relationships. In: C. Neal and D. Davies (Eds.). *Pink Therapy, Vol. 3: Issues in Therapy with Lesbian, Gay, Bisexual and Transgender Clients* (pp. 35–54). Buckingham, UK: Open University Press.

Pink Therapy. Gender and sexual diversity in the UK. https://pinktherapy.com

Pink Therapy. Online learning and CPD. https://pinktherapy.org

Pope, K. (2001). Sex between therapists and clients. *Encyclopedia of Women and Gender: Sex Similarities and Differences and the Impact of Society on Gender*, 2, 955–962. https://kspope.com/sexiss/sexencyc.php [last accessed November 2021]

Shlien, J.M. (1984). A counter-theory of transference. Client-centered therapy and the person-centered approach. https://adpca.org/wp-content/uploads/2020/11/A-Counter-Theory-of-Transference_John-M.-Shlien_1.pdf [last accessed 09.02.2022]

Vaughan, S. (2000). The hiding and revelation of sexual desire in lesbians: The lasting legacy of developmental traumas. *Journal of Gay & Lesbian Psychotherapy*, 3(2), 81–90. West Hazleton, PA: The Haworth Press.

Chapter 16

Berlant, L. (2011). *Cruel Optimism*. Durham, NC: Duke University Press.

Cannon, B. (2015). *Free without Excuses: Existential Issues in Therapy with Betty Cannon Ph.D.* https://youtu.be/mAvCUbVI6nY [last accessed 02.05.2022]

Harrington, A. (2019). *The Mind Fixers: Psychiatry's Troubled Search for The Biology of Mental Illness*. New York, NY: W.W. Norton.

Kimmerer, R.W. (2020). *Braiding Sweetgrass: Indigenous Wisdom, Scientific Knowledge and the Teaching of Plants*. London, UK: Penguin Random House.

Ladany, N., Mori, Y. and Mehr, K. (2013). Effective and ineffective supervision. *The Counselling Psychologist*, 41(1), 28–47.

Lorde, A. (2007). *Sister Outsider*. Berkeley, CA: Crossing Press.

McCully Brown, M. (2020). *Places I've Taken My Body*. New York, NY: Persea Books.

Munoz, J.E. (2009). *Cruising Utopia: The Then and There of Queer Futurity*. New York, NY: New York University Press.

Rich, A.C. (2003). *What Is Found There*. New York, NY: W.W. Norton.

Van der Kolk, B. (2014). *The Body Keeps the Score*. London, UK: Penguin Random House.

Vuong, O. (2019). *On Earth We're Briefly Gorgeous*. London, UK: Penguin Random House.

Wilde, O. (2016). *Only Dull People Are Brilliant at Breakfast*. London, UK: Penguin.

Yunkaporta, T. (2019). *Sand Talk: How Indigenous Thinking Can Save The World*. Melbourne, AUS: Text Publishing.

Glossary

Crenshaw, K. (1991) Mapping the margins: Intersectionality, identity politics, and violence against women of color. *Stanford Law Review*, 43(6), 1241–1299.

Index